OPERA RECORDINGS

OPERA RECORDINGS

A Critical Guide

By Kenn Harris

DAVID AND CHARLES
NEWTON ABBOT

3

789 · 913

HAR

00516 7049

0 7153 6362 X

© Kenn Harris, 1973

Filmset in 11 on 13 point Melior by
C. E. Dawkins (Typesetters) Ltd London SE1 1UN
and printed in Great Britain by
Redwood Press Limited Trowbridge Wiltshire
for David & Charles (Holdings) Limited
South Devon House Newton Abbot Devon

To my parents, George and Marion Harris.
I hope their faith in my abilities and their encouragement will
be justified by this book.

TABLE OF CONTENTS

PREFACE

Why does one become a collector of opera recordings? Just as the stamp enthusiast hoards rare and beautiful stamps, and as the lepidopterist cherishes his butterflies, the operaphile feels compelled to collect voices as captured on disc. To the casual opera-goer, any recording of CARMEN might suffice for an occasional playing, but to the enthusiast, every recording must be chosen with great care. To the true "buff" or, as in my case, the self-styled addict, a single recording of an opera rarely suffices. If there are six great Tosca's on disc, sooner or later we must hear them and, preferably, own them all. Even the existing recordings don't always suffice. It is not enough that, for example, Maria Callas and Joan Sutherland have recorded Bellini's NORMA. We dream, hope, and wait until Montserrat Caballé and Beverley Sills record the opera, too.

To the collector of operatic recordings, few activities are more pleasurable than assembling a group of fellow initiates in his home and trotting out his most prized treasures: a Tebaldi AIDA, the Nilsson SALOME, perhaps a "pirated" disc or two. Over wine, as the records play, memories are exchanged, legends enhanced, and, most thrilling of all to the zealot, perhaps a new convert to the artistry of one's favorite singer—or composer—is made.

This book is intended not only for those who already are collectors of opera recordings, although it is hoped that the opinions expressed herein will find some degree of favor with established opera buffs. Undoubtedly, they will stimulate controversy, for the soprano who impresses one listener with her poignant use of vibrato for so-called dramatic effect is apt to send another one into agony with her vocal wobble. Evidently, barring such blatant errors as singing the wrong note, every note hit by a singer and every tempo employed by a conductor effects each listener differently.

I make no advance apologies for the choices made in the following pages. Without doubt, they say much about my tastes, values, and concerns. *Soit.* My advice is not intended to be taken as gospel by even the newest and least experienced convert to opera. Hopefully, my opinions will serve as guidelines to others looking for the best in operatic recordings. We each have our own preferences. An artist who consistently fails to impress me either in the theatre or on disc may communicate brilliantly to many other listeners. Of course, my favorite might possibly be your *bête noir.* This, as I am very fond of reminding my friends who would lynch me because I don't share their admiration for Mme. A. or Mr. B., is what makes horse races.

This book should serve two purposes. One is, through the listing of all available recordings of each of the 76 operas covered herein to inform the reader of each of his possible choices. The second and principal one is, through the evaluations of many if not all of these recordings, to give the reader an idea of which of these recordings he should own and for what reasons.

No one should own anything, least of all an opera recording, solely because a critic tells him that he should. If your taste runs to the German works only, don't feel that you must display LA TRAVIATA and TOSCA prominently in your home just to prove how catholic your tastes are. By the same token, if you enjoy *verismo* and *verismo* only, don't waste your money buying FIDELIO and the RING. Go out and buy six recordings each of CHENIER and MADAMA BUTTERFLY and enjoy them!

People buy recordings for different reasons. Some fans simply wish to create a library of decent performances of the various operas. Others acquire every recording made by their favorite artists. Both of these approaches to record collecting are entirely reasonable. Prices being what they are, the finances of building up a large collection may well become rather difficult to manage, but assuming that the will is there, along with enough cash to take advantage of the material available, it is not too hard to amass a satisfactory collection. Fifteen or so years ago, the only operas that seemed to get recorded were the old chestnuts: AIDA, BOHEME, FAUST, and their ilk. One searched in vain for ARIADNE AUF NAXOS or even a good, complete DON CARLO. Now, this situation has changed to a great extent. Of course, the "bread and butter" operas dominate the scene, and there are at least ten different AIDA's, TRAVIATA's, and TOSCA's around, but there are now four full RING cycles, five NORMA's, and recent, stereo versions of ERNANI, NABUCCO, FEDORA and many other less generally popular works.

Record companies as a rule don't like to take risks with "unsafe" operas, and usually don't record them unless a star-studded cast can be assembled, the philosophy being that if you liked Tebaldi in TOSCA then you'll love her in LA WALLY. One international recording company, Phillips, is to be commended for its courageous policy of preserving contemporary works on discs, often with largely unknown casts. Thanks to this firm, there are recordings of such recent operas as THE DEVILS OF LOUDON and THE MIDSUMMER MARRIAGE, as well as the monumental first complete recording of Berlioz' LES TROYENS, to name only three recent achievements.

In opera of course, conservatism is no great vice, and Angel, London, and RCA deserve praise for preserving as many notable performances in the standard repertoire as they have already done. To those who ask "Do we really need another TOSCA, with performances by Callas, Tebaldi, Milanov, and Price already available?" I say, if the "other" Tosca is Birgit Nilsson, the answer is "yes."

The advent of the phonograph has done much to popularize opera in areas away from large cities. Thanks to recordings, even the most isolated listener can have access to outstanding performances of opera, Therefore, the recording industry has a great responsibility to issue high quality performances of the full spectrum of opera. Undoubtedly no producer sets out to create a bad or even mediocre performance, but pinching pennies and poor planning can lead to disaster in the studio.

Unless one is buying an opera set solely because a favorite artist appears in it, or because it is the only available performance of an important opera, it is advisable to hear the record before buying it or, at the very least, to read a few reviews, if only to discover if there is any sort of consensus of feeling about the set.

At the beginning of each article, all the complete recordings of the opera under discussion that were currently available at press time are listed. However, not all of those recordings are evaluated in the text which follows. You will also note that after certain catalogue numbers, there is an asterisk. The asterisk denotes that there is a highlight disc available for that album.

In this book, the recordings chosen for evaluation are either, in my opinion, generally distinguished or, if far less than perfect or even less than commendable, important due to the presence of one or more major artist in the cast. If there is a preponderance of generally favorable notices herein, it is only because the intent of the book is to indicate those albums that are worth hearing. I have taken the liberty of ruling out for discussion many albums that I consider to be inferior. By not mentioning them, I avoid wasting space and resist the temptation to be destructively nasty to artists who have in individual instances failed to conquer the musical demands made upon them.

It should also be noted that some of the recordings discussed in the book, especially budget reissues, are not available in the UK on a British label. I suggest that if you are particularly interested in such recordings that you look for them in the larger record shops that carry imported discs.

This book is dedicated to those who create opera as well as to those who enjoy it, and I fervently hope that the evaluations found in these pages stimulate readers to listen to recordings and attend live performances. If this much is achieved, I believe that the book will have succeeded.

Kenn Harris
New York City, 1973

AUTHOR'S ACKNOWLEDGEMENTS

Of the many people who aided (or at least, abetted) the creation of this book, a few must be listed for special thanks:

My editor, Mr. Harvey Silbert, whose painstaking work has helped so greatly to shape and focus the text.

Special thanks must also go to Ms. Gillian Hyde, who provided me with data concerning the availability of recordings in the United Kingdom, to Mr. Carl Ruderman, President of Drake Publishers Inc., New York, Mr. David St. John Thomas, Director of David & Charles, Ltd. in the UK and to Ms. Caroline Robbins, D & C's USA representative, each of whom encouraged and patiently waited for this book to be completed.

Kenn Harris
New York, 1973

CILEA: ADRIANA LECOUVREUR

Tebaldi, Simionato, del Monaco, Capuana cond.
Orchestra and Chorus of L'Accademia di Santa Cecilia
3 discs
London OSA 1331*
UK: Decca SET 221-3

Gavazzi, Truccato Pace, Prandelli, Simonetto cond.
RAI Orchestra and Chorus
3 discs
Everest/Cetra S430/2

Everyone has a pet project that he clings to in the face of all reason, and, I suppose, every opera buff loves at least one work that the critics and even much of the public despises. Mine is Cilea's ADRIANA LECOUVREUR, a *verismo* "epic" based on Scribe's fictionalized stage biography of the eighteenth century star of the Comedie Francaise. The details of the melodramatic plot need not be gone into here, but to give the uninitiated reader an idea of the general level of the proceedings, it suffices to say that Adriana dies in her lover's arms after inhaling the scent of violets poisoned by her rival.

Cilea, one of Puccini's lesser contemporaries and a noted musicologist of his day, composed a fragilely melodious score for ADRIANA that blooms when great singers take its leading roles. Masterpieces like BOHEME or NOZZE DI FIGARO can survive mediocre performances without severe damage, but ADRIANA requires first class artistry from its singers, as if to atone for the lack of divine inspiration on the part of its composer.

In recent years, Renata Tebaldi has been one of the two most prominent Adrianas (Magda Olivero being the other). It is said that Adriana is Madame Tebaldi's favorite role. She has enjoyed a number of successes in it in both Italy and America. In 1961, London-Decca recorded the opera with the soprano flanked by Mario del Monaco and Giulietta Simionato. Certainly after hearing the lush melodies given to Adriana, and noting that she has the lion's share of the major dramatic moments in the opera, one can recognize why Tebaldi enjoys the role so much. On the recording, she is in luminescent voice and she bathes the part in golden tone—especially in "Poveri Fiori." Her recitation of Phedre's monologue at the conclusion of Act Three (used in the plot as a means of insulting the villainess) is hammy but well within the style called for by the opera. Del Monaco is a strong Maurizio (Count of Saxony), supporting Tebaldi stylishly in the duets and delivering his one major aria, "L'anima ho stanco" with fervor. Giulietta Simionato is a splendidly wicked Princess Di Buoillion, easily matching Tebaldi's vocal opulence and authority. The soprano-mezzo duet with which Act Two concludes is a third rate imitation of the Aida-Amneris confrontation, but in the hands (or throats) of these two ladies, it is irresistible. The slightly less juicy role of Michonnet, Adriana's stage manager and confidant (and one of the few sympathetic baritone roles in all opera) is taken by a virtually unknown singer, Giulio Fioravanti, who, judging from this performance, should be delivered from his obscurity into the spotlight. Franco Capuana's expansive direction of the orchestra and chorus of the Accademia di Santa Cecilia helps greatly.

Although this recording is the preferred one, it is not the only ADRIANA set available. The budget-minded might appreciate the solid performance found on Everest-Cetra with a cast headed by the veteran soprano Carla Gavazzi and the tenor Giancinto Prandelli. This recording also features the RAI chorus and Orchestra conducted by Alfredo Simonetto. None of the singing approaches the level of the Tebaldi-Del Monaco set, but the performance has its own integrity and is grand fun to listen to as a complement to the London-Decca album.

VERDI: AIDA

Curtis-Verna, Corelli, Questa cond.
3 discs
Everest/Cetra S-401/3*

Nelli, Gustafson, Tucker, Valdengo, Toscanini cond.
NBC Symphony
3 discs
Victrola VICS-6113

Price, Bumbry, Domingo, Milnes, Raimondi, Leinsdorf cond.
London Symphony, John Alldis Choir
3 discs
RCA LSC-6198* UK: RCA SER5609-11

Nilsson, Bumbry, Corelli, Sereni, Mehta cond.
Rome Opera Orchestra and Chorus
3 discs
Angel S-3716
UK: HMV SLS-92⁹

Price, Gorr, Vickers, Merrill, Solti cond.
Rome Opera Orchestra and Chorus
3 discs
London OSA 1393
UK: Decca SET427-9

Tebaldi, Simionato, Bergonzi, MacNeil, von Karajan cond.
Vienna Philharmonic and Vienna Friends of Music Chorus
3 discs
London OSA 1313*
UK: Decca SXL 2167-9

Tebaldi, Stignani, del Monaco, Protti, Erede cond.
Orchestra and Chorus of L'Accademia di Sta Cecilia
3 discs
Richmond RS63004* (mono)

Caniglia, Stignani, Gigli, Bechi, Serafin cond.
Rome Opera Orchestra and Chorus
3 discs
Seraphim IC 6008 (mono)
UK: Seraphim SH153-5

Callas, Barbieri, Tucker, Gobbi, Serafin cond.
La Scala Orchestra and Chorus
3 discs
Angel 3525C (mono)

Milanov, Barbieri, Bjoerling, Warren, Perlea cond.
Rome Opera Orchestra and Chorus
3 discs
Victrola VIC 6119 (mono)

Leontyne Price, today's most popular exponent of this title role, has recorded the opera twice, both times for Victor-HMV. The earlier, 1960 version has recently been reissued by London-Decca. In 1960, Price was a spinto soprano, and, at that time, it was impossible to imagine her singing an impure note. Vocally, Price is heavenly ("Celeste Aida," indeed) in this recording. Her warm voice, so effortlessly produced, makes for an Aida of unparalleled allure. Dramatically, she was not then the fiery "lionessa" that she became in the role in later performances. The other principals on this recording are Jon Vickers, Rita Gorr, Robert Merrill, and Giorgio Tozzi. Jon Vickers is a strong sounding Radames even though his voice is just a bit on the cool side. Rita Gorr's expressive mezzo soprano with a vibrant dramatic projection makes an out-standing Amneris despite the fact that she has an edgy top range. Merrill is a high quality Amonasro, and Giorgio Tozzi is an estimable Ramfis. The Rome Opera Orchestra and Chorus are conducted by George Solti in his finest Italian operatic recording.

The later Price AIDA makes up in dramatic authority and security in the lower register what little it has lost in lustre on top. The earlier Price Aida was a young girl, the second one is very much a mature prima donna, but the performance is a most commendable one.

Placido Domingo is a more youthful and a more ardent Radames than Vickers, although one gets the feeling that Domingo is risking burning his voice out in so heavy a role as this. Grace Bumbry's Amneris is an accurate recreation of her stage performances heard frequently these days in the opera houses: warm, lively, and easily produced. Miss Bumbry's diction is somewhat blurred in this recording, however. Sherrill Milnes is the exciting Amonasro on this recording, while two fine basses, Ruggiero Raimondi and Hans Sotin, are lavished on the unrewarding roles of Ramfis and the King, respectively. Erich Leinsdorf conducts the Chorus and Orchestra of RCA Italiana with accustomed security in this recording that was issued to commemorate the opera's 100th birthday. It is a worthy tribute.

Angel-HMV presents two AIDA's. The newer version dates from 1967 and features the Rome Opera forces headed by Nilsson, Corelli, Bumbry, Sereni, and Giaiotti, with Zubin Mehta conducting. Birgit Nilsson has enjoyed considerable success as AIDA, although her glorious dramatic soprano is not noted for Italianate warmth. Mme. Nilsson conscientiously works on producing the desired "Italian" sound and on vocal terms, succeeds admirably. She has lightened her voice for this recording and offers immensely satisfying singing. Franco Corelli has always indulged his tendency towards sloppiness in this role onstage, and, unfortunately, his handsome voice is clouded by frequent scooping, sliding, inattention to dynamics, and general lack of sensitivity. Still, the voice itself is glorious, particularly during the "Nile Scene". Grace Bumbry sings Amneris in this recording. Her voice sounds smallish in comparison to Nilsson's, and this places her at a disadvantage in their duet in the first scene of Act Two. Elsewhere, her singing is pleasing, although she occasionally is sharp. Her dramatic flair helps her to create an interesting Amneris. Mario Sereni, a Metropolitan Opera regular for many years, is an artist who always sounds particularly fine on records. His Amonasro is more than adequate, as is the Ramfis of a very under-appreciated Italian basso, Bonaldo Giaiotti. The Rome Opera orchestra and chorus are well schooled in recorded Aida's (four) and respond idiomatically to Mehta's highly charged baton.

Renata Tebaldi, like Price, has recorded AIDA twice. Her most recent version, made in 1958 in Vienna, finds the soprano in splendid form, dramatically involved, and singing with regal beauty. Only the high C's emerge slightly ragged in "O patria mia." Tebaldi and Giulietta Simionato, the Amneris, render the listener breathless with their Act Two duet, and the Nile Scene duets with tenor and baritone come off exceedingly well. Carlo Bergonzi is a manly, eloquent Radames, packing power yet always singing stylishly, while Cornell MacNeil offers a brawny, resonant Amonasro. Simionato's Judgement Scene stands as the mezzo's crowning achievement on discs. Unfortunately, neither Arnold van Mill, the Ramfis nor the Vienna Friends of Music Chorus sing with much spirit. Herbert von Karajan's evident lack of sympathy for Italian opera makes for a heavy, pedantic reading of the score that works against the fine singing by the four principals.

Tebaldi's 1951 AIDA, originally released by London-Decca, is now part of that firm's Richmond series. The younger

Tebaldi created an Aida of great vocal beauty and gentle yet proud demeanor. Certainly, her voice sounded more youthful in 1951 than seven years later in Vienna. The soprano's colleagues here are all Italian "pro's" who are rather short on the fine points of phrasing but are capable of fiery, exciting singing. Mario del Monaco is a strong, brass-throated Radames, singing "Celeste Aida" as if it were a call to battle. He is awesomely compelling in his straightforward, iron-lunged work. Ebe Stignani, no longer in peak voice, still manages an imperious and often distinguished Amneris. Aldo Protti's Amonasro is competent if hardly polished, and Dorio Caselli's Ramfis fits well into the direct, unsophisticated performance led by Alberto Erede who directs the soloists and the Santa Cecilia forces with enthusiasm.

Among the older recordings in mono sound is the Angel-HMV La Scala set with Callas, Tucker, Barbieri, and Gobbi, conducted by Serafin. Callas, except for her tortured top notes, is heard to good advantage in the title role, although it is hardly her finest recorded performance. Callas is at her best when Aida is at her most distraught, as in the Second Act scene with Amneris who is powerfully sung by Fedora Barbieri. Richard Tucker in 1955 was somewhat light of voice for Radames, although he sings with his usual vigor. Gobbi is an Amonasro of uncommon power, while Serafin leads a stately performance that somehow never leaves the realm of high competence for the stratosphere of greatness.

Two RCA-Victrola sets are also worth investigating. One, which stems from an NBC radio broadcast of 1949 features Toscanini's highly charged and pristine reading of the score. However, the maestro's noble conception of the opera is flawed by terrible casting. Of the four principals, only Richard Tucker is of international quality, and in 1949, he was much too young to do the role Radames full justice. Herva Nelli is more or less adequate as Aida, fulfilling the minimum musical requirements of the score but falling far behind the work of Price, Tebaldi, Milanov, and Callas in the role. Eva Gustafson never should have attempted Amneris, but Giuseppe Valdengo turns in a fairly good Amonasro. The recorded sound is dry, and the whole set is valuable only for Toscanini's contribution. A novelty of the recording is Tucker's use of the alternate ending to "Celeste Aida" in which after bellowing "Un trono vicino al sol" on a high b flat, he repeats the words pianissimo an octave lower.

Finally, the other Victrola set preserves a Rome Opera effort from the mid-fifties which presents Zinka Milanov as a commanding Aida, Jussi Bjoerling in gorgeous voice as Radames, Fedora Barbieri as a very decent Amneris, and Leonard Warren as a compelling Amonasro. Jonel Perlea is the conductor, and he offers strong guidance from the pit.

MASCAGNI: L'AMICO FRITZ

Freni, Pavarotti, Sardinero, Gavazzeni cond.
Covent Garden Orchestra
2 discs
Angel S-3737
UK: HMV SLS938

Tassinari, Tagliavini, Mascagni cond.
RAI Orchestra
2 discs
Everest Cetra S429/2

Pietro Mascagni's one post-CAVALLERIA work to achieve any sort of international reputation is this three act pastoral set in a Jewish community in Alsace-Lorraine. The composer himself conducts the Everest-Cetra budget set which is of some historical interest for that reason as well as for the participation of Pia Tassinari and Ferruccio Tagliavini, but this set is out-distanced by the 1968 Angel-HMV performance.

The Angel-HMV cast is headed by Luciano Pavarotti as the women-hating Fritz and Mirella Freni as Suzel, the girl who eventually wins his heart. This is one of Pavarotti's first major recordings, and the unstinting flow of vibrant tone from the tenor is a positive joy! His characterization is genial and apt, while his third act aria (repeated again as the finale of the work) is almost reason enough to own the set.

Miss Freni brings sweetness and warmth to the slightly cloying role of Suzel. The soprano makes Suzel's first act aria "Son pocchi fiori" into a little gem and displays similarly winning qualities in the well known "Cherry Duet" with Pavarotti in the second act. Freni is partnered admirably in the

Bible reading scene by Vincente Sardinero who sings the matchmaking Rabbi David with a pleasant if not too large voice. The supporting cast is quite excellent, and the Covent Garden Orchestra plays mellowly under Gavazzeni's baton. The opera, as gentle and saccharine as CAVALLERIA RUSTICANA is powerful and bombastic, is hardly a masterpiece, but this recording presents it in as good a light as is possible today.

GIORDANO:
ANDREA CHENIER

Stella, Corelli, Sereni, Santini cond.
Rome Opera Orchestra and Chorus
3 discs
Angel S-3645*
UK: HMV SLS910

Tebaldi, Soler, Savarese, Basile cond.
RAI Orchestra and Chorus
2 discs
Everest/Cetra 5-412/2*

Tebaldi, del Monaco, Bastianini, Gavazzeni cond.
Orchestra and Chorus of L'Accademia di Sta Cecilia
3 discs
London OSA-1303*
UK: Decca GOS600-1

Caniglia, Gigli, Bechi, De Fabritiis cond.
Rome Opera Orchestra and Chorus
2 discs
Seraphim: IB-6019 (mono)

ANDREA CHENIER has remained a repertory item in Italy
and the United States. However, it is performed much less
frequently in other countries. This is surprising, for its lusty
melodies and fat roles for soprano, tenor, and baritone make
it a singers' opera if ever there were one, and, when given a

stylish and vocally high-powered performance, can send an audience climbing the walls with excitement.

There are four complete recordings of Giordano's verismo opera. Three offer the kind of singing needed if the opera is to succeed, while the fourth is notable only for the work of its soprano, Renata Tebaldi, who recorded the work for Cetra years before she sang the role of Maddalena Di Coigny for London-Decca in a generally more satisfactory performance.

This London set, with Mario del Monaco in the title role, Renata Tebaldi as Maddalena, and Ettore Bastianini as Carlo Gerard, is immensely enjoyable. Del Monaco's clarion tenor makes the character of the poet very much the revolutionary hero, if slightly to the detriment of the score's most tender moments. The "Improvviso" has the proper, slightly hysterical, tense quality, and "Si, fui soldato" is bravely hurled at Chenier's powerful enemies at court. The second act love duet is more difficult for del Monaco to act, but his singing is sensuous and persuasive. The final act gives del Monaco a chance to sing "Come un bel dí di Maggio" and the duet with Maddalena with power and dignity.

Tebaldi was eminently suited to Maddalena's music in the middle stage of her career when she could imbue the soprano part with meltingly limpid tone and bring to it her ever-expanding dramatic awareness and developing chest register. The second act duet with del Monaco reveals Tebaldi's artistry at its peak, with phrase after phrase stunningly voiced and projected with obvious sympathy for the character, as well as the music. "La mamma morta" in Act Three is tautly controlled and hauntingly vocalized, and the final duet "La nostra morte" remains one of the most thrilling pieces that she and del Monaco, who collaborated on so many discs, ever performed together. Ettore Bastianini's Gerard is mellifluously sung, with a full, dark tone and an impassioned, well-wrought characterization. The baritone makes the most of the opportunities provided by the third act showpiece "Nemico della patria." The uniformly good supporting cast includes the then unknown Fiorenza Cossotto as La Bersi. The Orchestra and

Chorus of L'Accademia di Santa Cecilia is enthusiastically led by Gianandrea Gavazzeni.

Angel-HMV's CHENIER features Franco Corelli in the title role, supported by Antonietta Stella and Mario Sereni as Maddalena and Gerard. Corelli is in victorious form here. His voice seems free from strain and is particularly bright and vibrant. The tenor sings both passionately and nobly throughout the score. Del Monaco brings a greater sense of maturity and physical strength to the role of Chenier, but Corelli is even more convincing than his London-Decca rival as a romantic and sensitive character. Unfortunately, neither of Corelli's principal colleagues quite match his performance. Stella is a worthy artist who, in this case, lacks in beauty of tone what she can so easily supply in power. Her voice is full but clouded and tremulous, and her high notes lack fire. Her interpretation is genteel but dull, and such an approach is deadly to the rough and tumble, anything but subtle opera at hand. Sereni sings with superficial ease, meeting the basic demands of the music but without equalling the superior artistry of Bastianini. One hardly senses anything of Gerard's complex, vacillating nature in Sereni's easy-going, generalized singing. The supporting cast is as competent as London's, and the Rome Opera forces are well-routined. Gabriele Santini's conducting is similarly adequate, although he fails to create a truly exciting atmosphere with his reasonable, considerate but unremarkable pacing of the score.

The remaining two CHENIER sets are budget priced reissues. Seraphim's set is from a 1940 Rome Opera production led by Olivero de Fabritiis, with Beniamino Gigli, Maria Caniglia, and Gino Bechi in the leading roles. The poet Chenier is said to have been Gigli's favorite role. It is easy to understand why Gigli, or any other tenor, would love the part, considering its four arias and two duets. Gigli, the most lyrical Chenier on discs, is in fine vocal estate, although he delights in holding many notes outrageously long (as does, of course, Corelli). No one on discs, though, can match his rendering of the fourth act "Come un bel dí di Maggio." This is certainly a performance that none of Gigli's admirers ought to miss. Caniglia's Maddalena is pleasingly impetuous. The soprano had a large voice that was more steelily commanding than beautiful. She was, however, an accomplished musician as well as a magnetic "presence", and, barring an occasional high note that is a little too cutting or opaque for comfort (and there are a number of such notes in the fourth act), Caniglia is an impressive heroine. Gino Bechi's rather tightly produced baritone was never an instrument of great beauty. Here, though, in a recording from his younger days, Bechi shows that he could sing with considerable richness of tone; furthermore, his characterization is arresting. Giulietta Simionato is heard briefly as the Countess Di Coigny, while Giuseppe Taddei turns up in a pair of brief comprimario roles. De Fabritiis conducts with notable élan (his tempi are slightly rushed at times), and the opera fits nicely on two discs, making it an economic bargain as well as a treat for nostalgic listeners.

Everest-Cetra's CHENIER also is squeezed on to two discs, but except for Tebaldi's ravishingly youthful Maddalena, there is little to recommend the set. The soprano sings "La mamma morta" with an elegance of phrasing and a dramatic intensity that she seldom surpassed in other recordings. If the early BOHEME and BUTTERFLY sets reveal Tebaldi at her lyrical best, this performance can be shown as pointing to her later emergence as a dramatic soprano. Unfortunately, the Chenier, Jose Soler, while evidently a sensitive artist, lacks both the range and the power for this role, contributing a barely adequate performance. Soler is painfully weak in each of the duets with the soprano. Ugo Savarese sings Gerard in a routine and disinterested fashion. Little is remarkable about the supporting cast, but Arturo Basile's conducting of the Radio Italiana forces is crisp and professional. Thus, this last CHENIER is not at all a distinguished over-all performance, but it offers a particularly lovely heroine in Tebaldi, and for this, it might be considered as a supplement to another recorded CHENIER.

R. STRAUSS:
ARIADNE AUF NAXOS

Janowitz, Geszty, Zylis-Gara, King, Prey, Schreier, Adam, Kempe
cond.
Dresden State Opera Orchestra and Chorus
3 discs
Angel S-3733
UK: HMV SLS936

Rysanek, Peters, Jurinac, Peerce, Berry, Leinsdorf cond.
Vienna Philharmonic and Vienna State Opera Chorus
3 discs
London OSA13100
UK: Decca 2BB112-4

Hillebrecht, Grist, Troyanos, Thomas, McDaniel, Böhm cond.
Bavarian State (Munich) Opera Orchestra and Chorus
3 discs
DGG 2709033
UK: Same

Of the three recordings of this charming opera, the Angel-
HMV offers the best balanced cast. Gundula Janowitz is a
languid, appealing Ariadne (and a flamboyant Prima Donna
in the prologue, in the bargain), succeeding admirably in her
long and arduous "Monologue". The Zerbinetta is Sylvia
Geszty, who copes with her character's grueling aria with
almost casual ease. Geszty's is a light coloratura soprano,
but one possessed of considerable tonal color. Moreover, her
technique is sound and her manner saucy. The Hungarian

soprano proves herself equal to the challenge posed by this role. James King, after a hilarious caricature of the haughty Tenor in the Prologue, settles down and acquits himself well as Bacchus, with his warm voice sounding particularly attractive as the god come down to earth to rescue Ariadne. Teresa Zylis-Gara is in lovely voice as the young Composer in the Prologue, although she does not make as much of the role as does Sena Jurinac on the London-Decca release. The *commedia dell'arte* players include, in addition to Sylvia Geszty, Hermann Prey as Harlequin and Peter Schreier as Scaramuccio, while Theo Adam is heard as the Music Master. These fine artists are conducted by Rudolfe Kempe in an expansive, lovely performance that fulfills Hofmansthal and Strauss' idea of mixing rustic comedy into a high flown *opera seria*.

The London-Decca ARIADNE, originally released by RCA, offers Leonie Rysanek in the title role. Although the top notes are excellent, Rysanek was not at her best here, and the lower register is breathy and dull in timbre. She does scale rare heights of ecstasy in the "Monologue" that neither Janowitz nor Hillebrecht (on DGG) reach, but one wishes that this recording had been made a little later when Rysanek had regained full control over her voice. Roberta Peters, a game and valiant Zerbinetta, performs the treacherous aria in a manner that, while not precisely effortless, is still musically accurate and pleasant to listen to most of the time. Her Zerbinetta is coquettish but not as excitingly feminine as Geszty's.

Jan Peerce, rather surprisingly cast as Bacchus, is somewhat dry of voice, and his medium-sized lyric tenor was not ideal for the role. His singing is rather perfunctory, hitting the notes accurately but performing without inspiration or security. Sena Jurinac's Composer is warmly vocalized and delightfully acted, while Walter Berry stands out as Harlequin. The Vienna Philharmonic is conducted here by Erich Leinsdorf, who seems less at home in this score than in Verdian or Wagnerian music. Leinsdorf imparts a sluggishness to the

performance that leaves the opera earthbound and heavy in
his hands.

The Deutsche Grammophon ARIADNE is blessed by the
incandescent conducting of Karl Böhm but is rather less
fortunate in the dry, pallid Ariadne of Hildegarde Hillebrecht
and the occasionally forced Bacchus of Jess Thomas. Reri
Grist's Zerbinetta sparkles with wit and a lovely voice skillfully deployed. Miss Grist's sound is slightly on the cold side,
but her voice is clearly produced and artfully handled, and
she triumphs in her aria. Tatiana Troyanos is a pleasant
Composer. The smaller roles are well cast, and the Bavarian
State Opera Orchestra gives its best to Dr. Böhm.

VERDI:
UN BALLO IN MASCHERA

Price, Grist, Verrett, Bergonzi, Merrill, Leinsdorf cond.
RCA Italiana Orchestra and Chorus
3 discs
RCA LSC-6179*
UK: RCA SER5556-8

Nilsson, Stahlman, Simionato, Bergonzi, MacNeil, Solti cond.
Orchestra and Chorus of L'Accademia di Santa Cecilia
3 discs
London OSA 1398*
UK: Decca SET215-7

Tebaldi, Donath, Resnik, Pavarotti, Milnes, Bartoletti cond.
Orchestra and Chorus of L'Accademia di Santa Cecilia
3 discs
London OSA 1398
UK: Decca SET484-6

Curtis-Verna, Tassinari, Tagliavini, Questa cond.
RAI Orchestra and Chorus
2 discs
Everest/Cetra S-428/2

Caniglia, Ribetti, Barbieri, Gigli, Bechi, Serafin cond.
La Scala Orchestra and Chorus
2 discs
Seraphim IB 6026
UK: Seraphim SH 131-2 (Mono)

Callas, Ratti, Barbieri, di Stefano, Gobbi, Votto cond.
La Scala Orchestra and Chorus
3 discs
Angel C/L 3557 (Mono)

RCA's 1967 BALLO is solidly cast, but it is only routinely conducted by Erich Leinsdorf under whose baton the RCA Italiana Orchestra and Chorus perform decently but without much commitment or Verdian excitement. Fortunately, the five principal artists find their own inspiration in the score, and the set is among the most richly vocalized of BALLO recordings.

Carlo Bergonzi is a dashing, graceful Riccardo who sings with elegance and warmth, blending his voice smoothly with those of his colleagues in an opera that greatly depends upon ensemble work.

Leontyne Price, justly renowned for her Amelia, which she added to her active repertoire the year before this set was released, is troubled only in the lower register, particularly in the second act finale where her chest tones are forced and surprisingly unlovely. In the heroine's two major arias, Price soars brilliantly to heights reached by few artists, singing with passion and freedom of sound, and the second act love duet with Bergonzi is thrilling and, moreover, finds Leinsdorf in better form than in most other sections of the opera.

Robert Merrill's voice, husbanded with so little attention to nuance or shading is, however, a still very attractive instrument. He makes for a stiff but vocally powerful Renato. Shirley Verrett finds some of Ulrica's music troublesome, but her high notes are fabulous, and she is an interestingly youthful-sounding fortune teller. Reri Grist's Oscar, delightful in its clear and exuberant phrasing, is the best on records.

Another interesting, if imperfect, BALLO is the most recent version, issued by London-Decca. Ebulliently paced by conductor Lamberto Gardelli, whose amiable tempi make the music sound as lovely as possible while missing some of the inherent drama in the score, this recording features a pair of veteran *prime donne* and a duo of young leading men. Luciano Pavarotti is an almost ideal Count. Voice and musicianship he has to spare, but he lacks the conviction and poise that will certainly come with further performances of this role. The Renato, Sherrill Milnes, as is the case with Pavarotti, makes the most of his wonderful music while only sketching in the personality of Renato (so admirably painted in full detail by Gobbi on the Angel-HMV version).

In contrast, the Amelia, Renata Tebaldi, is an artist who, although her instrument has lost its original sheen, benefits from the depth of resources gained through maturity. What impresses most about Tebaldi's performance in this recording is her intense identification with the role. Rarely has Amelia's despair been more excitingly communicated! Her voice sounds leaner than it has in the past but is sufficiently strong to make its way through the treacherous music of the trio in Act 1, Scene 2 and the quartet in the scene in Renato's house. Her two arias are sung with consummate beauty and the duet with Riccardo in the heath scene is equally stunning. All the more surprising, thus, is the fact that Tebaldi has never sung the role onstage. Of course, her twenty-five years of close association with Verdi operas has undoubtedly prepared her for the challenges of this role.

This recording is less fortunate in the other two ladies in the cast. Helen Donath sings Oscar prettily but without the requisite pertness the part so badly needs, while Regina Resnik's Ulrica is far below this artist's former standard of singing. The Orchestra and Chorus of the Accademia di Santa Cecilia are most commendable.

Another London-Decca BALLO was recorded in 1962 and is ignited by the conducting of Georg Solti who is the dominating but never oppressive force behind this set's excellence. His Riccardo, Bergonzi (again) sings with his customary finesse but is overpowered in the love scenes by Birgit Nilsson's tremendous voice, here deployed somewhat gingerly as Amelia. Never quite at her best in Verdi, Nilsson is secure in intonation but somewhat unidiomatic and dramatically a bit on the cool side as this long-suffering heroine. Cornel MacNeil's Renato is conventionally phrased but not without its moments of excellence, as in "Eri tu," for example. Giulietta Simionato's vibrant Ulrica is unmatched elsewhere on discs. Sylvia Stahlman is, however, not quite up to the demands of Oscar. Everyone else in the cast, though, is quite acceptable, and under Solti's electrifying direction, the performance emerges as a musical experience of the first order.

Deutsche Grammophon's BALLO is not quite on the same high level as the other sets described here. Antonietta Stella is a serviceable Amelia, bringing a sense of well-routined tradition to her performance. The soprano, however, seems a little tired, and her high notes are opaque and unexciting. Gianni Poggi lacks a sense of pitch, musical grace, and dramatic awareness, which more or less rules him out as a contender in the Riccardo stakes. Ettore Bastianini's resoundingly sung Renato is the chief virtue of the set, but La Scala's supporting cast is quite undistinguished, and Gianandrea Gavazzeni's efficient but unexciting conducting lends still another pedestrian quality to the performance.

Seraphim's budget BALLO, recorded in 1940, offers Beniamino Gigli's celebrated account of Riccardo. Here his voice is slightly strained at the top, and his idiosyncratic approach to his art robs the character of some of its nobility, but much of Gigli's singing is quite beautiful. Maria Caniglia sings Amelia with *slancio* and a sense of urgency, but her high notes are variable and are often lunged for, putting her more than a few steps behind Price or Callas. Gino Bechi is a sturdy Renato, singing "Eri tu" in a rough but effective manner. Fedori Barbieri is, as on the Angel set, an Ulrica to be reckoned with, although she lacks the brilliance of Simionato or the grace of Verrett. The rest of the cast is undistinguished. The Rome Opera Chorus and Orchestra perform in workman-like fashion for the slightly rushed Tullio Serafin (who probably pushed the score along in order to fit the set on as few 78 rpm discs as possible—this is the lone two l.p. BALLO).

Although the 1955 Scala BALLO has been withdrawn from

the Angel catalogue in the USA and that of HMV in the UK, it is still seen in the larger stores from time to time on Italian pressings, both in the original mono and in electronically rechanneled stereo. It warrants some discussion in that the contributions of Callas and Gobbi make it eminently worth searching for. The soprano's tautly controlled dramatic projection coupled with some of the best singing she ever did before the microphones would alone make the set worth acquiring. Callas' top notes were still in relatively good condition when this set was made, and the basically dark timbre of her voice is well suited to the unhappy Amelia. What is missing from Callas' performance is an ultimate sense of warmth. She offers an aristocratic heroine (and this is certainly fitting), but one who touches the intellect rather than the soul of the listener. Riccardo is sung here by Giuseppe di Stefano. The tenor's lyric voice is basically well suited to the role, but his sloppy musicianship mars his work from time to time. Tito Gobbi is a fascinating Renato from the dramatic point of view, offering an intelligent and powerful characterization. His voice loses quality on top, but both "Dalla vita che t'arride" and "Eri tu" are splendidly sung. Fedora Barbieri provides a gutsy if slightly unsteady Ulrica, while Eugenia Ratti portrays a pallid Oscar. She fails to do justice to either the personality or music of this most interesting operatic "transvestite". The Scala comprimarii perform knowledgeably, while Antonio Votto conducts in a somewhat rigid, uninteresting manner.

ROSSINI:
IL BARBIERE DI SIVIGLIA

Berganza, Ausensi, Benelli, Ghiaurov, Corena, Varviso cond.
Rossini di Napoli Orchestra and Chorus
3 discs
London OSA 1381*
UK: Decca SET285-7

Callas, Gobbi, Alva, Ollendorff, Zaccaria, Galliera cond.
Philharmonia Orchestra and Chorus
3 discs
Angel S-3559*
UK: Columbia SMS1002

de los Angeles, Alva Bruscantini, Wallace, Cava, Gui cond.
Royal Philharmonic Orchestra and Glyndebourne Chorus
3 discs
Angel S-3628*
UK: HMV SLS904

Peters, Valletti, Merrill, Corena, Tozzi, Leinsdorf cond.
Metropolitan Opera Orchestra and Chorus
4 discs
RCA LSC 6143
UK: Victrola VICS6102 (3 discs)

Simionato, Infantino, Taddei, Previtali cond.
RAI Orchestra and Chorus
3 discs
Everest/Cetra S-413/3

Simionato, Bastianini, Misciano, Siepi, Corena, Erede cond.
Orchestra and Chorus of Maggio Musicale Fiorentino
3 discs
Richmond RS63011 (Mono)

Berganza, Alva, Prey, Dara, Montarsolo, Abbado cond.
London Symphony Orchestra and Ambrosian Opera Chorus
3 discs
DGG 270904

There is ample opportunity for choosing from among the recordings of this favorite *opera buffa*. Whether one favors a soprano or mezzo for the heroine, or a slapstick or elegant treatment of the humor, one or the other of the available sets should meet one's tastes.

For the most smoothly sung BARBIERE, the listener might choose the budget priced Richmond reissue of London-Decca's 1955 vintage BARBIERE. In the title role, the late Ettore Bastianini is heard as a dashing, virile, and velvet-toned Figaro. Furthermore, his musical excellence is backed up by a flair for comedy, making Bastianini a Barber who offers a matchless combination of voice and wit. The Rosina, Giulietta Simionato, succeeds in establishing the heroine as a girl of great charm and piquant manner. The mezzo scales down her large voice and suggests the character's youth admirably. An outstanding singer of heavier music, Simionato quite under-standably is at a disadvantage in certain coloratura passages which emerge as a triumph of the will over nature. This is especially true in the case of "Una voce poco fa." The mezzo appears more at home in Rosina's music lesson.

Cesare Siepi sings Don Basilio's music with the same grace with which he performs Don Giovanni. As a result, the music teacher emerges as less of a caricature. His aria "La calunnia" has seldom sounded more impressive musically, with its tremendous humor coming not from heavy-handed distortion of text and note but naturally from the comic tension of the music.

Fernando Corena, in the first of his three recorded Bartolos, is the most manic member of the cast, blithely imitating Simionato in falsetto and adding any number of giggles, gasps, and squeaks to his role, all of which is, of course, fully in the traditional mode. Corena is hardly subtle, but his performance made me laugh out loud.

Heard as Count Almaviva is one Alvinio Misciano, an exceptionally light-voiced tenor who is not in the same league as his colleagues on this recording.

Alberto Erede conducts the Chorus and Orchestra of the Florence May Festival with grace, but his work lacks the requisite lightness needed to make the opera soar. Still, for pure *bel canto* singing from most of the principal artists and a delightful buffo performance from the Bartolo, this BARBIERE can't be surpassed.

London-Decca's stereo BARBIERE from the late 1960's is also very successful. The cast is headed by the Spanish baritone Manuel Ausensi who takes the role of Figaro. Ausensi owns a pleasant, medium-sized voice which he uses with considerable ability, although the picaresque qualities of the Barber don't evidently come to him naturally. In the "Largo et factotum," the baritone feels compelled to add several extra peals of laughter, as if this means were the only way of establishing that Figaro is a bit of a joker.

The Rosina is Teresa Berganza, a jewel of a coloratura mezzo, as everyone who has heard her even once must know. Every inch as charming as Simionato, Berganza is even more adept at negotiating the various tricks found in Rosina's music, and her relatively small voice adds a further dimension of grace to her work.

Nicolai Ghiaurov combines musical excellence with a heavier voice than Siepi's, giving Basilio something more of the forbidding air that one likes to associate with the part. Like Siepi, the Russian bass does not descend to cheap tricks in order to make the character more amusing but suggests the music teacher's various manias through the music alone.

Fernando Corena, perhaps taking his cues from Ghiaurov,

has toned his Bartolo down a few degrees from his earlier recordings, playing more at comic dignity than at excessive foolishness yet achieving his usual droll results.

Ugo Benelli is a gracefully lyrical Almaviva with a handsome, vibrant voice.

The Orchestra e Coro Rossini di Napoli is ebulliently conducted by Silvio Varviso, making this BARBIERE an eminently satisfying performance. Angel-HMV also features two BARBIERE sets in its catalogue, the older of which featuring Tito Gobbi, Maria Callas, and Luigi Alva, is a most interesting approach to the opera. For this recording, much of the traditional high-pressure slapstick business has been dropped in favour of a martini-dry and subtle conception of the opera. In the title role, Gobbi is suave and commanding. The baritone is in fine voice and has little trouble with the music, all the while creating a human and likeable protagonist. Soprano Callas opts for the mezzo version of her role and concentrates on the cool-headed, genteel aspects of Rosina's character, in a sense working at showing Rosina as the future Countess of *The Marriage of Figaro*. In her 1971 New York master classes, Callas stated that in "Una voce poco fa," Rosina should not overwhelm the listener with a "firework display" but should rather sing Rossini's music as written and rely on the text and score for full effect. Practising this sermon, Callas' recorded Rosina emerges as a well-bred young girl who hides a good bit of wilfulness under her nice manners. Musically, the Callas technique and sense of style is as secure as ever, but the voice exhibits its all too familiar tendency to become colorless yet strident in the upper register.

Luigi Alva's Almaviva is elegantly phrased and sung with a more than adequate if less than ravishingly beautiful tenor, but, even though his voice is not truly brilliant, Alva is an intelligent artist and a most welcome member of this ensemble.

Fritz Ollendorf may have a more beautiful voice than Corena, but he could well benefit from some of the latter's comic elan as Ollendorf's Bartolo is dull in comparison to Corena's. As Don Basilio, Nicola Zaccaria can muster neither the appropriate vocal weight nor a sense of character. The Philharmonia Orchestra is led with taste by Alceo Galliera.

The RCA set dates from 1959 and is one of a mere handful of survivors of that company's agreement with the Metropolitan Opera to make recordings of Met productions. Not only is this a more than acceptable performance in its own right, the RCA-Met BARBIERE is a valuable aural souvenir of a "typical" Metropolitan presentation of the opera in the 1950's and early 60's.

In the title role, Robert Merrill exudes high spirits, and his voice, here captured in its prime, seldom has sounded fresher or more attractive. No match for Bastianini in terms of sensual richness or personality, Merrill is, however, a likeable and musical Figaro.

Roberta Peters is a healthy example of the light voiced, "chirpy" coloratura soprana Rosina to which audiences had grown accustomed since the days of Lily Pons and Galli-Curci. (The original, mezzo version came to the forefront again in the mid 1950's and 60's in the hands of such artists as Simionato, Horne, and Berganza, not to mention sopranos Callas and de los Angeles who preferred the lower line in this role.) Miss Peters, always a technically accomplished musician and an appealing performer, uses her voice with skill and works successfully towards making her character believable and sympathetic. In 1959, Miss Peters' voice was smoothly produced and uniformly pleasant, and her pert handling of her music results in a more than competent Rosina, albeit one that falls below the standards set by her competition on other recordings.

Cesare Valetti is probably the best Count Almaviva on records. With his handsome voice, stylish musicianship, and (particularly in the Act Two Finale and the "Pace e Gioia" nonsense in Act Three) elegant handling of the comedy, he surpasses his counterparts on the other recordings.

Giorgio Tozzi's voice lacks the velvety smoothness of Siepi's as well as the incisiveness of Ghiaurov's. Still, Tozzi creates a vividly nasty, old Don Basilio, and his sense of operatic fun makes him a worthy partner for the Bartolo of Fernando Corena.

The Orchestra and Chorus of the Metropolitan Opera perform capably under the steady and buoyant baton of Erich Leinsdorf, making for a lively, musical performance of the opera.

BELLINI:
BEATRICE DI TENDA

Sutherland, Veasey, Pavarotti, Opthof, Bonynge cond.
London Symphony Orchestra and Ambrosian Opera Chorus
3 discs
London OSA 1384*
UK: Decca SET320-2

Bellini's penultimate opera, BEATRICE DI TENDA, was written in between NORMA and I PURITANI but has never achieved anything like the popular and critical admiration showered upon either of those operas. The performances given by Joan Sutherland and friends in various opera houses and concert halls and preserved thanks to London-Decca reveal that BEATRICE is a work of consummate beauty. It lacks the pathos and grandeur of NORMA and the over-whelming melodiousness of PURITANI, but still possess some very enjoyable material. Its complicated, gloomy plot need not trouble us in evaluating the performance, especially since the singers and conductor do not seem to be terribly concerned with this drama of marital discord, treachery, and patient suffering.

London-Decca summoned some of the finest bel canto singers of the mid-1960's and, as a result, put together a performance of vocal distinction.

Joan Sutherland, as the sinned-against Duchess Beatrice, is in brilliant technical form. The heroine is of the type that the

Australian soprano sings best. Gentle and unhappy, Beatrice does not demand the type of histrionic adroitness that has eluded Joan Sutherland, and thus the diva's performance is effective and, in its way, moving. Orombello, Beatrice's unfortunate lover (he spends much of the opera being tortured offstage), is sung by the then very young Pavarotti who displays a true understanding of this type of singing and a seamless lyric tenor voice with which to carry out his intentions. Josephine Veasy sings Agnese, "the other woman" in the opera, with a well-schooled and pleasant sounding mezzo soprano, complementing Sutherland's own achievements in this recording. Cornelius Opthof is a slightly grainy sounding Fillipo. He does not match the work of his colleagues. Richard Bonynge conducts The London Symphony Orchestra with sensitivity, but his fondness for slow tempi prevents the admittedly phlegmatic drama from ever igniting. Still, as there is no other recording of BEATRICE DI TENDA in the planning stages at this writing, one ought to be grateful for this largely successful recording.

PUCCINI: LA BOHEME

Tebaldi, d'Angelo, Bergonzi, Bastianini, Siepi, Corena, Serafin cond.
Orchestra and Chorus of L'Accademia di Santa Cecilia
2 discs
London OSA 1208*
UK: Decca SXL2170-1

Freni, Adani, Gedda, Sereni, Mazzoli, Schippers cond.
Rome Opera Orchestra and Chorus
2 discs
Angel S-3643*
UK: HMV SLS907

Moffo, Costa, Tucker, Merrill, Leinsdorf cond.
Rome Opera Orchestra and Chorus
2 discs
RCA LSC-6095*

Carteri, Tagliavini, Santini cond.
RAI Orchestra and Chorus
2 discs
Everest/Cetra S-402/2*

Albanese, McKnight, Peerce, Valentino, Moscona, Baccaloni,
Toscanini cond.
NBC Symphony Orchestra and Chorus
2 discs
Victrola VICS-6019

Tebaldi, Gueden, Prandelli, Corena, Erede cond.
Orchestra and Chorus of L'Accademia di Santa Cecilia
2 discs
Richmond RS62001* (Mono)

de los Angeles, Amara, Bjoerling, Merrill, Tozzi, Corena, Beecham
cond.
RCA Orchestra and Chorus
2 discs
Seraphim IB 6000
UK: Seraphim ALPI 409-10 (Mono)

Albanese, Menotti, Gigli, Poli, Berretoni cond.
La Scala Orchestra and Chorus
2 discs
Seraphim IB 6027 (Mono)

Callas, Moffo, di Stefano, Panerai, Zaccaria, Votto cond.
La Scala Orchestra and Chorus
2 discs
Angel 3560 B/L*
UK: HMV 33CX1464-5

LA BOHEME has fared extremely well on disc. London-Decca's 1960 recording of the opera probably qualifies as the most lavishly cast. Carlo Bergonzi and Renata Tebaldi are paired as Mimi and Rodolfo, and their sweet, full voices blend with one another. Mimi has always been a most congenial role for Mme. Tebaldi and although the stiffness of the competition on other recordings prevents one from choosing her performance as "absolutely the best" of all Mimi's, one would certainly be hard-put to find fault with either her singing or her characterization. Bergonzi is perhaps the most idiomatic Rodolfo on records, edging out his chief competition by being more tasteful than Gigli and a shade more powerful than

Bjoerling. Few could dispute the claim that Bergonzi has the most beautiful tenor voice to have come from Italy since World War Two.

Gianna D'Angelo contributes a soubrettish Musetta but one whose occasional wanderings from pitch comprise the set's chief flaw (although many will count Serafin's slow and saccharine tempi on the debit side as well).

Ettore Bastianini is the set's rich voiced Marcello, Cesare Siepi is its mellow Colline. Chief among the supporting artists is Fernando Corena in the double assignment of Alcindoro and Benoit, tasks that he fulfills with aplomb.

Seraphim's first BOHEME is a monaural version from the 1950's led by the late Sir Thomas Beecham. In a written preface to the recording, the conductor tells of a meeting between himself and Puccini in which the composer confided to the maestro that he preferred BOHEME to be slowly paced. Dedicating his interpretation to Puccini's wishes, Beecham indeed leads the longest BOHEME on records, one which takes nearly fifteen minutes longer than Toscanini's 1946 recording. Although Beecham's tempi cloy even more than Serafin's, casting an uncalled for angelic, sugary glow over the opera, the set is redeemed by some very lovely singing. Bjoerling's Rodolfo is one of the Swedish tenor's finest recorded achievements, sung with great warmth and a voice that Caruso would have envied. Victoria de los Angeles is a tasteful and somewhat reserved Mimi who suggests the character's goodness at the expense of her charm. As Mirella Freni and Licia Albanese demonstrate elsewhere on records, Mimi need not be played as a sexless angel. She is a lively young woman who wholeheartedly embraces Bohemian life. She is not a brazen hussy, but no one would be likely to confuse Mimi with a nun or a saint. Furthermore, de los Angeles' top notes were already shrill and pinched when this set was recorded. Lucine Amara, in one of her infrequent recordings, is an attractively youthful Musetta, ably matched by the Marcello of Robert Merrill. Giorgio Tozzi is an imposing Colline, and John Reardon is an adequate Schaunard. As with the London-Decca set, on this recording the roles of Benoit and Alcindoro are taken by Fernando Corena. The pick-up chorus and orchestra are reasonably good, obedient as they are to Beecham's unflaggingly anemic pacing.

Seraphim's "other" BOHEME is a reissue of a 1938 La Scala performance made "historic" through the presence of Gigli and the very young Licia Albanese as the two lovers. Gigli's gorgeous voice makes up for his generally obtuse musicianship and rather narcissistic tendencies as a performer. In particular the "Racconto" is glowingly sung. Albanese offers here a delicately feminine Mimi. She was already by this time a fine Puccini stylist. The supporting cast is undistinguished, but the performance still has validity and a relevance for today's listeners. The conducting by Umberto Berretoni is quite incisive, making for a highly listenable performance. This BOHEME was recorded in the very early days of complete opera recordings and there are a number of ad libs evidently designed to show the listening audience what is happening "onstage." The most amusing example is Gigli's spoken "Mimi, c'e la cuffietta" ("Mimi, here is your bonnet") in the fourth act.

Angel-HMV lists two BOHEMES in its catalogue. The older, mono version is a 1957 Scala production with Callas, Moffo, di Stefano, Paneai, and Zaccaria—Votto, conducting.

Maria Callas was never particularly identified in the public ear with the role of Mimi. Apart from the usual Callas wobble above the staff, the soprano sings the role well, paying full attention to projection of the text. She is rather more successful in capturing Mimi's sadder moments. Like de los Angeles, she fails to see Mimi as a vivacious and charming girl in the first two acts.

Anna Moffo, beginning her international career, offers quite the loveliest Musetta I have ever heard, while Rolando Panerai is a sonorous and commanding Marcello, and Nicola Zaccaria an unimpressive Colline.

In the role of Rodolfo, Giuseppe di Stefano forces his beautiful voice rather cruelly and indulges in some provincial mannerisms, including a scream at the end of the opera that belongs in a Neapolitan back ally brawl. In fairness, di Stefano's performance is not bad, but, given his splendid voice, it surely could have been better were he a finer musician and a more tasteful singer. Antonio Votto leads a well paced and generally enjoyable performance that fails to achieve greatness in spite of the many fine elements that make it up.

The newer Angel version dates from 1965 and features Mirella Freni and Nicolai Gedda in the leading roles. Both artists have beautiful voices and are excellent operatic actors, making them a most attractive and convincing pair of lovers. Mariella Adani and Mario Sereni are strongly cast as Musetta and Marcello, while Thomas Schippers leads the Rome Opera forces with intelligence and strength.

No discussion of BOHEME recordings could omit mention of the Toscanini performance dating from the February 1946 broadcast by NBC radio that eventually was released as a recording. This recorded broadcast commemorated the fiftieth anniversary of the premiere of LA BOHEME. Despite wretched sound, this recording emerges as one of the most exciting performances of any opera ever recorded. Arturo Toscanini was nearing eighty when he led this performance, but his tempi are as youthful as they must have been when he conducted the opera's world premiere in 1896. Licia Albanese sings still another delightful Mimi, and Jan Peerce, though lacking the vocal talent of Bjoerling or Bergonzi, manages to provide a well sung, if slightly hammy Rodolfo. Anne McKnight and Frank Valentino are adequate as Musetta and Marcello. The highly competent supporting cast features Salvatore Baccaloni as Benoit and Alcindoro. The NBC Symphony Orchestra and Chorus perform with gusto, inspired by the genius who directed them. Other BOHEMES feature more beautiful vocalism (as Toscanini grew older, he favored casts that would follow his every command at the expense of choosing the most gifted singers available) and finer recorded sound, but the brilliance of Toscanini's conception as well as historical ties to the work, make it a cornerstone of any record collection.

One more mono BOHEME is worthy of attention. Richmond's reissue of the London-Decca monaural set made in the early 1950's features radiant singing from Tebaldi as Mimi. As good as many of her later recordings are, the soprano has never surpassed the sweetness and fullness of line and the easy vocal production that marked her first recordings. Giancinto Prandelli, a lyric tenor of great talent who never really "clicked" in opera houses outside of Italy (he did sing a few performances at the Met during the 1950's) is a fine Rodolfo. His was a handsome, clear voice that lacked only the ultimate intensity of projection that might have made him into a major operatic personality. In this recording, he emerges as a personable, ardent Rodolfo in a performance that stands up fairly well against much of the competition.

Hilde Gueden offers a delightful Musetta, singing with clarity and creating a subtly attractive and unshrewish grisette, as well. The other soloists are at the very least solid, with an added surprise in that Fernando Corena is heard not as Benoit or Alcindoro, but in the baritone role of Schaunard. Alberto Erede's conducting of the Orchestra and Chorus of L'Accademia di Santa Cecilia stresses the sentimentality of the opera in a pleasant if unremarkable reading of the score.

MUSSORGSKY:
BORIS GODUNOV

Christoff, Lear, Uzunov, Cluytens cond.
Paris Opera Orchestra and Sofia Opera Chorus
4 discs
Angel S-3633*
UK: HMV903

Ghiaurov, Talvela, Spiess, Vishnevskaya, von Karajan cond.
Vienna Philharmonic and Vienna State and Sofia Opera Choruses
4 discs
London OSA1439
UK: Decca SET514-7

Changlovich, Bugarinovich, Andrashevich, Baranovich cond.
Orchestra and Chorus of Belgrade National Opera
3 discs
Richmond RS63020 (Mono)

Moussorgsky's BORIS GODUNOV, which exists in at least four versions, has been recorded several times in what is generally known as the Rimsky-Korsakov edition, with any number of individual changes, cuts and/or restorations made at the discretion of the individual conductors.

The two major recordings that have survived into 1972 were made twelve years apart; Angel-HMV's in 1958 and London-Decca's in 1970. Given the vast demands made by this score, it is no wonder that neither recording is perfect. The Angel set lacks strong supporting singers but is made unforgettable by the triple triumph enjoyed by bass Boris Christoff. The

London set offers a more musically polished performance but with a loss of dramatic vividness.

My personal preference leans toward the Angel BORIS, all the while acknowledging the many excellences of the London album.

The fact that Boris Christoff undertook not only the title role but also Pimen and Varlaam for Angel is due perhaps as much to the shortage of first rate Russian-singing basses as to the remarkable artistry and versatility of the Bulgarian singer. Although Chaliapin often sang Boris and Varlaam in performances, the task of singing Boris and Pimen at the same performance is physically impossible, as the two appear face to face during Boris' death scene. On records, of course, the seemingly unachievable can be made to happen, and Christoff carries out the three assignments with musical distinction and practically no loss of dramatic credibility.

Since a fine Boris alone can dominate a performance of this opera, imagine the influence that a singer of the stature of Boris Christoff in the three leading bass parts will exert! Christoff is a high strung, larger than life Czar who is as frightening in his rage as he is pathetic in his guilty anguish. The rough hewn, distinctive Christoff sound has never been wrought with so little strain or such subtle coloration than here. In contrast to the paranoid Boris, Christoff's Pimen is almost unearthly in his quiet dignity. Lightening and reducing the size of his voice in Pimen's scenes, Christoff makes his noble instrument seem as graceful and physically beautiful as, for example, that of a *basso cantante*. In what surely is the most challenging scene for Christoff, the confrontation between Boris and Pimen, an unknowing listener would swear that two different men were singing, at least until the final moments of Pimen's description of the miracle when Christoff allows his voice to regain its accustomed magnitude and thus causing the loss of some character differentation.

As for his contribution in the lesser role of Varlaam, Christoff sings this part with a zest and bumptuousness that he seldom is allowed to display in other roles. The monk's song in the Inn is carried off with a leering dash that practically leaps up off the disc itself!

With the exception of the sumptuous voice of Evelyn Lear in the role of Marina, the supporting singers in this BORIS GODUNOV fall below Christoff's standard. Miss Lear, in what was her first major recorded performance, shows sufficient temperament and ample voice to make the rather wooden Princess into a major figure in this opera. The composer, it should be remembered, added the "Polish Act" in a revised version of BORIS in order to provide a female role for the formula-conscious audiences of his day. Marina's music, while pleasant and suitably voluptuous, does not begin to equal the writing for Boris, and dramatically her scenes don't even do much to make the false Dmitri a more intense or three dimensional figure. However, as sung by Miss Lear, Marina injects a bit of sensual contrast to the Czar's torments and the suffering of the Russian people, the dual themes of the opera.

As Dmitri/Grigory, Dimitir Ouzunov projects a steadier, larger voice than he did during his appearances with the Metropolitan Opera in the years between 1959 and 1965. The tenor's singing is not polished, and the top notes lack sheen, but his work has undeniable power. Ouzunov seems determined to be involved with his character, making the monk turned pretender into a figure of clarion strength if little subtlety.

After giving credit to Anton Diakov for his sleazily elegant Rangoni, and noting that John Lanigan is an oily, sycophantic Shuisky, and Kiril Dulguernov is a suitably pathetic Simpleton, the rest of the supporting cast earns little praise, with some singers evidently chosen only because they could sing in Russian. The Choirs of the National Opera of Sofia was flown to Paris for this recording and there paired with the Paris Conservatoire Orchestra under Andre Cluytens' baton. The Chorus sings with dramatic strength although it lacks the musical stature of, for example, the La Scala chorus. The orchestra is adequate but not brilliant. Cluytens conducts with a sense of restraint and misses a fair percentage of the score's raw power. Interestingly, Cluytens is most at home in the eclectically romantic third act. The recording places Boris' death at the end of the score, thus focusing perhaps more attention on the Czar's plight than on that of the people. Unrevolutionary as this decision may be, ending the opera with Boris' death allows for a more dramatic finish and avoids the anti-climax of the ironic and bitter scene with the Simpleton which gains in effect from occurring before Godunov's racking death.

London-Decca's BORIS is led by Herbert von Karajan who is lucky in being able to use the Vienna Philharmonic and the Vienna State Opera Chorus combined with the Sofia chorus used in the Angel recording. Working towards bringing the most orchestral detail possible from the score, the conductor achieves some worthy moments, particularly in the Dmitri-Marina duet. Unfortunately, he also opts for needlessly slow tempi that prevent the drama from soaring to any kind of height.

As Boris, Nicolai Ghiaurov displays his splendid, satiny voice. Lacking Christoff's, savage, almost primitive intensity, Ghiaurov makes the Czar more of an Italian courtier than a Russian tyrant. Although in the Clock Scene, Ghiaurov achieves a sense of horror that is transmitted to the listener, elsewhere he fails to equal Christoff's characterization. Where Christoff is tortured and agonized, Ghiaurov is merely noble and melancholy. Ghiaurov's death scene is particularly lacking in bite.

Pimen is sung here by Martti Talvela, whose inky voice ought to someday make him an eloquent Boris. At present, however, Talvela shows little inclination to act, letting his sense of legato and the rich sound he produces carry the day.

Ludovic Spiess is an impressive Dmitri. He sings with ease and warmth. His big, spinto voice is less tight sounding here than in his "live" performances at the Metropolitan. Galina Vishnevskaya, in the role of Marina, is in disappointing voice, sounding shrill, tremulous, and more petulant than alluring, but Zoltan Kéléman is an especially fine Rangoni. Anton

Diakov, Angel's Rangoni, is heard here as Varlaam, a role
that he sings acceptably but one in which he is outclassed by
Christoff. Again, the smaller roles are sung with little distinction although Aleksei Maslennikov, who undertakes both
Shuiski and the Simpleton, is an excellent lyric tenor. He is,
however, an insensitive actor and thus makes little dramatic
impression in either part. As this recording includes the rarely
performed St. Basil scene in Act 4, Maslennikov has to sing
both his roles opposite one another in the important
encounter between Boris, the Simpleton, and Shuiski. In this
case, unfortunately, a listener unfamiliar with the scene would
think that only two characters faced each other. Karajan, by
using the St. Basil scene, places Boris' Death before the
"Revolution" episode, offering an alternative to Cluytens'
ending of the opera. This recording, incidentally, preserves
one of the most acclaimed of von Karajan's Salzburg Festival
productions, although to my way of thinking, the flaws in
both Karajan's concept and his singers' performances at
times threaten to outweigh the not inconsiderable virtues of
the recording.

BIZET: CARMEN

Bumbry, Freni, Vickers, Paskalis, Frubeck de Burgos cond.
Orchestra and Chorus of Paris Opera
(1875 Opera-Comique version)
3 discs
Angel S-37-67*
UK: HMV SLS952

Price, Freni, Corelli, Merrill, von Karajan cond.
Vienna Philharmonic and State Opera Chorus
3 discs
RCA LSC6199*
UK: RCA SER5600

Callas, Guiot, Gedda, Massard, Pretre cond.
Paris Opera Orchestra and Chorus
3 discs
Angel S-3650X*
UK: HMV SLS913

Resnik, Sutherland, del Monaco, Krause, Schippers cond.
Suisse Romande Orchestra
3 discs
London OSA 1368*
UK: Decca SET256-8

de los Angeles, Micheau, Gedda, Blanc, Beecham cond.
French National Radio Orchestra and Chorus
3 discs
Angel S-3613*
UK: HMV SLS755

Juyol, Micheau, De Luca, Wolff cond.
Orchestra and Chorus of the Opera-Comique
3 discs
Richmond RS63006* (Mono)

Horne, Maliponte, McCracken, Krause, Gramm, Bernstein cond.
Metropolitan Opera Orchestra and the Manhattan Opera Chorus
3 discs
Deutsche Grammophon 2709043
UK: Same

Taken as a whole, the most striking feature of recorded
CARMEN performances is the fact that three of the most distinctive Carmens (Price, Callas, and de los Angeles) have
never sung the role onstage. In each case, one senses the loss
to the opera-going public.

RCA's 1964 release features Leontyne Price in the title
role. The soprano is in fine voice in this recording, and thus the
Gypsy's music is performed with ease and considerable
abandon. Price uses her chest tone abundantly, proving that
the role is not beyond the means of a spinto soprano. A
particularly successful touch is her interpolation of a high A
in the second verse of the Seguidilla at precisely the moment
when Don José capitulates to Carmen's wiles.

Price makes a real attempt at acting her role. She sounds
brazenly angry when quarrelling with Don José in Act Two,
and the card scene is similarly intense. The soprano's French
diction is clearer than that of her colleague's in the major roles
in this set, and the only criticisms that may legitimately be
applied to her performance concern some eccentrically mannered vocal attacks and a too heavy reliance on register
breaks for "dramatic" effect.

Franco Corelli in the role of Don José abuses his beautiful
voice by sliding into and out of far too many phrases, and his
insistence on belting out prolonged high notes does grate after
a short while. Furthermore, his French would never earn him
an A at Berlitz. Still, the tenor provides his quota of thrilling

moments, including a blazingly sung "Flower Song" and a stirring final confrontation with Carmen.

Mirella Freni's Micaela is modestly and sweetly sung, although she shares Corelli's linguistic difficulties. Her vowels, while not quite Italian, are certainly not French.

Robert Merrill is an excellent Escamillo. The baritone is in fine voice, and his jaunty, almost arrogant manners are fully appropriate to the role. The supporting roles are sung with high competence by a team of singers loaned by the Paris Opera. The Vienna State Opera Chorus, Vienna Philharmonic, and Vienna Boys Choir are each impressive, but Herbert von Karajan is the wrong conductor for this opera. His heavy tempi and graceless, deliberate approach to the music create an atmosphere less of Spain than of Valhalla. This is the longest CARMEN on discs.

Several months after the RCA CARMEN with Price was issued, Angel-HMV produced a CARMEN that starred Maria Callas, whose gypsy, as Price's, is a studio creation. As with the vast majority of her performances, the Callas Carmen is excellently interpreted by the soprano. She provides allure in the first act, sexiness in the second, and strength and bravado in the final two acts. These qualities, to which may be added the soprano's clear if slightly cautious French, amount to an extraordinary account of the role. Her only dramatic miscalculation occurs in the second act when she becomes bitchy with José to an extent that approaches the ludicrous. The performance, however, is marred by Callas' almost pathetic vocal estate in 1964. The sound is at best lean, with virtually every high note coming out in tatters. Still, one cannot fail to be moved by Callas' gypsy, even though one will wish after hearing it she had not waited so long to attempt the part.

Nicolai Gedda, the Don José of this Angel-HMV album, is a tenor whose musical and linguistic gifts are of the same mettle as Callas'. He is an intelligent, sensitive José who lacks only the ultimate vocal thrust provided by del Monaco on the London-Decca set discussed below or by Corelli on the

RCA set. Corelli, however, lacks Gedda's musicianship while del Monaco lacks his vocal ease.

Janine Guiot is a small, rather white of voice Micaela who is nowhere near to being a match for this Carmen, but Robert Massard is a stylish Escamillo. The supporting artists are from the Paris Opera and sing excellently. Georges Pretre's conducting of the orchestra and chorus of that theatre is exemplary. The performance is quite effective, although the music is performed elsewhere on records with more vocal beauty.

Angel-HMV has released two other CARMEN sets in addition to the Callas version. Of these, the most interesting is the 1970 album that, for a change, stars a CARMEN who has sung the role on stage, television, and film—Grace Bumbry. The album also stars Jon Vickers as José, Mirella Freni as Micaela, and Kostas Paskalis as Escamillo. While all the other CARMEN recordings employ the Guiraud recitatives that replaced the spoken dialogue of the original opera-comique production of CARMEN, this recording's producers have opted for a return to the 1875 edition of the score. Thus, the by-now familiar Guiraud music is missing, replaced by abridged dialogue that serves to carry the plot forward between musical numbers. It is a refreshing change to hear the opera in its pristine state, but the producers, fearing the discordance that might have occurred due to the difference in the international cast's spoken French, have substituted the dissonance caused by using a cast of actors to perform the dialogue of the four major characters. As the supporting cast is French, these artists speak, as well as sing, for themselves.

A further merit of this set, though, is the inclusion of some music usually cut from performances, including the entire duel scene for Escamillo and José and a short piece for Morales in the opening scene for which the music has evidently been gathering dust in a Paris archive for nearly a century.

The performance itself is one of the best on records. Bumbry is a sensuous Carmen, fully capable of assuming each of the gypsy's many faces. Now sultry, now kittenish, ulti-

mately angry and defiant, Bumbry comes close to perfection.
A mezzo noted for her flights into the soprano repertoire,
Bumbry sounds at home on top of the staff as well as
beneath it and follows Leontyne Price's "tradition" of insert-
ing a high A into the Seguidilla.

Jon Vickers' fine voice and highly strung characterization
make him a good choice for the role of José. Occasionally, he
pushes his voice dangerously, but in general he has the
resources to carry the role off successfully. Although the
voice is less smooth and mellow than Corelli's, Vickers' impassioned delivery of the "Flower Song" makes it almost
unbearingly moving, furthermore the tenor is magnificently
strong in his battles with the heroine in the third and fourth
acts.

Mirella Freni once again provides an ingratiating Micaela,
and her French diction is considerably better than that on her
first recording of the role. Completing a quartet of distinguished principal artists, Kostas Paskalis is a velvety voiced,
rather aristocratic Toreador. The ubiquitous (in CARMEN
recordings, anyway) forces of the Paris Opera are led by Rafael
Fruhbeck de Burgos who offers elastic, sensitive support to
his cast of singers. His sunny tempi move the opera swiftly.

Angel-HMV's third CARMEN set dates from the late 1950's
and offers a polished yet eccentric and not entirely satisfying
performance conducted by Sir Thomas Beecham. The accent
on this recording is on elegance and grace, which are two
elements that in themselves don't add up to a riveting
CARMEN. Much of the blame must fall on the lovely
shoulders of the Carmen, Victoria de los Angeles. Her phrasing is noble and her singing is consistently lovely, however,
her Carmen hardly seems capable of so vulgar an action as
taunting a co-worker in a factory, let alone stabbing her.
Nicolai Gedda, in this his first recording of the role, is a
striking José, while Janine Micheau is an unduly pallid
Micaela. Ernest Blanc contributes a rousingly sung Escamillo,
and the French National Radio orchestra plays well for
Beecham whose benign approach to the opera washes out the

vivid primary colors of the score.

With RCA's wonderful old (1951) mono CARMEN that featured Rise Stevens, Jan Peerce, Licia Albanese and Robert Merrill, each in optimum voice under the strong direction of the late Fritz Reiner no longer available, the next major CARMEN recording to consider is the 1962 London-Decca version with Regina Resnik in the title role. Few singers today are endowed with Resnik's ability to get inside a character and project it vocally and dramatically. Never noted for limpid beauty of voice, Resnik in '62 was, however, equal to virtually all the musical demands of Bizet's gypsy (a few high notes are prophetically wobbly). The American singer also offers a knowing characterization that emphasizes Carmen's wickedness.

Mario del Monaco was not in good voice during the taping sessions for this recording, and while his José is intensely acted, it is also sung with coarse, often badly strained production and little attention to the role's subtleties. Joan Sutherland makes a mish-mash of Micaela's words and little sense of her character, but sounds pretty if somewhat nasal. Tom Krause is a sensual, dark voiced Escamillo who sounds provocatively younger than his Carmen. The Orchestra and Chorus of the Suisse Romande are sympathetically led by Thomas Schippers.

Budget-minded shoppers have a choice between a complete if ancient Carmen on Richmond with an undistinguished cast led by Suzanne Juyol and Libero de Luca or highlights on Seraphim sung in German by Christa Ludwig (an enticing Carmen), Rudolph Schock, and Hermann Prey. These excerpts are taken from a complete recording released in Europe by Odeon. It's surprising and disappointing that no more recent French language CARMEN is available at a low price, but one can hope that the old RCA set will return on the Victrola label.

Deutsche Grammophon's 1973 release of CARMEN documents the production, conceived by the late Goran Gentele, that opened the regime of General Manager Schuyler Chapin at the Metropolitan Opera in September of 1972.

Under the musical direction of Leonard Bernstein, the production (and recording) delved even further into the original score than did the 1970 Angel recording and arrived at a thrillingly powerful version of the opera that utilizes much of the original spoken dialogue as well as much previously unknown new music. Although the recording omits the scene for Morales in the first act, it reinstates the men's choral passages directly before Carmen's first entrance, includes the complete scene in Act Two in which Carmen mocks José, and opens a large standard cut in the fight scene between José and Escamillo. Most strikingly, it also utilizes different and vastly more effective music from the Toreador Song at the end of Act Four. This sharpens the tension and, as Carmen is now stabbed as soon as José sings "Eh bien, damnée," one no longer must contend with the dubious spectacle of José's stalking, cornering and killing the gypsy in a sort of dumbshow of the offstage bullfight.

Aside from the significance of the making of the Metropolitan's first professional recording in nearly fifteen years, this is under any circumstances a worthwhile set to own. The performance is dominated as much by Bernstein as by Marilyn Horne who performs the title role. The conductor opts for slower, broader tempi than one usually encounters, and these may well annoy on first hearing. On repeated playings however, it must be conceded that Bernstein creates a marvelously dramatic background on which the drama unfolds. Furthermore, the Met's orchestra has rarely played so well.

Marilyn Horne's Carmen is earthy as opposed to glamorous, and in many instances more jolly than wicked. This approach is not going to please every listener, nor is it necessarily definitive. However, it works brilliantly for Horne, who lavishes her uniformly smooth voice on the part, using her chest register tastefully and, in general, with effectiveness. Horne's "Habañera" is one of the best I have ever heard, and her final moments with Don José are electrifying. James

McCracken brings raw vocal power to Carmen's unhappy lover, yet in this instance the tenor is capable of moments of tenderness, as in the "Flower Song." Tom Krause is an attractive Escamillo, and Adriana Maliponte is a charming Micaela. Of the supporting artists, Donald Gramm's Zuniga and Andrea Velis' Remendado stand out as being particularly fine. The French diction is acceptable, and the chorus (not the Met's but a "pick-up" group assembled when a contractual dispute prevented the Metropolitan Chorus from participating) is quite adequate. In sum, this is an important and in most ways a highly satisfying performance.

MASCAGNI: CAVALLERIA RUSTICANA

Simionato, del Monaco, MacNeil, Serafin cond.
Orchestra and Chorus of L'Accademia di Santa Cecilia
2 discs
London OSA 1228*
with PAGLIACCI OSA 1330
UK: Ace of Diamonds GOS588-90 (with PAGLIACCI)

Suliotis, del Monaco, Gobbi, Varviso cond.
Rome Opera Orchestra and Chorus
2 discs
London OSA1266*
UK: Decca SET343-4

de los Angeles, Corelli, Sereni, Santini cond.
Rome Opera Orchestra and Chorus
2 discs
Angel S-3642
UK: HMV SLS902

Cossotto, Bergonzi, Guelfi, von Karajan cond.
La Scala Orchestra and Chorus
3 discs (Available only with PAGLIACCI)
Deutsche Grammophon 2709020*
UK: Same as above

Simionato, Braschi, Basile cond.
RAI Orchestra and Chorus
2 discs
Everest/Cetra S-410-2

Milanov, Bjoerling, Merrill, Cellini cond.
RCA Orchestra and Robert Shaw Chorale
2 discs
Victrola VICS6044
UK: Same as above

Callas, di Stefano, Panerai, Serafin cond.
La Scala Orchestra and Chorus
2 discs
Angel 3509
UK: HMV 33CX1183

Rasa, Gigli, Mascagni cond.
La Scala Orchestra and Chorus
2 discs
Seraphim IB-6008

Nicolai, del Monaco, Protti, Ghione cond.
Milan Orchestra and Chorus
2 discs
Richmond RS62008

As is the case with its "sister" opera, PAGLIACCI, Mascagni's
one act masterpiece has been recorded on numerous occasions, often though not always being issued as half of a twin
bill package with Leoncavallo's popular work. The list of
singers who have chosen to record CAVALLERIA is long and
distinguished, and there are several really fine recordings
available.

Deutsche Grammophon's version, available only with PAG-
LIACCI, features a Scala cast led by Fiorenza Cossotto, Carlo
Bergonzi, and Giangiacomo Guelfi, under the baton of Herbert
von Karajan. Cossotto, a mezzo-soprano Santuzza, is in
satiny voice, spinning out phrase after phrase effortlessly, and
at an intensity level that approximates molten lava. Resisting
the temptation to be a sulky, tempestuous heroine, Cossotto

finds an element of proud if scorned beauty in the unlucky girl's make-up and creates from this a moving and vocally sumptuous heroine. Bergonzi is an uncommonly well bred Turiddu, finding little difficulty with the music. No one—not even Bjoerling—surpasses Bergonzi's Brindisi. Hearing the tenor and Cossotto in the central duet is to experience two of the finest Italian voices to which one is likely to be exposed in this or any day. Not one to indulge in superfluous sobbing or grunting, Bergonzi still manages to seem preoccupied and guilt-ridden in the "Addio alla mamma." Guelfi is an imposing Alfio, full of strength and apparently all too capable of doing Turiddu in. Lola is pleasantly sung by Adriana Martino, and Mamma Lucia is capably impersonated by Maria Gracia Allegri. The Scale orchestra is able in Karajan's sensitive hands, to make Mascagni's music seem more substantial than perhaps it really is. The chorus also proves itself once more to be peerless. Karajan's tendency toward slow tempi, however, rob the opera of some of its natural vitality. In terms of the singing, though, this performance is difficult to match.

Angel's mono CAVALLERIA, also a La Scala effort, is hard to locate these days but is worth searching for as Maria Callas has perhaps never turned in as fine a recorded performance as her Santuzza of this album. Her voice is evenly produced, and the wobble is virtually absent. The burning intensity of Callas' Santuzza is enough to melt the disc on which it is preserved. Favoring a more vituperative characterization than Cossotto's, Callas here is a very real and desperate woman, sounding in the "Voi lo sapete" as if on the brink of an abyss. Callas is fortunate in her Turiddu, Giuseppe di Stefano, whose beautiful voice (as yet unharmed by poor management of his talents) and easy, natural involvement in his role make him an exciting match for La Divina. Rolando Panerai belts out Alfio's music with great verve. Anna Maria Canali's Lola and Ebe Ticozzi's Mamma Lucia are most helpful. The opera is superbly paced by Tullio Serafin.

London-Decca offers two relatively recent "CAV's." One, dating from the early 1960's, offers the impassioned and vocally heavenly Santuzza of Giulietta Simionato, who is especially fine in the "Regina Coeli" ensemble. Mario del Monaco indulges his weakness for bleating at times in this recording. However, there is undeniable power and even brilliance in much of his singing. Cornell MacNeil is this set's rough and ready Alfio. Conducting the Orchestra and Chorus of L'Accademia di Santa Cecilia, Tullio Serafin once again brings off a brisk and lively performance.

London's most recent CAVALLERIA surrounds a decidedly tired Mario del Monaco with the Santuzza of Elena Suliotis and the Alfio of Tito Gobbi. To say that this is the Greek soprano's best recording since *Nabucco* in 1966 is to comment sadly on the decay that has so prematurely ravaged her voice. Since Santuzza lies fairly low and calls for the sort of abandoned, emotional singing that appears to be Suliotis' forte. She carries the role off without too many bad moments, but the voice sounds quite strident and unattractive on top. Del Monaco falls far below his usual standard here, and the performance is chiefly redeemed by Gobbi's skilfully wrought Alfio. Silvio Varviso leads the Orchestra di Roma in a rather cold performance that, while never actually bad, fails to shed any new light on this familiar opera.

The best of the several budget priced CAVALLERIA's is the Victrola set made in the early 1950's as a companion to the PAGLIACCI that has since been reissued by Seraphim.

Zinka Milanov was closely linked with Santuzza in the mind of the United States public. Her stately, rather "generalized prima donna" approach to the role lacks the electricity of Callas' or Cossotto's work, but few could fail to be swayed by the power and beauty of her singing. Although Milanov occasionally is bothered by a vibrato in this recording (her "Voi lo sapete" will not go down as the best piece the soprano preserved in the studio), much of her work here is quite distinguished, the bitter duet with Alfio being a case in point.

Jussi Bjoerling, who also recorded the role in a 1958 RCA set with Tebaldi and Bastianini that has been unaccountably and regrettably withdrawn, is here a smooth voiced, dandified Turiddu. Never the most dynamic of actors, Bjoerling instead concentrates on making Turiddu irresistibly attractive through means of his burnished singing—a line of attack that proves to be most successful. There has never, with the possible exception of Caruso's recordings, been a "Siciliana" that surpasses Bjoerling's. Robert Merrill is the album's dashing Alfio, and two old friends from the Metropolitan Opera's recent past, Margaret Roggero and Thelma Votipka, are heard to excellent advantage as Lola and Mamma Lucia respectively. The RCA orchestra responds well to Renato Cellini's rather languid beat, and the Robert Shaw chorale does nicely with Mascagni's choral passages.

The composer's own interpretation of CAVALLERIA RUSTICANA, stemming from a World War Two vintage Scala recording made two years before his death, has been re-issued on the Seraphim label. Mascagni, at least in his declining years, seemed unwilling to conduct the work with the animation that it requires to succeed as a *verismo* drama. Indeed, the novelty of an opera being conducted on disc by its composer seems the only distinction that can be conferred on Mascagni's slack, dull reading of the score. Beniamino Gigli's Turiddu is the keystone of this recording, finding the tenor in generous voice. In this role, Gigli's primitive acting is not terribly inappropriate, Turiddu being, after all, a swaggering small town lout. The Santuzza, an obscure soprano named Lina Bruna Rasa, is unsteady, uninteresting, and generally unequal to the role's demands. Gino Bechi is a vigorous, solid Alfio, and a surprise in casting finds the very young Giulietta Simionato in the role of Mamma Lucia which she sings with characteristic intelligence. (The dubious virtue of hindsight would lead one to say that her performance boded well for Simionato's later successes.) This set, however, is mainly notable for "historical" value and does not compete very well with more recent CAVALLERIAs.

OFFENBACH:
LES CONTES D'HOFFMANN

de los Angeles, Schwarzkopf, d'Angelo, Gedda, London, Blanc,
Cluytens cond.
Orchestra de la Societé des concerts
3 discs
Angel S-3667*
UK: HMV SLS918

Sutherland, Domingo, Bacquier, Tourangeau, Plishka, Bonynge
cond.
Orchestra and Chorus of the Suisse Romande
3 discs
London OSA 13106
UK: Decca (Catalogue number unavailable)

Sills, Burrows, Treigle, Marsee, Castel, Rudel cond.
London Symphony Orchestra
3 discs
Audio Treasury ATS 20014

The HMV-Angel recording of Offenbach's lone opera, having
held the position of sole recorded version of the work since
1965, has recently been joined by two new recordings of
HOFFMANN. The first set, distinguished in its own right and
boasting the finest singer of the title role (Nicolai Gedda) now
faces stiff competition from both the London-Decca and ABC-
HMV albums.

Less evenly cast than the newer HOFFMANN discs, the
Angel set features much singing of high order and, wonder of

wonders, there is even a good deal of French style present, thanks to the use of a French supporting cast, a French chorus and orchestra, and the late Andre Cluytens' conducting. Nicolai Gedda's poet is well known to American and European audiences, and let it thus suffice to say that the Swedish tenor's elegantly phrased and ripely sung performance is well preserved here. Gedda's voice is seamlessly produced, while dramatically he embodies Hoffmann's ardent and highly strung personality. There being no one lady who wished to sing all three of the poet's romantic interests back in 1965, the producers divided the parts among Gianna D'Angelo (Olympia), Elisabeth Schwarzkopf (Giulietta), and Victoria de los Angeles (Antonia). Somewhat less understandably, the four villains were distributed among three artists, of whom two, George London (Coppelius and Dr. Miracle) and Ernest Blanc (Dappertutto) could well have performed the entire quartet alone.

As Olympia, Gianna D'Angelo is appropriately light and chirpy, singing with poise if not with warmth or abundant sheen. Victoria de los Angeles' Antonia is also a blessing, except when she is straining for high notes. In the main, though, de los Angeles is a gently effective heroine. Elisabeth Schwarzkopf, then nearing the end of her days as a great singer, is quite cruelly miscast as the courtesan Giulietta, a role whose tessitura is best suited to mezzo-sopranos. Schwarzkopf lacks here the necessary power in the lower register to do full justice to the music. Furthermore, her tone is not sufficiently sensuous to suggest the character of the frankly voluptuous Giulietta. It cannot be said that Mme. Schwarzkopf really sings poorly on this recording, but her voice does sound tired and strained.

Turning to the villains, George London, like Schwarzkopf, had already begun his vocal decline when this set was made. Heard as Coppelius and Dr. Miracle, London's voice is distressingly rough, particularly in Act One. The third act sessions found the bass-baritone in better form, and his characterization of Dr. Miracle is spine-chilling. Nicolai Ghiuselev is

acceptable in the relatively ungrateful role of Lindorf. Unquestionably the best of the three artists who share these
roles is Ernest Blanc in the role of Dappertutto. His dark and
supple voice and jauntily nasty characterization scintillate
like the diamond to which Dappertutto addresses his aria.
This recording follows the Parisian practice of assigning the
role of Nicklaus to a baritone, Jean-Christophe Benoit in this
instance, instead of to a mezzo. Benoit carries off the assignment well enough. He doesn't sing the "Barcarolle" though. In
that, the mezzo line normally sung by Nicklaus is handled
capably by Jeanine Collard. A further eccentricity of this set is
the use of both "standard" versions of the Epilogue (Bonynge
employs still a third, as will be discussed below), providing
the listener with a rather confusing, "two-headed" finale. The
chorus is exceptionally good, and the orchestra's work can
not be carped at either. Cluytens conducts with élan and a
sense of the score's theatricality that adds to the lustre of the
performance.

In the Fall of 1972, London-Decca's HOFFMANN appeared,
followed less than a month later by the ABC version.

London's album features Placido Domingo in the title role.
Joan Sutherland sings the four ladies (in Bonynge's reconstruc-
tion of Offenbach's original score, Stella sings, too) and
Gabriel Bacquier takes on the four villains. In a lengthy preface to the libretto, Bonynge enumerates the many liberties
taken with Offenbach's music since the opera's first production. Bonynge has painstakingly cut out music added by other
composers (much by Ernest Guiraud who completed the
orchestration after the composer's death several months
prior to the premiere) and what emerges is an opera-comique
with much spoken dialogue.

All this would make the recording of more value to students
of Offenbach's work than to the "average" listener were the
performance not as buoyantly and musically performed. In
truth, this is one of the most satisfying of the Sutherland-
Bonynge recordings, although Domingo disappoints just a
little in the title role. The tenor is in perfectly fine voice, but he

is becoming increasingly devoted to sobs and "belted" high notes à la Corelli (or perhaps Ethel Merman), furthermore, there is a general sloppiness of attack and a coarsening of musical sensitivities that has begun to creep into his work. This Hoffmann evidently prefers beer to wine, while one might say the opposite of Gedda's hero.

Miss Sutherland has a field day as Olympia, adding her incomparable trills and breath-taking ornamentation to the "Doll's Song," which she sings without her customary scooping or well known mannerisms. There is also an adroit sense of humor at work here, and Miss Sutherland thus confirms what LA FILLE DU REGIMENT suggests as far as her gifts for comedy are concerned. Giulietta, though, is a strange character for this soprano who rarely has to attempt sexiness in her work. Although diction is a problem, Sutherland summons a robust tone for the lower phrases and acts the role with sophistication and real charm. One of Bonynge's changes in the score is to drop the ensemble from this act, moving it to the Epilogue. This, even if it was Offenbach's original intention, works less well than the conventional version, as the "Venetian Scene" is thus robbed of its musical climax, while the already anti-climactic Epilogue is prolonged. A more successful restoration is the original ending of this act in which Giulietta accidentally takes poison and is chided by Dappertutto's "Giulietta, maladroite." Sutherland's Antonia is still another of her sad, sweetly and wanly suffering ladies. This role is warmly sung if somewhat unaffecting dramatically.

Gabriel Bacquier is a perfect choice for the "Evil Genius" characters, bringing a witty, sardonic personality to bear on the roles, in addition to singing them most handsomely. Bacquier aims more to amuse than frighten in the first three roles, allowing only Dr. Miracle to sound really menacing. This is all to the better, since the other characters are hardly as demonic as Méphistophèles, for example.

The supporting artists include the Metropolitan's enormously talented Paul Plishka as Crespel, and Huguette Tourangeau as a rather dark voiced Nicklaus. Bonynge's direction of the Orchestre de la Suisse Romande is quite commendable. Favoring brisk tempi, the conductor injects a verve and a drive into the entire opera, giving the work a cohesion and sense of excitement that are most exhilarating.

The second new HOFFMANN, led by Julius Rudel, uses the standard edition of the score, Guiraud additions (and subtractions) and all. Stuart Burrows, one of the finest young tenors to be found these days, sings Hoffmann with a grace and delicacy matched only by Gedda, but he plays Hoffmann more callowly than he might. This Hoffmann is more naive than passionately foolish. Aside from this dramatic inhibition, Burrows' singing is admirable in every respect.

Beverly Sills, like Joan Sutherland, is a superb Olympia. The American soprano uses rather less ornamentation in Olympia's song than does Sutherland, but Sills is a particularly mischievous and extroverted puppet, making her singing utterly delightful. Giulietta taxes Sills somewhat more than do the other two roles, but Antonia is another triumph for the soprano. One can hardly imagine Antonia's little song more movingly performed, and Sills rises to the challenges hurled at her by the trio with Dr. Miracle and the Mother's voice.

Norman Treigle provides "star quality" for the four villains, singing with abandon and marvellously full tone. He rather overplays Dr. Miracle, suggesting an almost Miltonian Demon, but this larger-than-life quality is hardly to be resented.

Susann Marsee is a sweet-voiced Nicklaus, and Nico Castel provides some jolly moments in the four brief comic tenor roles. Rudel's conducting is marked by taste and ebullience.

Thus, belatedly, LES CONTES D'HOFFMANN has come into its own on discs, with three enjoyable, distinguished performances from which to choose.

MOZART: COSI FAN TUTTE

Schwarzkopf, Ludwig, Steffek, Kraus, Taddei, Berry, Böhm cond.
Philharmonia Orchestra
4 discs
Angel S3631*
UK: HMV SLS901

della Casa, Ludwig, Loose, Dermota, Kunz, Schoeffler, Böhm cond.
Vienna Philharmonic
4 discs
Richmond 63508
UK: Ace of Diamonds GOS543-5

Price, Troyanos, Raskin, Shirley, Milnes, Flagello, Leinsdorf cond.
Philharmonic Orchestra
4 discs
RCA LSC 6416
UK: RCA SER575-8

Casapietra, Burmeister, Geszty, Schreier, Leib, Adam, Sultner cond.
Orchestra of German State Opera, Berlin and Staatskappelle, Berlin
4 discs
Eurodisc 80 408 XR

M. Price, Minton, Popp, Alva, Evans, Sotin, Klemperer cond.
New Philharmonia Orchestra
4 discs
HMV C 191-02 249/52 (UK only)

This most brittle and cynical of the Mozart-Da Ponte collaborations is currently served by five meritorious albums (two of which are not on US labels), one of which is a budget reissue. Of these, perhaps the most well-balanced and handsomely sung version is that found on Angel-HMV.

The two sisters are sung by Elisabeth Schwarzkopf as Fiordiligi and Christa Ludwig as Dorabella. Schwarzkopf, here rather late in her operatic career, sings diligently and with careful musicianship. Her delicate and witty shading of both the music and the text creates a charmingly synthetic character. One cannot, of course, take Fiordiligi's protestations of love, grief, or remorse terribly seriously, and Schwarzkopf understands this, too, and spares us a heavy-handed, languid heroine. Vocally, her top notes are occasionally hard-pressed, but pitch is accurate, and most of the soprano's work in this recording is of high quality. "Come scoglio," with its inhuman range, presents difficulties to any soprano who attempts it. Schwarzkopf manages both the highest and lowest lying passages with skill, and even a sense of ease.

Ludwig, recording Dorabella here for the second time, is luscious in the part. Properly flighty, even sensuous, Ludwig provides an apt musical and dramatic foil to her "sister," Schwarzkopf. Furthermore, Ludwig's voice is equal to every one of the considerable demands of the role, and she succeeds in lightening her voice appropriately.

Hanni Steffek is a worthy Despina, handling both the music and the comedy of the character with aplomb and resorting to less hamming and distortion in the scenes where Despina pretends to be a doctor and a notary than one usually has to contend with.

Alfredo Kraus' Ferrando is cleanly sung and hilariously acted, while Giuseppe Taddei is an equally successful, if rather intentionally gruffer Guglielmo. As Don Alfonso, Walter Berry both injects the requisite cynicism and mischievousness into the role and delivers a smoothly sung account of the music.

These soloists are brought together and led through the intricacies of the score by Karl Böhm. His delicate touch is apparent everywhere, supporting the artists in their solos, guiding them merrily through the many concerted passages, and eliciting excellent work from London's Philharmonia throughout.

RCA's COSI dates from 1968 and is built around the Fiordiligi of Leontyne Price, who had previously sung the role in an English-language Metropolitan Opera revival in 1965. Singing in Italian for the recording, Price is in exciting voice except when forced into her lower register which is too husky. Price's characterization is less interesting than Schwarzkopf's, but her lovely singing is reason enough to justify her performing the role. Price lacks the ultimate agility of voice for the role, but there are many happy moments in her performance, particularly in the "Farewell Trio" and the charming duet with Dorabella, "O guarda sorella" which opens Act One, Scene Two.

With the exception of Sherrill Milnes' smooth and manly Guglielmo, none of the other soloists match their counterparts on the Angel set. George Shirley is a dry voiced, rather uninteresting Ferrando, failing to make a positive impression in his arias or when singing with his colleagues. Tatiana Troyanos' Dorabella is also rather dry of tone and indifferently projected, and Ezio Flagello lacks humor—a crucial ingredient—as Don Alfonso. Judith Raskin is also rather weak as Despina.

Under Erich Leinsdorf's baton, the performance proceeds with predictability rather than sparkle. If this recording is hardly a total failure, neither is it pre-eminently successful.

The Richmond COSI, also led by Karl Böhm, would be worth full price—as a budget item, it is practically irresistible. Lisa della Casa, always a distinguished Mozart singer, is an elegant Fiordiligi, suffering in comparison to Schwarzkopf only in the "Come scoglio," where she is hopelessly adrift in the lower sections. Elsewhere, the Swiss soprano is buoyant and charming, and her musical instincts are of the highest order.

Christa Ludwig sings Dorabella here also. Her voice is appropriately youthful, and her manner is as saucy as a proper

Neapolitan lady's could dare be. Emmy Loose is a sprightly Despina, while the trio of gentlemen could hardly be bettered: Anton Dermota as a forthright yet musically gracious Ferrando, Erich Kunz as a deft and likeable Guglielmo, and Paul Schoeffler as a dark-voiced, elegant, and very human Don Alfonso. Dr. Böhm conducts the Vienna Philharmonic with firmness and clarity, shaping, once more, a vibrant and brisk performance.

VERDI: DON CARLO

Tebaldi, Bumbry, Bergonzi, Fischer-Dieskau, Ghiaurov, Talvela, Solti cond.
Covent Garden Orchestra and Chorus (5 act version)
4 discs
London OSA 1432*
UK: Decca SET305-8

Caballé, Verrett, Domingo, Milnes, Raimondi, Foiani, Giulini cond.
Covent Garden Orchesta and Chorus (5 act version)
4 discs
Angel S-3774
UK: HMV SLS956

Stella, Cossotto, Labò, Bastianini, Christoff, Santini cond.
La Scala Orchestra and Chorus (5 act version)
4 discs
Deutsche Grammophon 271103

Caniglia, Stignani, Picchi, Silveri, Rossi-Lemeni, Neri, Previtali cond.
RAI Orchestra and Chorus (4 act version)
4 discs
Everest/Cetra S-414-4

Stella, Nicolai, Fillipeschi, Gobbi, Christoff, Neri, Santini cond.
Rome Opera Orchestra and Chorus (4 act version)
3 discs
Serephim IC 6004 (Mono)

There are three separate versions of DON CARLO: The original, five act French edition which has not been recorded, and the four and five act Italian versions which are well represented in the catalogues of the various companies. A generation ago, the four act DON CARLO was a relatively unfamiliar visitor to the stages of most opera companies in the USA and Britain. Today, the opera is almost a staple at the Met and Covent Garden and is frequently performed elsewhere. Some adventurous companies have even performed the five act version, reinstating the short but tremendously important Fontainbleu Scene (Act I) that adds a new dimension to the score and increased dramatic meaning to the libretto.

The DGG recording of the five act version (the first on records) with Antonietta Stella, Flaviano Labò, and Boris Christoff has become difficult to obtain, leaving two competing editions of the complete opera and two budget-priced, mono recordings of the more common and less satisfactory four act abridgement. Each of these sets is worth owning, although the two mono albums are far less attractive than the newer, uncut, stereo recordings.

Angel's 1971 release is a very fine performance, although the London set, made roughly six years earlier, offers keen competition. These are "all star" recordings in which each of DON CARLO's six leading roles is filled by a major voice. It is uniquely difficult to state which of the two performances is the better, and personal taste will have to dictate the listener's choice.

Certainly Angel's cast includes several of the most beautiful and well-schooled voices of the present day. Placido Domingo offers a flowing line and a rich tenor voice in the title role, all the while sounding appropriately youthful as the Prince. Domingo is particularly fine in the Fontainbleu aria and the subsequent love duet with Elizabeth. Montserrat Caballé delivers herself of the tragic queen's music with great taste and a velvety soprano that, except for a slight sense of strain at the very top when she is singing *forte,* is ingratiatingly smooth. At her best in tender passages, Caballé excels in the

"Non piangere mia compagna," and the duet with Carlo that precedes this aria. All that is lacking is dramatic bite in such places as the encounter with Philip in Act Four, Scene One, and, in general, a more forthright approach to the character would be appreciated. However, in terms of musicianship and vocal splendor, Cabellé's Elizabeth is ideal.

Sherrill Milnes, in spite of some pitch problems, is a resonant and sympathetic Rodrigo (Marquis of Posa) and Shirley Verrett is an Eboli of decidedly regal temperament and lovely voice. Miss Verrett's voice is smaller in size than those of other contemporary Ebolis, but her singing is secure and powerful. Verrett meets every vocal demand made on her in both of the Princess's showpieces and offers exciting high B flats in the "O don fatale."

Although some may find the voice of Ruggero Raimondi somewhat youthful in timbre for King Philip, there can be little exception taken to his uncommonly beautiful singing. This Italian bass is sinister in his encounter with Posa, pathetic yet dignified in "Ella giammai m'amò" and desperate in the scene with the Grand Inquisitor, creating a compelling human being out of the Spanish king's moody and none too sympathetic character. The Inquisitor is sung by the young Giovanni Foiani who comes close to equalling Raimondi's darkly arresting sound, although failing to suggest the character's terrible vindicativeness or great age. Simon Estes is a sonorous Friar. The Orchestra and Chorus of The Royal Opera, Covent Garden are led with unfailing power and a deep sense of drama by Carlo Maria Giulini who keeps the long, difficult score flowing and offers brilliant leadership to his fine cast. London's cast is headed by Carlo Bergonzi who surpasses even Domingo (if only by a hair) in terms of musicianship and Verdian style. This Don Carlo is a sensitively sung Prince. Bergonzi resists any urge to be unduly flamboyant, controlling his lovely tenor with unfailing taste and singing with great skill. His Queen is sung by Renata Tebaldi. In this role, Tebaldi must bow to Cabellé in terms of ease of vocal production, but the Italian soprano imparts a sense of anguish to the role that Caballé is unable to equal, especially in the duet with Carlo in Act Two, Scene Two. Grace Bumbry is a powerful Eboli distinguished by her clear and even command of the music. Nicolai Ghiaurov is a rather vicious King Philip who makes little attempt to soften the brutal aspects of the character. His huge, dark voice is well suited to his conception of the role. Martti Talvela's enormous voice and superb enunciation of the text make him a fearsome Grand Inquisitor. Dietrich Fischer-Dieskau is a warm, if somewhat small-voiced Rodrigo. His hesitant Italian diction, though, stands out from the more even pronunciation of his colleagues. Georg Solti conducts the Royal Opera Orchestra and Chorus with a firm hand that moves the music forward with rather less passion than does Giulini, but with a sweep and grandeur of its own. The recorded sound on both these albums is excellent, with London's being a shade warmer than Angel's.

The four Act DON CARLO has been given at the Metropolitan ever since Rudolph's Bing's debut as General Manager in 1950. Less adventurous or budget minded listeners may be content with either of the mono recordings of this edition.

Seraphim offers the only three disc set which, although benefiting from the exciting singing and acting of Boris Christoff as Philip and Tito Gobbi as Rodrigo, suffers from the completely inadequate Don Carlo of Mario Fillipeschi. Antonietta Stella is in this instance a competent if hardly outstanding Elizabeth, and Elena Nicolai's rather harsh sounding Eboli is no match for Shirley Verrett or Grace Bumbry. Giulio Neri and Plinio Clabassi complete the cast as the Inquisitor and Friar, respectively and sing with some distinction. The Rome Opera Orchestra is conducted with little energy by Gabriele Santini.

The Cetra set, well over twenty years old, is notable chiefly for the singing of Maria Caniglia and Ebe Stignani in the roles of Elizabeth and Eboli. Each lady had a huge voice used with great dramatic force. Others in the competent Cetra cast are Nicola Rossi Lemeni as Philip, Mirto Picchi as a weak Don Carlo, and Paulo Silveri as a dignified and handsomely sung Rodrigo. Giulio Neri is also the Inquisitor of this album. The

RAI Orchestra and Chorus is conducted by Fernando Prevatali who fails to be inspired by this great score.

In the early 1960's, Deutsche Grammophon issued the first five act DON CARLO in a Scala recording in which Antonietta Stella and Boris Christoff duplicated their 1951 assignments as the King and Queen of Spain. They were joined this time by Flaviano Labò as Carlo, Ettore Bastianini as Rodrigo, Fiorenza Cossotto as Eboli, and Ivo Vinco as the Inquisitor, with Gabriele Santini, also familiar from the previously mentioned Rome Opera set in the pit.

Labò, a diminutive but conscientious tenor, finds Carlo's music rather heavy going. His tone is often breathy and strained, and he never equals Bergonzi's or Domingo's handling of the role. Dramatically, Labò at least tries to breathe some sense of action into his work, but the general impression he makes in the role is that of a good but second-rate singer.

The years between Stella's two Elisbettas brought the Italian soprano more dramatic authority but robbed her voice of its fresh sound. Here the voice sounds harsh on top and rather tough in the lower register. Bastianini's coarse, grainy tone as Rodrigo foreshadowed, of course, his untimely death from throat cancer in 1967. Lest this recording be written off as totally inferior to the two later complete sets, Boris Christoff's intense King Philip should be noted, as should the emergence of Fiorenza Cossotto as a major artist. This set was among the first to employ the mezzo in a leading role (Eboli). Cossotto's "Veil Song" is supply produced, her denunciation of Carlo in the Garden Scene is a marvel of Verdian malevolence, and her "O don fatale," if still a trifle lightweight in comparison to what Cossotto does with the piece today, stands up very well to those sung by Verrett and Bumbry. Cossotto's real-life husband, Ivo Vinco, makes for a satisfactory Grand Inquisitor, but Santini's pedestrian conducting further weakens the set.

MOZART: DON GIOVANNI

Danco, della Casa, Gueden, Siepi, Corena, Dermota, Berry, Boehme,
Krips cond.
Vienna Philharmonic and State Opera Chorus
4 discs
London OSA 1401*
UK: Ace of Diamonds GOS604-6 (3 discs)

Nilsson, Arroyo, Grist, Fischer-Dieskau, Flagello, Talvela, Böhm
cond.
Prague Opera Orchestra and Chorus
4 discs
Deutsche Grammophon 2711006
UK: Same

Sutherland, Schwarzkopf, Sciutti, Waechter, Taddei, Alva, Giulini
cond.
Philharmonia Orchestra and Chorus
4 discs
Angel S-3605*
UK: Columbia SMS1009

Sutherland, Lorengar, Horne, Bacquier, Gramm, Krenn, Bonynge
cond.
English Chamber Orchestra and Ambrosian Opera Chorus
4 discs
London OSA 1434*
UK: Decca SET412-5

Watson, Ludwig, Freni, Ghiaurov, Berry, Gedda, Klemperer cond.
New Philharmonia Orchestra
4 discs
Angel S-3700
UK: HMV SLS923

Curtis-Verna, Taddei, Valletti, Rudolf cond.
RAI Orchestra and Chorus
3 discs
Everest/Cetra S-403/3

In general, the recording companies have done well by this Mozart opera, and today there are five major sets to be found. At the risk of being atavistic, my personal favorite is the oldest of these. It was made in the 1950's by London-Decca. This ablum stars Cesare Siepi in his most famous role, as Don Giovanni. His voice and artistry are preserved here in full bloom—his "Champagne Aria" has the requisite brilliance, his "Deh vieni, alla finestra" the perfect allure, and "La ci darem la mano" is as suavely and delightfully seductive as any recent account of the duet. Not one to hog the spotlight, Siepi blends his talents evenly with his colleagues here, never dominating the action at another artist's expense.

Fernando Corena, long Siepi's onstage companion as Leporello in many major opera houses, brings his incisive conception of the role to this recorded production and is the perfect complement to Siepi's Don. Singing with more voice than, alas, he can muster now, Corena adds a dimension of devilish wit to the proceedings, and a wonderful combination of roguishness and cowardice that never degenerates into vocal slapstick.

Anton Dermota offers a strong Don Ottavio, if not a truly brilliant one. There is some sense of strain in "Il mio tesoro," but Dermota's polished voice and commanding sense of style are assets of the recording. Walter Berry, who has since become a fine Leporello, exhibits an excellent sense of character here in the role of Masetto and sings effectively, too. Kurt

Boehme's rough bass voice makes for a properly flinty Commendatore.

Turning to the three ladies, a better matched trio has seldom been assembled for a DON GIOVANNI recording. Although she sings Donna Anna here, Susanne Danco might have been better cast in the more lyrical role of Donna Elvira. Her voice is quite lovely, and her technique is sure, but Donna Anna's formidable tessitura at times presses Danco's strength to its limits. Not quite heroic, Danco's conception of Donna Anna is refreshingly human and even feminine, and at her best, the French soprano is quite persuasive in the role.

Lisa della Casa has been a great Donna Elvira, and here her cool, limpid voice and authoritative impersonation work well. Both of her arias come off with distinction, and throughout the performance, della Casa is a mainstay of vocal skill. Hilde Gueden is a precious Zerlina with a slightly darker voice than one often hears in the part, making this peasant lass appear to be a little wiser than one might expect, but appealing all the same. Joseph Krips inspired conducting of the redoubtable Vienna Philharmonic and the Vienna Opera Chorus add a glowing background on which Mozart's *dramma giacosa* is played out on this recording.

EMI presents two rival DON GIOVANNI sets, available, as usual, in the USA on the Angel label and in the UK on the HMV label.

The older set finds Eberhard Wachter to be a dashing, light-voiced Don Juan who, if lacking Siepi's total identification with the character, is courtly, witty, and musically skilful. Giuseppe Taddei, a baritone Leporello, is similarly adept at providing a vivid character and sings with aplomb, creating a funny if less clever servant than Corena's. Luigi Alva is a youthful, accurate Don Ottavio who makes this difficult-to-enact gentleman seem even more bloodless than usual, while Gottlob Frick is an imposing Commendatore.

The leading ladies are a distinguished group. Joan Sutherland was on the threshold of world acclaim when she recorded this first of her two Donna Anna's. Her voice has seldom been more pleasant to the ear, and her diction in those days was A GREAT DEAL BETTER THAN IT IS TODAY!!! Her characterization is reserved, but far less mannered than many subsequent Sutherland performances. Elisabeth Schwarzkopf's Elvira is elegantly sung with delicate phrasing and full benefit of the soprano's many vocal resources. Graziella Sciutti's slightly nasal, light soprano is well enough suited to Zerlina, but she does less with the role than some of her competition. Piero Cappuccilli sings Masetto here with a sturdy, confident sound well suited to the character. The Philharmonia Orchestra and Chorus perform well under the ebullient baton of Carlo Maria Giulini who paces the opera brilliantly, offering consideration for the singers as well as an understanding of Mozart.

Good conducting is the element most conspicuously absent from EMI's second DON GIOVANNI, led by the eminent, venerable Otto Klemperer, whose ponderous tempi and refusal to allow any sparkle at all to permeate the stony conception of the opera that he has chosen to commit to discs comes close to ruining the performance. It is a pity, for his singers are among the strongest found on DON GIOVANNI recordings. Nicolai Ghiaurov, in the title role, is a dark voiced and very attractive seducer whose reading of the lines is as amusing as his singing is ingratiating. As does Siepi, Ghiaurov offers a courtly yet passionate rake. One rarely hears so large and impressive a voice so agilely controlled. A particular delight is Ghiaurov's "La ci darem la mano." The success of this duet is not only due to Mr. Ghiaurov's own singing but also to the winning efforts of Mirella Freni, a completely successful Zerlina whose eagerness to succumb to the Don is matched only by her tender, if sporadic, concern for her Masetto. Freni's voice has a healthy sensuous quality to it that enables her to transform each of the many operatic soubrettes that she portrays into real, living human beings, and her Zerlina is one of her best achievements.

I also admire Claire Watson's Donna Anna. Her voice hardens when she sings loudly, and some of the fioritura of

"Or sai chi l'onore" poses difficulties for her, but Watson's vengeful, neurotic conception is strong and comes across most interestingly. Christa Ludwig is a mezzo Elvira, and while she has no trouble at all with her music, her characterization is at times a little too forceful. Elvira is an *ensoi*, a victim, and when properly handled, a rather pathetic figure. If she comes on too strongly, she is apt to appear ridiculous—something that Ludwig never quite allows to happen, but still, this great artist might have been better cast as Donna Anna.

Walter Berry is an exceedingly musical, good natured Leporello who displays the proper agility for the "Catalogue" aria, as well as a dry irreverence for his master and the other characters. Franz Crass is quite good as the Commendatore—in fact, except for Paolo Montarsolo's weak Masetto, the entire cast is exemplary which makes Klemperer's abyssmally dull conducting even more of a shame.

London-Decca's second DON GIOVANNI focuses much attention on the Joan Sutherland—Richard Bonynge team who serve here as Donna Anna and conductor, respectively. Miss Sutherland suffers in this recording from muddy diction and occasional pitch problems, as well as sounding hollow of tone in the lower register. Bonynge's beat is generally weak, and while the finales are quickly paced, they lack drive and power. Bonynge has allowed, evidently even encouraged his singers to embellish their music, and Mozart seems to gain little from this practice. In fact, Mozart wrote the variations he desired in the repeats of his arias right into the score. Thus, when a singer embellishes those repeats, Mozart's own musical development is lost.

Gabriel Bacquier is the Don. A gifted singer and a sensitive artist, he is gentlemanly and musical but suggests little of the Don's sensuality. Don Giovanni does not need to be portrayed as a particularly youthful man, but a stronger, more dashing characterization than Bacquier's is necessary. Donald Gramm is an excellent Leporello, musically fleet and icily funny. Werner Krenn is a relatively unknown artist, but his supple, attractive Don Ottavio promises much for the future. In

"Dalla sua pace," the tenor indulges in some superfluous ornamentation, but in fairness, Krenn carries this off with ease. Pilar Lorengar sings Elvira with her accustomed charm. Moreover, her vibrato is held in check here and thus her voice is captured in top condition. Marilyn Horne, a mezzo Zerlina, sings with refinement, and her beautiful voice is used with charm and comic inventiveness. She is the most lively of the three women, as well befits her character, and her performance is in many ways the most enjoyable on the recording. Leonardo Monreale and Clifford Grant complete the cast as Masetto and the Commendatore respectively. Bonynge employs the English Chamber Orchestra in an effort to create a more intimate atmosphere for Mozart's score. Bonynge is a very gifted musical scholar who deserves much credit for his work in re-introducing bel canto works to today's public. Unfortunately, he seems unable to carry his often excellent ideas over into performances.

Deutsche Grammophon's DON GIOVANNI is marked by the powerful conducting of Karl Böhm who creates in the opening chord of the overture, an atmosphere of tension which remains throughout the opera. His Don Giovanni, Dietrich Fischer-Diskau, is a shade tight of voice but is more comfortable here than in some of his other excursions into Italian language works. Ezio Flagello offers a sound, rather bumptuous Leporello whose "Catalogue Aria" ranks with the best. Peter Schreier is heard to good advantage as Ottavio, and Alfredo Mariotti is a competent Masetto. Martti Talvela's tremendous voice would make him an imposing Stone Guest even without the use of an electronic echo chamber which the DGG producers elected in order to fortify the bass' second act appearances.

Birgit Nilsson offers a steely, powerfully sung account of Donna Anna's music. Her Amazonian soprano is not at its most comfortable state when the soprano is braving Anna's two arias' coloratura moments, but Nilsson is a furious and fearsome lady here—and no easy mark for poor Don Giovanni!

Martina Arroyo, herself a noted Donna Anna at the Metropolitan Opera, sings Donna Elvira with silken opulence if little of Nilsson's force of personality. As noted earlier, Elvira should not be a hellion, but some sense of character would be helpful. On purely musical terms, though, Arroyo's "Mi tradi" is quite well done.

Reri Grist is in superb voice as Zerlina, whom she endows with a youthful sweetness that never is allowed to cloy. Her voice is none too large, but here, at least, it is projected well, and Grist's clean diction, sense of fun, and musical excellence make her Zerlina one of the nicest attributes of a generally well sung and outstandingly conducted performance. The orchestra and chorus are none other than those of the Prague Opera. (Prague is the city where DON GIOVANNI had its premiere.) Under Dr. Böhm's direction, the musicians do themselves and Mozart proud.

DONIZETTI: DON PASQUALE

Sciutti, Oncina, Corena, Krause, Kertesz cond.
Vienna Opera Orchestra and Chorus
2 discs
London OSA 1260*
UK: Decca SET280-1

Noni, Valletti, Bruscantini, Rossi cond.
RAI Orchestra and Chorus
2 discs
Everest/Cetra S-404-2*

Although this *opera buffa* is indisputedly one of the most shining examples of its genre, as well as being an unfailing audience pleaser, DON PASQUALE has fared very poorly on discs. There are two complete recordings available, although one of them, the Cetra version with Sesto Bruscantini, Cesare Valetti, and Alda Noni, conducted by Mario Rossi is rather difficult to locate. Thus, for all practical purposes, London-Decca's 1965 recording has the field to itself.

With the exception of Fernando Corena, an inimitable Pasquale in the opera house and on records, this performance is second-rate. The supporting cast, which includes Juan Oncina as Ernesto, Tom Krause as Dr. Malatesta, and Graziella Sciutti as Norina is competent, but falls far below Corena's level of performance. In the hands of Corena, Don Pasquale is in turn irritating, foolish, pathetic, and lovable. Furthermore, in addition to being a skilled—indeed—an inspired comic actor, Corena is an excellent singer among whose finest gifts is his tremendous agility, enabling him to whip through the staccato blusterings of the old man in Act

Three in a fashion that is as technically amazing as it is hilarious to encounter. In 1965, Corena's tone was more rounded than it is today, and thus he does full justice to Pasquale's music as well as his comedy.

Corena's colleagues could profit from emulating the basso's ebullience. Graziella Sciutti is a well-schooled lyric soprano with a pleasant if smallish voice. However, her Norina is disappointingly kittenish. Her work is rather hesitant and one seldom gets the feeling that Sciutti is singing with full voice. In those scenes where Norina pretends to be shrewish, this quality is not sufficiently established. Much more can be done with Norina and it is a pity that this soprano hasn't discovered the means to flesh out the character, vocally as well as dramatically.

Juan Oncina is a light-voiced, pleasant-sounding, and attractive Ernesto, contributing the best vocalism found in the performance. Oncina lacks animation, though. Tom Krause comes closer to Corena's level of comic adroitness but sounds uncomfortable in Malatesta's more florid passages. Still, his duet with Pasquale is the comic highpoint of the set, even more so than the insane ensemble with which the second act concludes, as that number is tepidly performed by soprano and tenor.

The Vienna Opera Orchestra and Chorus (the latter is especially good) are conducted by Istvan Kertesz who perhaps must shoulder most of the blame for the tameness of the performance. His tempi are graceful but bland, and instead of sparkling like a good *spumante*, this DON PASQUALE all too often cloys like warm sauterne.

RICHARD STRAUSS: ELEKTRA

Nilsson, Collier, Resnik, Krause, Stolze, Solti cond.
Vienna Philharmonic and State Opera Chorus
2 discs
London OSA-1269*

Borkh, Schech, Madeira, Fischer-Dieskau, Uhl, Böhm cond.
Dresden Opera Orchestra and Chorus
2 discs
Deutsche Grammophon 2707011
UK: Same

Konetzni, Mödl, Ilitsch, Mitropolous
Orchestra and Chorus of the Maggio Musical Fiorentino
2 discs
Everest/Cetra S-459-2

London-Decca's ELEKTRA, released in 1967 with a cast headed by Birgit Nilsson, Regina Resnik, Marie Collier, and Tom Krause, with Georg Solti conducting the Vienna Philharmonic, comes as close to perfection as any record of any opera that I know of. Not only are the performances well matched for vocal quality, but there is exciting acting from each member of the cast, and Solti's conducting is firmly supportive, building from scene to scene until the unbearable tension explodes in the double murder of Klytaemnestra and Aegisth and in Elektra's dance unto death.

Mme. Nilsson's many excellences as an artist need little description at this point. Let it merely be said that the soprano

is in full control of her mammoth yet supple voice from beginning to end, and that she colors her singing spectacularly, suggesting the inky pits of Elektra's despair in the opening monologue, her cunning manipulation of both her mother and sister,
her joy at discovering that Orestes lives, and, of course, her
final, psychotic giddiness as her enemies are slaughtered.
Nilsson's vocal chords seem made of steel, for she never seems
to tire. No one, however, can justly claim that her voice is
metalically cool here. Rarely has the diva seemed more involved
in a character than in her Elektra.

Chrythosthemis, Elektra's sister and foil, is sung here by
the late Marie Collier. Collier was a spinto soprano with a
warm voice that when pressed took on a noticeable vibrato.
In this recording, Collier's singing is richly feminine and
definitely unheroic. Thus, this mild-tempered, vocally modest
Chrythosthemis is an excellent complement to Nilsson's super-
charged heroine.

Regina Resnik sings Klytaemnestra with the remnants,
intelligently deployed, of a voice that at its best was serviceable if not beautiful. High notes are tremulous and the register
breaks are quite distinctive. Resnik's strengths in recent
seasons have been found in her resourceful acting, and in this
recording she is completely convincing and surprisingly sympathetic as the bedraggled, moribund queen. Resnik's growled
lower notes and her tortured reading of the lines conjure up a
heady vision of the guilt-ridden, suffering Klytaemnestra. Her
death shrieks, while undeniably blood-curdling upon first
hearing, seem excessive after repeated hearings. Lower-
pitched gasps would have been equally effective.

Tom Krause is a youthful, vigorous Orest, a bit hard-pressed
for volume when singing with Nilsson but nonetheless attractive in the role. Gerhard Stolze is a raspy, dissipated Aegisth
whose brief scene with Elektra is blackly comic as performed
by the tenor and Nilsson. Featured among the serving-women
in the opening scene are such major voices as those of Felicia
Weathers and Yvonne Minton, while their Overseer is
Pauline Tinsley, the British soprano who gave Beverley Sills a

run for her money singing Queen Elizabeth to Sills' Maria Stuarda at the New York City Opera in 1972. The Vienna Philharmonic plays with accustomed power and clarity, shedding stark musical sunlight on Strauss and Von Hommansthal's recreation of Euripides drama.

DONIZETTI:
L'ELISIR D'AMORE

Freni, Gedda, Sereni, Capecchi, Molinari-Pradelli cond.
Rome Opera Orchestra and Chorus
2 discs
Angel S-3701

Sutherland, Pavarotti, Malas, Cossa, Bonynge cond.
English Chamber Orchestra and Ambrosian Opera Chorus
3 discs
London OSA 13101
UK: Decca SET503-5

Gueden, di Stefano, Corena, Molinari-Pradelli cond.
Orchestra and Chorus of the Maggio Musicale Fiorentino
3 discs
London OSA 1311*
UK: Ace of Diamonds GOS566-7

Carteri, Alva, Taddei, Panerai, Serafin cond.
La Scala Orchestra and Chorus
2 discs
Seraphim S-6001

Valletti, Bruscantini, Gavazzeni cond.
RAI Orchestra and Chorus
3 discs
Everest/Cetra S-415/3

This perenially admired comedy has been recorded at least five times, with three currently available performances being of special interest to the collector. These include the Angel-EMI, Seraphim, and new London-Decca recording. I would dearly love to include the older London edition with Hilde Gueden, Giuseppe di Stefano, and Fernando Corena, but this seems to have disappeared from most major record departments and stores.

Of the trio of remaining L'ELISIR sets, I like best the 1966 Angel-HMV recording which finds in Mirella Freni an Adina of high spirits and fine musicianship who projects the bubbling farce as well as she sings Adina's sprightly music. Miss Freni is joined by Nicolai Gedda who infuses his voice with an added degree of warmth which enables him to become a Nemorino of charm and, most surprisingly, dignity, although Gedda creates a likeably comic character for Adina's suitor. Gedda's "Una furtiva lagrima" is strongly sung and tops off a handsomely vocalized performance. Renato Capecchi is a knowledgeable and smooth Dr. Dulcamara, and Mario Sereni is a properly vain Belcore, furthermore, he is one who is able to sing the sergeant's music with finesse. Mariella Adani completes the small cast as Gianetta. Francesco Molinari-Pradelli leads the chorus and Orchestra of the Rome Opera in a crisp and lively performance.

In the spring of 1972, London-Decca issued a new L'ELISIR set in which the opera receives the by now all too familiar "Bonynge Treatment" in which Joan Sutherland is surrounded by the group of artists that seems to turn up in most of her current stage appearances and recordings are conducted by Miss Sutherland's husband, Richard Bonynge in a curiously mannered and limp fashion. Although there are a number of virtues to this performance, these do not, unfortunately, include idiomatic conducting, brightness of performances, or uniformly good casting, all of which are found in the Angel set.

Joan Sutherland sings with grace and taste, and her voice has seldom seemed more attractive. However, Miss Sutherland is simply not a soubrette. Her voice, best at radiating sweet sadness, an attribute which makes Sutherland a winner as, for example, Amina in Bellini's LA SONNAMBULA, but which puts her Adina quite out of the running after conceding that the singing itself is very beautiful.

A large part of the blame for the lifelessness of this recording, though, must be shouldered by Bonynge whose slow, dull tempi effectively flatten every bit of buoyancy in this score. Bonynge's chief contribution to the performance, and this is considerable, is his reinstatement of much music generally omitted from modern performances of the opera. Indeed, it is this "new" music (which includes a different *cabaletta* for the heroine in the last act) that constitutes one's chief inducement to own the set.

Luciano Pavarotti is heard here as Nemorino. He sings the role to perfection, with a larger, warmer sound than Gedda, but is unable to match that tenor's gifts as a comedian, and, again thanks to the terribly languid tempi, his Nemorino lacks humor or sparkle. I suppose, though, that on hearing Pavarotti sing "Una furtiva lagrima", these considerations will be washed away in the floodtide of his voice!

Dominic Cossa is a Belcore of uncommon delicacy of phrasing and is more successful than anyone else in the cast in terms of characterization. Spiro Malas is a gifted bass whose aspirations to the buffo roles are hampered by his lack of agility and comic inventiveness. His Dulcamara does not begin to equal Capecchi's or Corena's work. Maria Casula is heard to no great advantage as Gianetta. The Ambrosian Opera Chorus and English Chamber Orchestra are each composed of talented musicians, but Bonynge's execrable conducting fails to show these groups off in the best light. Incidentally, between the cuts opened by the conductor and his soggy tempi, the opera is spread onto three discs, as compared with Angel and Seraphim's two, making this set as economically unattractive as it is musically disappointing.

Seraphim offers a mid-1950's La Scala performance sparklingly conducted by Tullio Serafin and featuring Rosanna

Carteri and Luigi Alva as the lovers (if that term can be applied to this couple). Both artists had pleasant, rather light voices in those days and are appealing in their roles, although one could ask for more vocal weight from Alva. Giuseppe Taddei is quite wonderful as Dulcamara, and Rolando Panerai is a resonant Belcore, adding up to an enjoyable set that is well worth its bargain price.

VERDI: ERNANI

Price, Bergonzi, Sereni, Flagello, Schippers cond.
RCA Italiana Orchestra and Chorus
3 discs
RCA LSC-6183*
UK: RCA SER5572-4

Mancini, Rossini, Previtali cond.
RAI Orchestra and Chorus
3 discs
Everest/Cetra S448/3

Verdi's fifth opera, the melodious and vibrant if rather crude ERNANI has, in this century, been but a sporadic visitor to the repertoires of US and British opera companies. It has been recorded twice, but as the old Everest-Cetra version is of less than top quality, the only sane choice is the RCA-HMV version made in the late 1960's in Rome and which features Leontyne Price, Carlo Bergonzi, Mario Sereni, and Ezio Flagello, with the RCA Italiana Chorus and Orchestra led by Thomas Schippers.

Carlo Bergonzi is, on records at least, an ideal Ernani. His lack of physical stature need not concern the listener who is thus free to enjoy his smooth and silvery voice, peerless style, and noble musicianship. Few tenors share Bergonzi's ability to be both eloquent and virile in this role. Bergonzi makes his dramatic points without resorting to shouting or forcing his voice, and one could find no more lyrical a singer to express Ernani's love for Elvira than this tenor from Parma.

Leontyne Price has had several years' experience singing Elvira, the slightly more florid-voiced, older sister of the

TROVATORE Leonora. Except for finding some of the fioritura of "Ernani involami" and its *cabaletta* to be rather heavy
going, Price is in optimum voice, matching Bergonzi in the love
scenes and elsewhere finding herself completely at home in
Elvira's music.

Mario Sereni is in particularly strong voice as Don Carlo,
making the most of the generous opportunities for the baritone
with which this role is endowed. His "O verd'anni miei" and
"O somma Carlo" are powerfully vocalized, and he is, on the
recording, worthy to stand beside Bergonzi and Price.

Ezio Flagello, another Metropolitan stalwart, is in this
instance a weak link, singing a dull-voiced Silva that realizes
little of the role's musical potential. He also fails to satis-
factorily convey this character's monumental ego or rigidity.
Silva is a one-dimensional character but hardly the bore that
Flagello makes of him in the part.

Thomas Schippers is to be applauded for recording
ERNANI virtually uncut, but his tempi are characterized by
speed without purpose and consequently the performance is
hampered by the maestro's lack of true sympathy for the
music. Still, the contributions of Price, Bergonzi, and Sereni
make this recording a worthwhile acquisition that true
Verdians will want to own. The Chorus and Orchestra of
RCA's Rome studios perform with commendable vigor.

VERDI: FALSTAFF

Ligabue, Simionato, Elias, Freni, Evans, Merrill, Kraus, Solti cond.
RCA Italiana Orchestra and Chorus
3 discs
London OSA 1395
UK: Decca SET2BB104-6

Schwarzkopf, Barbieri, Moffo, Merriman, Gobbi, Panerai, Alva, von Karajan cond.
New Philharmonia Orchestra and Chorus
3 discs
Angel S-3552
UK: Columbia SMS1001

Ligabue, Resnik, Sciutti, Rossl-Majdan, Fischer-Dieskau, Panerai, Oncina, Bernstein cond.
Vienna Philharmonic and State Opera Chorus
3 discs
Columbia M3S-750
UK: Columbia 72493-5

Carteri, Taddei, Rossi cond.
RAI Orchestra and Chorus
3 discs
Everest/Cetra S-416-3*

Although the RCA FALSTAFF conducted by Arturo Toscanini is no longer available in most shops, the loss of this classic performance is compensated for by three more recent recordings.

Leonard Bernstein's Columbia set, recorded in 1966 in Vienna, preserves that maestro's highly successful revival of Verdi's last opera at the Vienna State Opera, a revival that duplicated his 1964 Metropolitan triumph with the opera. Bernstein's strong control over soloists and orchestra as well as his quicksilver tempi make for a deft and lively FALSTAFF. His soloists are an intelligent and generally gifted group, although the Falstaff, Dietrich Fischer-Dieskau seems, once again, miscast in an Italian opera. The German baritone finds Falstaff's music easily within his vocal range but runs into trouble with characterization, being able to suggest little of the fat knight's excesses. Nor does he imbue Sir John with the sly charm that endears him to listeners. The monologues are attractively sung, but proper weight and vocal coloration are missing.

Ilva Ligabue is heard on this recording (as she is on London-Decca's complete FALSTAFF and that company's older set of excerpts made with Fernando Corena) as Mistress Alice Ford, displaying a pleasant, secure voice and a proper measure of charm in this tricky role. Graziella Sciutta sometimes allows her tone to spread on high notes, but in the main offers a lovely Nanetta, to whom Juan Oncina is deftly matched as a clean-cut, lightweight Fenton.

Rolando Panerai provides a comically dour Ford and sings a rousing "È Sogno?", while Hilde Rossel-Majden is a competent although undistinguished Mistress Meg Page.

The real vocal heroine of this set, though, is Regina Resnik who sings a chesty but musical Mistress Quickly, and one who makes the most of her many opportunities for scene-stealing. Quickly has long been one of Resnik's finest opera house creations, and it is faithfully preserved here.

Outstanding in the supporting role of Dr. Caius is Gerhard Stolze. He brings to Verdi's comedy the same pithy sense of character that he more frequently lavishes on such roles as Mime or Herod.

The London-Decca FALSTAFF was originally released by RCA in 1964. Georg Solti, like Bernstein, opts for an animated reading of the score, furthermore, he is even luckier than the American conductor in his choice of soloists. Solti's cast is headed by Sir Geraint Evans whose basically dark, rather gruff baritone is well suited to the coarse, dissipated characterization that he provides. This Falstaff is more successful when looking forward to future conquests, as in the opening scenes of the first two acts, than in recapturing his past glories, as may be heard by comparing, for example, Evan's marvelously lusty singing of the "Honor" monologue with his rather pedestrian "Quando ero paggio." Still, the Welsh baritone's Falstaff may be counted as a resounding success on the basis of these discs.

Ilva Ligabue once more pleases as Alice, although she could do well to cultivate more comic spirit. Ligabue is more matronly than mischievous as Alice, Mirella Freni, in one of her first major recordings, is a sweet, clear-voiced Nanetta whose radiant soprano is as much a reason for owning this recording as Solti's ebullience or Evan's colorfulness.

Alfredo Kraus is appropriately youthful sounding in the role of Fenton, with his voice blending quite nicely with Freni's in the several short duets that they share. Robert Merrill is a particularly sonorous Ford, and imparts more meaning to the text than one has grown to expect from him, while Rosalind Elias is enormously alluring as Meg Page. Giulietta Simionato is quite the richest-voiced Quickly found on records, and in what for her is a rare appearance in a *buffa* role, reveals an engaging sense of comedy.

All these fine vocal elements are framed by the work of the RCA-Italiana forces, and under Solti's direction, it may be said that a good time was had by all—cast, musicians, and listener.

Angel-HMV's FALSTAFF album dates from the middle 1950's and was made in London with the Philharmonic Orchestra and Chorus led by Herbert von Karajan whose approach to the music is slightly more subdued than either Bernstein's or Solti's, but who nonetheless permits the score to crackle with excitement in vital moments such as the end of the second act when Sir John is thrown into the Thames.

Karajan's cast, led by Tito Gobbi in the title role, is well chosen and offers serious competition to the other recordings Gobbi's Falstaff is rather a different man than Evans' knight. Seemingly more intelligent and more aware of his own condition, Gobbi's Sir John is less gross and more likeable than Evans'. Moreover, Gobbi's command of the Italian language is absolutely complete, and he is able to give virtually every word its own pointed thrust with a result that is more subtle than anything achieved by Geraint Evans in his undeniably entertaining performance.

Elisabeth Schwarzkopf is surprisingly light voiced in the role of Alice Ford, but she is more successful than Ligabue in presenting Alice as a vixenish, light hearted woman. Nan Merriman, Dame Quickly in Toscanini's FALSTAFF, here sings Meg Page with ample voice and high spirits. Quickly herself is puckishly sung by Fedora Barbieri. This album gives her an opportunity to show that she can be as effective in a character role as in Verdi's more heroic mezzo roles. Anna Moffo, in her first recording, is an utterly charming Nanetta, well partnered by the Fenton of Luigi Alva who has made quite a specialty of this role in opera houses around the world. Rolando Panerai is heard once more as Ford, and his heavy baritone is once again effectively utilized.

Altogether Verdi's great comedy has been exceedingly well served by the recording industry. Besides these three almost equally excellent, complete sets available, there are Toscanini's recording which is worth hunting for in record emporiums and a Cetra-Everest budget set which will serve the economy minded. There is also London's 1964 highlight disc (the only set of excerpts available) which is notable for the richly comic Falstaff of Fernando Corena who is allowed to perform Falstaff's two great monologues plus "Quando ero paggio" and the entire first scene of Act Two. Regina Resnik is heard again as Dame Quickly and is in top form. Ligabue turns up again briefly as Alice Ford, and other artists in the various roles include Renato Capecchi as Ford, Luigi Alva as Fenton, and

Lydia Malimpietri as Nanetta. The conductor is Edward Downes.

PUCCINI:
LA FANCIULLA DEL WEST

Tebaldi, del Monaco, MacNeil, Tozzi, Capuana cond.
Orchestra and Chorus of L'Accademia di Santa Cecilia
3 discs
London OSA 1306*
UK: Ace of Diamonds GOS594-5

Gavazzi, Bertocci, Basile cond.
RAI Orchestra and Chorus
3 discs
Everest/Cetra S453-3

With the disappearance of the Angel-EMI set featuring, of all people, Birgit Nilsson as Minnie, the only generally available version of Puccini's horse opera is the London-Decca set, made in the late 1950's with the services of Renata Tebaldi, Mario del Monaco and Cornell MacNeil in the principal roles. When performed onstage, US audiences have been known to snicker at the Italian speaking cowboys found in FANCIULLA. The medium of the phonograph removes this problem, as one can close one's eyes and pretend that the opera is set in other times or places. However, this is snobbish, and if the work is approached on its own terms and with tongue properly in cheek, its many fine qualities including glorious orchestration, some unforgettable vocal climaxes, and some nice "American touches" such as a Stephen Foster folk song in Italian.

Renata Tebaldi recorded the opera a decade before she was to sing the role onstage for the first time (Metropolitan Opera, 1970). However, she was no stranger to Puccini, of course, and thus sings with engaging sympathy for the music and with

her customary warm tone. Even the high C's come off easily
in this performance. Del Monaco also was in fine voice, and
his manly sound gives Ramerez a.k.a. Johnson the proper
sense of *machismo*. Cornell MacNeill, in this early recording,
offers a particularly sumptuous reading of the villainous
Rance, although one could look in vain for a menacing
characterization. In the brief role of Jake Wallace, the blind
storyteller who sings the Foster adaptation, Giorgio Tozzi is
most eloquent. London's sound effects department has a field
day in this recording, creating effects ranging from pistol
shots to blizzard winds and cards thrown on the table. All
these effects aid in producing an idiomatic and appropriately
hammy performance. Francesco Molinari-Pradelli ably conducts the Santa Cecilia Orchestra and Chorus who offer first-
class work.

GOUNOD: FAUST

de los Angeles, Gedda, Christoff, Cluytens cond.
Orchestra and Chorus of Paris Opera
4 discs
Angel S-3622*
UK: HMV SLS816

Sutherland, Corelli, Ghiaurov, Bonynge cond.
London Symphony Orchestra and John Alldis Choir
4 discs
London OSA 1433*
UK: Decca SET327-9

Seemingly indicative of the sudden and extreme drop in
popularity that FAUST has suffered in recent years is the fact
that this once perennially beloved work is represented by only
two complete recordings. Neither is perfect, but the Angel-
HMV set is, in general, a more balanced and cohesive performance than the London-Decca release.

Made in Paris in 1958, Angel's FAUST is actually a
"remake" of a monaural performance issued a few years
earlier by RCA. The three principals, Gedda, de los Angeles,
and Christoff, as well as the conductor, Andre Cluytens, and
the Paris Opera Orchestra and Chorus repeat their RCA
chores on the Angel set.

It would be difficult to find a better Faust than Nicolai
Gedda who might properly be dubbed "the thinking man's
tenor." Gedda's musical intelligence is, moreover, backed up by
an exceedingly beautiful voice that, if perhaps lacking the
ring a Bergonzi or a Pavorotti, is still capable of doing full
justice to virtually any role composed for a lyric tenor voice.

Even when not directly comparing Gedda's Faust to that of his miscast rival on the London-Decca recording, the Swedish tenor's performance would be notable for its limpid sound, flawless enunciation, and musical purity. Able to sustain ample high notes, Gedda somehow doesn't let these become circus stunts. The difference between Gedda's "Salut De-meure" and Corelli's rendering of that aria is that between a cultivated artist and a gloriously endowed musical savage. Elsewhere, Gedda imparts an ardent quality into Faust's measures without ever forcing his voice beyond its natural strength.

Similarly well cast is Victoria de los Angeles as Mar-guerite. Always a passive vocal actress, the soprano sings with characteristic skill, lacking only an ultimate sense of security on the high notes and, unlike Sutherland on the competing version, a trill in the "Jewel Song." De los Angeles performs the ballad of the King of Thule with an affecting musical elegance, and her modesty in the church scene is a splendid foil for the brash arrogance of Boris Christoff's Méphistophèles. Her soaring lines in the final trio would seem sufficient to earn the mercy of the Almighty.

Boris Christoff's voice, characterized by a rough edge and a uniquely black quality, is well suited to Mephisto's music. Furthermore, the bass is a powerful actor, and thus he creates a Devil who is indeed a force with which to be reckoned —at one moment a suave temptor of virtue and in the next a frightening persecutor. Christoff's diction is, as is de los Angeles', above reproach.

Ernest Blanc is a worthy Valentin, strong of voice and noble in characterization of one of the greatest "stuffed tunics" in all opera. Rita Gorr is a charming and musical Dame Martha, as one might expect of an artist who has sung Amneris and Dalila. Liliane Berton, though, is an edgy Siebel.

Andre Cluytens conducts with great consideration for the singers but is unable to infuse much fire into Gounod's tapioca pudding of a score. His orchestra is quite competent, but the Paris Opera choristers are in this instance deficient in energy and vocal strength.

Before discussing London's FAUST in any detail, I would like to share a remark made by a ranking executive of that firm backstage at the Metropolitan Opera. Upon being congratulated for London's then new, all star GIOCONDA set, this gentleman acknowledged with all due modesty that Ponchielli had been well served by that recording. "Of course last year," quipped the executive, "we did very well with Ponchielli's FAUST, too!" This wry reference to the 1967 overcast and underconducted version of the Gounod work smacks of hindsight, for seldom has an opera been more systematically smothered than on this recording which stars Franco Corelli, Joan Sutherland, and Nicolai Ghiaurov. Lest I be considered too harsh on this earnest attempt at a relevant, strongly sung FAUST, let me say that the set is not without considerable virtues, not the least of which is· its near completeness—the first scene of Act Four which contains arias for Marguerite and Siebel is restored here, as is a portion of the prison scene. Furthermore, the order of scenes in the fourth act goes back to the original score, with the death of Valentin preceding the Church Scene. These considerations, of course, are rather academic and take nothing away from the colossal miscasting of Corelli as Faust. The tenor's true-blue admirers will not fail to be pleased by Corelli's on-pitch, secure vocalism. These excellences though, are offset by the fact that he simply overwhelms the music, taking "Salut demeure" too loudly and elsewhere belting out phrases that should best be gently spun, particularly in the love duet. Furthermore, Corelli's French is substandard.

Joan Sutherland is, if not really miscast, simply too much her usual, droopy operatic self in the role of Marguerite. Granted, Sutherland trills magnificently in the "Jewel Song," but this is perhaps the only exciting moment in her portrayal. If one constantly scrutinizes the text while listening to Sutherland sing here, one will barely understand some of her words. With the "Jewel Song" excepted, Sutherland's Marguerite emerges as one long scoop.

Nicolai Ghiaurov is the lone example of adroit casting among the principals. No less charismatic than Christoff, Ghiaurov is a more suavely insinuating Mephisto, with a sensual air lightly cloaking his wickedness. Ghiaurov's delivery is, paradoxically, the saving grace of this recording.

Robert Massard's Valentin is quite satisfactory, as are the contributions of Margreta Elkins as Siebel and Monica Sinclair, a first-rate "character" mezzo, as Martha. The Ambrosian Opera Chorus and Highgate School Singers outclass their Parisian rivals. Conducting the London Symphony Orchestra, Bonynge paces the opera crisply if not brilliantly, though he all but ruins the trio and apotheosis with a sudden and uncalled-for lethargy.

GIORDANO: FEDORA

Olivero, del Monaco, Gobbi, Gardelli cond.
Monte Carlo Opera Orchestra and Chorus
2 discs
London OSA 1283*
UK: Decca SET435/6

Caniglia, Prandelli, Bertocci, Rossi cond.
RAI Orchestra and Chorus
2 discs
Everest/Cetra S452/2

It is strange that in the USA where ANDREA CHENIER has for years enjoyed a fair degree of popularity, Giordano's other operas have languished in relative obscurity. Of course, in England even CHENIER has not established itself, and English verismo buffs must content themselves with recordings of those operas. FEDORA was Giordano's second opera, and it has always been popular in Italy. Adapted from a Sardou melodrama, which like its sister work, TOSCA, became a vehicle for Sarah Bernhardt, FEDORA is a lusty tale of murder and revenge tempered by love. Strange as it seems, in spite of the inherent crudity of its dramaturgy, FEDORA, given a strong cast, works like dynamite in the theatre or opera house.

In 1970, London-Decca issued a recording of this Giordano work that introduced many listeners to the phenomenal Magda Olivero.

Olivero has sung Fedora all across Italy and in the USA, while, due to the paucity of FEDORA productions, del Monaco and Gobbi have performed their roles chiefly in Italy. Mme.

Olivero on these discs emerges as something of a revelation.
Her voice is medium sized and somewhat wiry but strikes the
ears as would a wave of molten lava—hot liquid, and over-
powering. Even in the later stages of her career, Olivero's voice
is superbly controlled, and her high notes are perfectly secure.
Thus, she is a wonderful choice for the title role. On stage,
Olivero's gestures and bearing are often painfully old-
fashioned. On discs, the sincerity and conviction of her
approach to her role are unmarred by these mannerisms, and
thus her Fedora is even more effective on records than in the
opera house. Those who do not sympathise with verismo music
and the style of singing that it created will perhaps take
exception to Olivero's frequent use of the *coup de glotte* and
other assorted sighs and gasps, but the melting power of "Su
questa santa croce" in the first act, the duet with Loris (del
Monaco) in Act Two, and her long death scene in Act Three
provide some of the greatest moments that I have ever spent
listening to records.

Mario del Monaco must once have been a fine Loris. His
"Amor ti vieta" is still impressive, but by the time this
recording was made, he had lost whatever ability to sing below
fortissimo that he ever possessed, and the bellowing eventually becomes monotonous. Still, few other tenors past or present could send a chill down the spine the way del Monaco
does with his cry of "Fedora io t'amo" at the end of Act Two.

The immense talents of Tito Gobbi are lavished on the
benign de Siriex, whose chief reward to the baritone is the
opportunity to toss off the pseudo-Russian aria "La donna
russa" at Fedora's soiree in Act Two. A young coloratura
soprano, Lucia Cappolino does nicely with the role of Fedora's
scatterbrained friend, Countess Olga. FEDORA is an opera
with many comprimario roles, and these are expertly handled
on this recording. Special mention should go to Robert Binder
who sings Cirillo, the bereaved servant in Act One, and to Kiri
te Kanawa who sings the travesto role of Dmitri. This brief
appearance by the young soprano who caused a sensation at
Covent Garden in 1972 as the Countess in *Le Nozze Di*

Figaro may well go down as a footnote to a most distinguished career. The orchestra and chorus of the Monte Carlo
Opera are more than adequate and are idiomatically led by
Lamberto Gardelli. FEDORA is no masterpiece, but when
sung as well at it is on this recording, one longs to see a fully
staged production.

Those wishing to compare this performance with an alternative version must turn to the vintage Everest-Cetra set that
stars Maria Caniglia and Giancinto Prandelli.

The Cetra set is quite easy to listen to. Maria Caniglia was, in
her heyday, a dramatic soprano to be reckoned with, and her
big, exciting voice and self-assured manner make her a good
choice for the title role. If she never reaches the high tension
electricity of Olivero in her portrayal, she nonetheless sings
very well and her death scene is especially effective. Prandelli
is no match for del Monaco's virile, charismatic interpretation
of Loris, but his voice is a good deal smoother than del
Monaco's, and at times is much more pleasant to hear. Scipio
Colombo and Carmen Piccini are competent if undistinguished
singers in the roles of Di Siriex and Countess Olga. The minor
roles are handled with more skill than is often encountered
on Cetra recordings. The Milan-RAI Orchestra and Chorus
are led by Mario Rossi and play with reasonable sonority.

DONIZETTI:
LA FILLE DU REGIMENT

French Version:
Sutherland, Pavarotti, Malas, Sinclair, Bonynge cond.
Orchestra and Chorus of Covent Garden
2 discs
London OSA 1273*
UK: Decca SET372-3

Italian Version: (LA FIGLIA DEL REGGIMENTO)
Pagliughi, Valletti, Rossi cond.
RAI Orchestra and Chorus
2 discs
Everest/Cetra S-417-2*

A French language version of this delightful comic opera which Donizetti wrote for Paris was unavailable till London-Decca recorded the 1966 Covent Garden production led by Richard Bonynge with, need one even mention, Joan Sutherland in the title role.

LA FILLE is one of the Bonynges most successful collaborations. Miss Sutherland finds this character to her dramatic tastes, and she is delightfully appealing in "Au bruit de la Guerre", vocally stunning in "Salut a la France", and droopy and scoopy only in "Il faut partir." Bonynge also conducts with more verve, thank heaven, than usual. Luciano Pavarotti who, at this writing, is the toast of New York for his Tonio in the Met's importation of the Covent Garden Fille production, shows why on this recording. His effortless top notes and beautiful phrasing and generally golden singing are not soon forgotten. Spiro Malas is a competent Sulpice and Monica Sinclair is a charming Marchioness. All told, this recording is a delight.

The Italian version of this opera, LA FIGLIA DEL REGGI-MENTO, is often performed in Italy and the USA, too. The only existing recording is a Cetra gem from the late 1940's, now available on the Everest label.

Lina Pagliughi is not nearly as gifted a singer as Miss Suther-land, but her pleasant, sparkling coloratura only rarely becomes shrill on the top. She sings with little variety (the rueful "Convien partir" is interpretively undifferentiated from the jocular "Apparve la luce"), Furthermore, her diction is not even as clear as Joan Sutherland's! Everything considered, though, Miss Pagliughi does make an acceptable Maria.

As for the other members of the cast, Cesare Valetti is a light-voiced and articulate Tonio, lacking only the gifts of Pavorotti in terms of sheer sound. Sesto Bruscantini is a bumptuous and forthright Sulpizio (better than Malas, actually), and Rina Corsi is a rough voiced, undistinguished Marchese. The con-ducting, like the orchestral and choral work, is jaunty but pedestrian. This is not nearly as polished a performance as the Bonynge's French language version, but is well worth the bargain price and is an interesting contrast to the London-Decca version.

BEETHOVEN: FIDELIO

Dernesch, Donath, Vickers, Keleman, Ridderbusch, von Karajan cond.
Berlin Philharmonic and Deutsche Oper Chorus
3 discs
Angel S-3773
UK: HMV SLS954

Jones, Mathis, King, Schreier, Talvela, Adam, Crass, Böhm cond.
Dresden State Opera Orchestra and Chorus
3 discs
Deutsche Grammophon 2720009 or 2709031
UK: Same

Ludwig, Berry, Frick, Vickers, Klemperer cond.
Philharmonia Orchestra and Chorus
3 discs
Angel S-3625*
UK: Columbia SMS1014

Nilsson, Sciutti, McCracken, Krause, Prey, Boehme, Maazel cond.
Philharmonic and State Opera Chorus
2 discs
London OSA 1259
UK: Decca SET272-3

Mödl, Jurinac, Windgassen, Poell, Frick, Schock, Furtwangler cond.
Vienna Philharmonic and State Opera Chorus
3 discs
Seraphim IC 6022 (Mono)
UK: HMV PLS2

Excluding the Toscanini led FIDELIO recording which is no longer available and the budget priced Seraphim edition with Martha Modl in the title role and with Furtwangler conducting, there are at least four worthy, modern recordings of Beethoven's lone opera.

Deutsche Grammophon's most recent effort with the work, released in 1970 to coincide with the 200th anniversary of the composer's birth, boasts the most eloquent, rousing conducting of any recorded FIDELIO in my experience, with the honors going to Karl Böhm. Dr. Böhm invariably manages to bring out the best in any orchestra with which he works, and in this set, the Dresden State Orchestra distinguishes itself by the clarity and loveliness of the sound that it produces. If Böhm errs at all, it is in allowing the performance to sound almost *too* joyous, as if the conductor were so eager to share with his listeners the wonderful sense of righteousness and freedom gleaned from the final scene, that he embues the entire opera with this quality from first note to last—this however, is quibbling of the worst order and ought not to diminish one's admiration for Karl Böhm's work by one iota.

Dr. Böhm is, of course, aided by the work of his strong cast of singers. To the title role, Gwynneth Jones brings what is perhaps less than a truly heroic voice, but, as captured in this set, Jones' soprano is a warm and darkly beautiful instrument, and although one is conscious of some degree of strain during both the "Abscheulicher" and the "Rescue Scene" confrontation with Pizarro, Jones is in control of her resources at virtually all times. Her nearly uniformly fine singing and particularly moving, feminine interpretation serve to create a memorable Leonore.

James King's Florestan is very competently sung. One might search for a more freely produced, ringing, or larger voice than King's or hope for a more impassioned account of the text than the American tenor seems able to provide, but King meets the musical challenges of the part squarely and with considerable success. As Pizarro, Theo Adam sings with an appropriately rough, menacing tone. Furthermore, Adam skilfully suggests the Governor's fiendish nature, shading his words along with his music in order to create a vivid dramatic personality. This FIDELIO is particularly blessed in its casting of the opera's supporting roles. Franz Crass is a dignified and sympathetic Rocco who can command a clean legato line. Edith Mathis, perhaps the most celebrated interpretor of Marzelline in Europe and the United States, proves to be a delightful foil for Jones' Leonora, singing prettily yet never cloying on the senses as some Marzellines do. Peter Schreier, to whom leading roles in Mozart operas are often entrusted, is an engaging Jaquino. Martti Talvela's voluminous bass is lavished on the role of Don Fernando, in whose booming tones the forces of goodness are personified in a forthright manner. The chorus of the Dresden State Opera is more than equal to the many demands Beethoven makes upon it here. This recording, unlike the Karajan, Maazel, and Klemperer ones, includes the Leonore overture No. 3 between the two scenes of Act Two.

The older Angel-HMV recording of FIDELIO has, in spite of the ploddingly methodical and generally bloodless conducting of Otto Klemperer, a number of virtues. Christa Ludwig, a mezzo Fidelio, invests that role with the velvety richness of her lower and middle registers, and a slightly steely, vaguely uncomfortable top that, in its brave and by and large successful attempt to surmount the difficult tessitura of the role, adds a special quality of courageous audacity that befits the role. As Mme. Ludwig was married to Walter Berry, the Pizarro, at the time this recording was made, the diva was able to hurl "Abscheulicher" and other choice epithets squarely at her spouse, and for posterity! More seriously, Christa Ludwig possesses in both her vocal and histrionic make up, the ability to be an exciting and beautiful interpreter of this role.

Jon Vickers, heard here in the first of his two recorded Florestans (both for Angel-HMV), proves to be quite the best exponent of the part. His cries of "Freiheit" in his aria bring tears to this listener's eyes, and his noble singing and vigorous acting in this role have not been equalled on discs to date.

Walter Berry is excellently cast as Pizarro, singing with more vocal beauty than any of his competitors and yet managing to be as pompous and nasty as the role demands him to be. Berry makes Pizarro's aria "Ha! Welch' ein Augenblick" into far more of a musical highlight than it often is when sung with less attention paid to the music. Gottlob Frick is a sonorous and human Rocco, while Franz Crass, the Rocco on Böhm's recording, turns up here as a highly competent Don Fernando. Ingeborg Hallstein is a fresh-voiced if rather small scale Marzelline, while Gerhard Unger is a dry-voiced, undistinguished Jaquino. The Philharmonia Orchestra and Chorus provide top grade support, even though Otto Klemperer conducts with a singular lack of dramatic emphasis. The finale of the second act, though, is most dynamically directed.

Angel-HMV's most recent FIDELIO stems from Herbert von Karajan's 1971 Salzburg Easter Festival production with the transplanted Berlin Philharmonic Orchestra and Chorus of the Deutsch Oper. The conductor is extraordinarily successful in musically suggesting the darkness and terror of Pizarro's world. The march and Pizarro's aria have never seemed quite so awesome, and the music with which Act Two opens evokes Florestan's dungeon all too .vividly. Curiously, von Karajan seems less at ease in the last scene which is choppily conducted and in which the final chorus sounds almost graceless.

Von Karajan has been, in this case, less than totally fortunate in his choice of singers. In the title role, Helga Dernesch displays a pleasant voice when singing softly, but one that turns both hard and wooden on top, particularly during *forte* passages. This drawback diminishes Miss Dernesch's effectiveness in nearly every one of Leonora's big moments, once the canon "Mir ist so wunderbar" has come and gone. Jon Vickers is below his best vocal form here, sounding musically haggard and dry in his aria. Vickers' characterization is even more intense than previously, and one ultimately accepts and admires the tenor's work even with serious reservations and indeed fears about the Canadian tenor's vocal estate, much as one is enthralled by a late Callas performance.

Zoltan Kéléman is a vocally strong and dramatically forbidding Pizarro, and is firmly supportive of what appears to be
von Karajan's thesis that Pizarro is the dominant force in the
opera. Karl Ridderbusch is similarly effective as Rocco. Helen
Donath is a pleasant sounding, if one dimensional Marzelline,
partnered by Horst R. Laubenthal's square jawed Jaquino.
Jose van Dam copes nicely with Don Fernando's brief measures. The Berlin Philharmonic and Deutsch Oper chorus
respond in a precise, well disciplined manner to their conductor. This recording presents a generally studied, carefully
prepared performance that lacks the animation of Böhm's
performance and the vocal splendor of Klemperer's.

London-Decca's FIDELIO showcases the Leonore of Birgit
Nilsson. Minus the Leonore No. 3 overture and some of the
dialogue, the performance fits neatly onto two discs (whereas
the other three sets discussed here occupy three records each).

Of any soprano singing today, Mme. Nilsson alone possesses
the vocal strength to scale the vocal heights of the role of
Leonore. No one attacks high notes with Nilsson's cool faith
and easy production. Yet the character of Leonore calls for a
sense of vulnerability as well as raw courage, and it is this
tension that is lacking in Nilsson's recorded Leonore. One
feels at times that this Leonore has been merely programmed
to succeed vocally, and this, of course, Nilsson does. One
would, however, like to be made aware of somewhat more of
Leonore's desperation.

James McCracken sings Florestan here. His huge tenor voice
that loses nothing in terms of volume or amplitude above the
staff is a major asset in this role. Dramatically, McCracken is
involved, although he is a less subtle an actor than Vickers.
Tom Krause is in disappointing voice as Pizarro, infusing the
part with little vocal color and insufficient dramatic bite.
Kurt Boehme is a dry-voiced and uninteresting Rocco, while
Herman Prey injects some vocal distinction into the final scene
in the role of Don Fernando. Graziella Sciutti's Marzelline
suffers from unsteady intonation and an unbecoming vibrato.

Donald Grobe, however, is an uncommonly fine Jaquino. Although Maazel's direction is uninspired, the Vienna Philharmonic Orchestra and State Opera Chorus perform with their customary expertise, making this a less than first-rate FIDELIO, but one that Nilsson's many admirers will certainly enjoy.

WAGNER:
DER FLIEGENDE HOLLANDER

Rysanek, Elias, London, Tozzi, Liebl, Dorati cond.
Covent Garden Orchestra and Chorus
3 discs
London OSA 1399
UK: Decca 2BB 109-11

Schech, Wagner, Fischer-Dieskau, Frick, Schock, Konwitschny
cond.
Deutsche Oper Orchestra and Chorus
3 discs
Angel S-3616*
UK: World Record Club SOC156-8

Silja, Burmeister, Adam, Talvela, Kozub, Klemperer cond.
New Philharmonia Orchestra and BBC Chorus
3 discs
Angel S-33730
UK: HMV SLS934

Varnay, Uhde, Weber, Keilberth cond.
Bayreuth Festival Orchestra and Chorus
3 discs
Richmond SRS63519

Jones, Stewart, Ridderbusch, Esser, Böhm cond.
Bayreuth Festival Orchestra and Chorus
3 discs
DGG 2709040
UK: Same

There are four modern recordings of Wagner's first really characteristic work—two from EMI-Angel, one on DGG and one now available on London-Decca (although it was originally an RCA set). It is this latter recording that is in most ways the most effective performance. Of the three *maestri* who direct the opera on discs, Antol Dorati, in one of his only operatic recordings, comes closest to fully capturing the brooding, Romantic qualities of the work and to shaping a theatrically effective reading.

The cast is taken entirely from the mid-1960's revivals of THE FLYING DUTCHMAN that rank among the best achievements of the Bing regime at the Metropolitan Opera; George London, Giogio Tozzi, and most especially, Leonie Rysanek recreate here with great success the parts that brought them acclaim in New York.

George London's tragic and premature vocal decline is perhaps already foreshadowed in this recording. Despite his assured technique, which keeps his singing from sounding painfully strained, and the still handsome sound of his bass-baritone voice, London's Dutchman lacks sonority and the sense of control that would be present were the voice in top condition. London is seldom able to let his voice ring out, even in the First Act monologue. Furthermore, when he does sing at full volume, the voice takes on a harshness that underscores his declining powers. London's characterization, though, is marked by a welcome tenseness and a communication of the phantom captain's spiritual anguish.

Leonie Rysanek's Senta is one of her finest roles. In the the early 1960's, the Austrian soprano underwent an extended period of vocal unease from which she eventually emerged with a surer control of her low notes while retaining her always incredible top notes. Mme. Rysanek exhibits on this set a number of unfortunately weak and unsteady moments in the lower register, and, although her Act Two Ballad surpasses those sung by her competitors on the other recordings, it is performed with less than her customary abandon. Where Rysanek triumphs, however, is in the creation of a really credible and touching heroine. Neurotic and remote, yet brave and unswerving in her loyalty to the Dutchman, this is a Senta who leaves her listeners breathless. Although Rysanek begins the part somewhat cautiously, she handles the treacherous music of the final scene, high C's and all, as if it were child's play, building in intensity and gaining in vocal ease as the opera progresses.

Giorgio Tozzi has made something of a specialty of the role of Daland over the years at the Metropolitan. In smooth voice when this recording was made, Tozzi cuts a surprisingly youthful, rather roguish figure as Senta's greedy father. He sings with grace and acts the part in a droll manner that offers a welcome contrast to the sombreness that pervades the work.

Karl Liebl is an effective Eric—surely Wagner's least grateful tenor role. Although lacking a truly beautiful sound, the German tenor seems at home in the music and even manages to inject a sense of helpless despair in the Third Act. Rosalind Elias is a properly, and for her, surprisingly matronly Mary, and Richard Lewis is a callow Steersman. The Covent Garden Chorus and Orchestra match their Metropolitan soloists in musical distinction. The Overture is played with beautiful tone and, in Dorati's hands, a gripping sense of the drama to come.

EMI's early DUTCHMAN, available on Angel in the USA and as a budget-priced World Record Club reissue in the UK, is dominated by Dietrich Fischer-Dieskau in the title role. More a lyric than a heroic baritone, Fischer-Dieskau packs the power called for by Wagner without losing the tender richness of voice that illuminates the Second Act duet with Senta. Vividly delivering the text, the baritone is a dignified, sensitive Dutchman who deserves a more attractive Senta than that offered by Marianne Schech. Mme. Schech is a dramatic soprano with an ample but unfocused voice. Her tone spreads when singing above mezzo-forte, and her intonation, particularly in the upper register, is not always true to pitch. She offers little more than a conventionally agitated interpretation of her role and in general blights the proceedings at every appearance. Gottlob Frick is a strong, rather curt Daland who sees few of the lighter aspects of the role that are apparent to Tozzi. His is a steady, well-routined performance. Rudolf Schock is a doleful, very romantic Eric, with the smoothest, most lyrical voice of the three tenors who sing the role on these recordings. The aptly named Sieglinde Wagner is a vigorous if also tremulous Mary, while Fritz Wunderlich puts in a welcome appearance as the Steersman. The Orchestra and Chorus of the (West) Berlin Opera are conducted by Franz Konwitschny who shapes a strong if rather austere reading of the opera which emphasizes the darkest, most mysterious aspects of the opera but loses some of the contrasting sense of Senta's all-consuming and redeeming love.

EMI's latest DUTCHMAN, found in the USA on Angel and in the UK on HMV, employs the original, 1842 Dresden version of the opera, making it the longest DUTCHMAN on discs. Theo Adam, one of the most successful of the younger Wagnerian singers, is heard in the title role. Adam has no trouble with the music, and his sense of character and "presence" is strong, but I have personally always found the timbre of his voice to be unpleasantly dry. This Dutchman tends to bark a fair amount of the time, and his dourness might make even Senta nervous.

Senta is sung on this recording by Anja Silja. At this point in her career, Miss Silja is better in a staged performance than on a recording, as her voice has grown undependable and often acutely unpleasant, whitish, and strident. Occasionally referred to as the "German Callas," Silja does the original Callas little credit. Why is it that every attractive girl with a good stage presence and a flawed voice is called a new Callas? Maria Callas was, even during the pit of her vocal decline, a superb technician and a uniquely gifted artist. Miss Silja, though the possessor of very real musical gifts and an excellent actress to boot, is simply not in the same league. It is hard to imagine her singing the variety of roles that Callas sang when Silja has difficulties in the German dramatic repertoire that she has staked out for herself. The Ballad is unbeautiful, to say the least, and Senta emerges as quite a spinsterish, unromantic figure. By the third act, Silja is in better command of her artistry, but she never establishes control of the role.

Martti Talvela is in top form as Daland, providing the finest singing of the album. Fine singing is not to be heard from Ernst Kozub, an Eric who seems straight from the forests of Norway. Annelies Burmeister is a competent Mary, and Gerhard Unger sings the Steersman. The BBC Chorus proves equal to the music it is required to perform, and the Philharmonia Orchestra plays well under Otto Klemperer's guidance. The veteran Klemperer's tempi are in general more animated than his recent recorded standard, and his powerful shaping of the opera is quite effective. One wishes only that the level of the singing were on a similar level.

VERDI:
LA FORZA DEL DESTINO

Tebaldi, Simionato, del Monaco, Bastianini, Siepi, Corena, Molinari-Pradelli cond.
Orchestra and Chorus of L'Accademia di Santa Cecilia
4 discs
London OSA 1405*
UK: Ace of Diamonds GOS5979 (3 discs)

Price, Verrett, Tucker, Merrill, Tozzi, Flagello, Schippers cond.
RCA Italiana Orchestra and Chorus
4 discs
RCA LSC-6413*

Arroyo, Casoni, Bergonzi, Capuccilli, Raimondi, Evans, Gardelli cond.
London Philharmonic and Ambrosian Singers
4 discs
Angel S-3765*
UK: HMV SLS948

Caniglia, Stignani, Masini, Pasero, Erminero cond.
RAI Orchestra and Chorus
3 discs
Everest/Cetra S-418-3*

Callas, Nicolai, Tucker, Tagliabue, Rossi-Lemeni, Capecchi, Serafin cond.
La Scala Orchestra and Chorus
3 discs
Angel 3531 C (Mono)

Milanov, Elias, di Stefano, Warren, Tozzi, Mantovani, Previtali cond.
Orchestra and Chorus of L'Accademia di Santa Cecilia
4 discs
UK only: RCA SER4516-9

One of Verdi's most complex operas, calling for a large cast of singers, LA FORZA DEL DESTINO has fared better than many of Verdi's works on discs, there being several truly distinguished sets available, as well as one or two others of marginal interest.

Perhaps the best of the lot, and by any standards a vocally well balanced, explosive performance, is the London-Decca set.

Leonora Di Vargas is sung here by Renata Tebaldi (who stopped singing the role within weeks of participating in the tragic Metropolitan Opera performance during which Leonard Warren collapsed and died). Although one can understand the soprano's unwillingness to sing a role connected with so grim an event, one regrets Tebaldi's decision since, as shown by this recording, she was an excellent Leonora, singing with passion and urgency while preserving purity of tone and spinning a lovely Verdian line. The supple, effortless grace of Tebaldi's "Convent Scene" knows no equal on records, and the soprano's "Pace, pace mio dio" ranks with those of Muzio, Milanov, and Callas.

Alvaro is sung with characteristic thrust by Mario del Monaco. He sounds rather breathy in Alvaro's first entrance (as well any Alvaro might, after supposedly scaling a balcony to gain access to Leonora) but finishes the scene with power, creating a somewhat rough hewn but sympathetic character.

Del Monaco is partnered by Ettore Bastianini in the role of Don Carlo (di Vargas). Bastianini is in optimum form on this recording. The three tenor-baritone duets are ample reason in themselves for owning the set. Bastianini, as might be expected, offers an "Urna fatale del mio destino" of tonal beauty and dramatic aptness, singing with full command of his instrument and the Verdian idiom.

Cesare Siepi sings Padre Guardiano with dignity yet almost a too youthful sounding a voice. Siepi atones for this slight lack of "fatherly" authority with the sheer glory of his singing. Fernando Corena recreates his humorous and all too human Fra Melitone, while Giulietta Simionato makes one wish that Preziosilla were a larger role. The comprimario artists could hardly be better, and Francesco Molinari-Pradelli leads the Orchestra and Chorus of the Accademia di Santa Cecilia energetically and tastefully in a performance that ought to change the mind of any one who claims that FORZA is not one of Verdi's greatest works.

RCA has recorded two complete FORZAs. The earlier version, while still current in England, has been deleted in the USA. This Rome Opera performance finds Zinka Milanov at somewhat less than her best in one of her most celebrated roles. Although occasionally sounding tired and at times afflicted with a heavy vibrato, Milanov's Leonora is still authoritative, skilfully sung, and, at best, quite exciting. Her "Pace, pace mio dio" is quite beautiful, and Milanov is dramatically intense during the "Convent Scene," as well. Admirers of this great soprano would do best, though, to search for the single disc of excerpts from the opera that Milanov, along with Peerce and Warren, made for RCA in 1955. On the complete set, Milanov's colleagues include Giuseppe di Stefano, whose voice was beginning to fray and who resorts to a good deal of excess sobbing which serves to obscure some of the fine work he contributes—particularly in the duets with Leonard Warren. Warren, in one of his last recordings, sings with resonant authority, and his immense voice, if a little harsh at the top of his range, is still an extraordinary instrument.

Rosalind Elias is a pretty if light-voiced Preziosilla, and Giorgio Tozzi and Dino Mantovani sing Guardiano and Melitone with competence (however they fall short of the standard set by Siepi and Corena in the same roles). Fernando Previtali leads the opera with clarity and a sense of the musical drama at hand. Unfortunately, this set is crudely cut in Act Two— the dramatically crucial second duet for Alvaro and Carlo is omitted.

RCA's more recent FORZA is centered upon the Leonora of Leontyne Price who in recent years has made the role rather a specialty of hers. Singing with her customary opulence of sound, Price is a sweet-voiced, rather placid heroine who at the very least imbues the heroine with gorgeous sound. One might wish for more bite in her singing, however. Don Alvaro is sung by Richard Tucker who mars his often extremely impressive vocalism with sobs and gulps that call to mind the Italian provinces instead of the stages of the Metropolitan and La Scala. Robert Merrill, in splendid voice, does a great deal musically with Don Carlo, although he makes little effort to create a character. Shirley Verrett is a delightful Preziosilla, singing with a tantalizing mischievousness. Giorgio Tozzi sings Guardiano here with more power than in his earlier recording, while Ezio Flagello offers a rather grumpy, heavy-sounding Melitone. The RCA Italiana forces are conducted by Thomas Schippers who, while by no means ungifted, does not manage to propel the opera to any sense of dramatic purpose. His beat is often flabby, and climaxes don't seem to get anywhere.

HMV-Angel boasts a pair of FORZA recordings. The earlier set, a 1955 mono production, fits on to three discs (whereas the other sets take four) by cutting the opening scene of Act Four between Melitone, the mendicants, and Padre Guardiano. More importantly, though, the role of Leonora, sung here by Maria Callas, is unabridged. Callas' Leonora may well be her best Verdi recording. Although her tone here often exhibits Callas' unique, "veiled" quality, this is by no means unattractive, and, since her high notes are, in general, most secure, Callas is musically exemplary. Furthermore, the soprano's ability to express the emotional content of music has seldom been in greater evidence. Thus, the Callas Leonora is highly strung, aristocratic, and very real in her suffering. Unfortunately, aside from the knowing, sensitive conducting of the La Scala Orchestra and Chorus, by Tullio Serafin, the performance falls short of the rival FORZA sets. Richard Tucker, fresher of voice here than on the 1964 RCA set, still manages to sob and sigh in crude fashion. Carlo Tagliabue's vocally over-the-hill Don Carlo constitutes the set's major weakness, while Nicola Rossi-Lemeni's Guardiano is colorless and dramatically flat. Elena Nicolai's Preziosilla is heavy-set but lively, and, among the supporting singers, only Renato Capecchi's Melitone might be judged as first rate. The La Scala Chorus, though, is particularly good throughout this recording.

Angel's 1970, four disc FORZA displays Martina Arroyo's Leonora, the Alvaro of Carlo Bergonzi, and the Padre Guardiano of Ruggiero Raimondi among its principal assets. Arroyo is a singer of taste and considerable vocal ability, but her Leonora is dramatically dull and cold. Arroyo manages some lovely moments, particularly in the "Convent Scene," but her performance is outclassed by those of Tebaldi, Price, Callas, and Milanov. Bergonzi, in absolutely top form, is the finest Alvaro on discs, singing with honeyed tone and musical grace, ever a model of style and intelligence. Piero Cappuccilli's lean, rather harsh tone enables him to portray a suitably tough, unyielding Don Carlo, but he too falls short of the work of much of his competition. Raimondi is an excellent Guardiano, except for some rough going in the lower register. Bianca Maria Casoni is a very light-voiced and unalluring Preziosilla. Melitone is vividly portrayed and attractively sung by Sir Geraint Evans. The Royal Philharmonic Orchestra and Ambrosian Opera Chorus provide high quality support under the very fine direction of Lamberto Gardelli.

The only budget priced FORZA is a rather workaday 3-disc Everest-Cetra edition, whose principal glories are the intense (if occasionally strident) Leonora of Maria Caniglia, and the truly magnificent work of Tancredi Pasero, a rarely recorded artist who is considered by some to be among the great singers of the century, as Guardiano. Ebe Stignani has some fine moments as Preziosilla, but the rest of the cast, including Galliano Massini as Alvaro and Carlo Tagliabue as Don Carlo, is quite routine. The RAI Chorus and Orchestra are conducted here by Bruno Erminero who performs with little distinction.

R. STRAUSS:
DIE FRAU OHNE SCHATTEN

Bjoner, Borkh, Mödl, Thomas, Fischer-Dieskau, Hotter, Keilberth cond.
Bavarian State Opera (Munich) Orchestra and Chorus
4 discs
DGG 2711005
UK: Same

Rysanek, Goeltz, Höngven, Hopf, Schoeffler, Boehme, Böhm cond.
Vienna State Opera Chorus and Vienna Philharmonic
4 discs
Richmond RS64503
UK: Ace of Diamonds GOS534-7

The Strauss-Hofmansthal fantasy, as difficult to stage well as it is to cast well, received a tremendous boost in popularity in the United States when the Metropolitan gave the work in an opulent, imaginative production during its first season at its new Lincoln Center house in 1966. With an international cast including Leonie Rysanek, Christa Ludwig, Irene Dalis, James King, Walter Berry, and Karl Böhm, the opera became a sellout, was broadcast coast-to-coast three times, and has become a frequent visitor to the repertoire of the Met. Covent Garden has also successfully staged the work in recent seasons.

Neither of the two recordings are totally satisfactory. DGG's performance was recorded live at the opening of Munich's rebuilt National Theatre in 1963. Its cast is uneven and the score is heavily cut, while the conductor, Joseph Keilberth, had to drag out tempi in the interludes to accommodate the admittedly difficult scene changes.

Ingrid Bjoner's not so dramatic soprano was mercilessly tried by the demands of the role of the Empress. Her top tones are occasionally quavery, and while she often sings with a certain sweetness, there is little personality or authority to her work. Inge Borkh is a marvelously bitchy Dyer's Wife, but her voice, too, is forced beyond its natural limits by the role. Top notes are strident, and bottom notes deficient in beauty, but Borkh's commitment to the character is noteworthy. The third major female role, that of the Nurse to the Empress, is taken by Marthe Mödl, here well past her vocal prime (in truth in very ugly voice). This "quality," however, is well suited to the malevolent hag that Mödl sings, and thus the veteran soprano makes do with her withered resources, singing fiercely but, like Borkh, fully within the spirit of the role. Turning to the men, Jess Thomas is a manly, lyrical Emperor, rising to the occasion during his long scene in the second act, while Dietrich Fischer-Dieskau's warm and mellifluous Barak-the-Dyer is a true pleasure to hear. Hans Hotter's tremendous personal authority makes the role of Keikobad's Messenger into a cameo to treasure. The supporting players are variable, and the orchestra is occasionally overwhelmed by the music it was called upon to perform. Opening night nerves and mishaps may have contributed a great deal of rough spots that mar the recording. A work of this complexity really ought to have been done under studio conditions.

The other FRAU is now a Richmond-Ace of Diamonds bargain in stereo. This set features Leonie Rysanek, in her early prime, in one of her greatest roles, the Empress. In more recent years, the soprano's lower register has filled out somewhat, but even in the 1950's, Rysanek's top notes were more exciting than virtually anyone else singing the Strauss operas —and no one can match the raw emotion of Rysanek's Empress in her third act ordeal at the fountain. Chrystel Goltz is a serviceable Dyer's wife, but Elisabeth Höngven is somewhat pallid as the Nurse. Hans Hopf does his best with the Emperor, but his top notes are scrawny and rough. Paul Schoeffler is a mature but sensitive Barak, and Kurt Boehme sings with competence as the Messenger. Karl Böhm's reading of the score is vivid.

While these two recordings certainly have their respective virtues, a new, studio recording of this opera with a "dream cast" featuring Rysanek, Ludwig, Brilioth, Berry, and perhaps Hans Sotin, led again by Dr. Böhm, is needed and makes something very nice to dream about.

PONCHIELLI: LA GIOCONDA

Tebaldi, Horne, Bergonzi, Merrill, Dominguez, Ghiuselev, Gardelli
cond.
Orchestra and Chorus of L'Accademia di Santa Cecilia
3 discs
London OSA 1388*
UK: Decca SET364-6

Callas, Cossotto, Miranda-Ferraro, Cappuccilli, Vinco, Votto cond.
La Scala Orchestra and Chorus
3 discs
Seraphim S-6301

Cerquetti, del Monaco, Simionato, Bastianini, Siepi, Gavazzeni
cond.
Orchestra and Chorus of the Maggio Musicale Fiorentino
3 discs
Richmond 63518
UK: Ace of Diamonds GOS609-10

Callas, Barbieri, Poggi, Votto cond.
RAI Orchestra and Chorus
3 discs
Everest/Cetra S419-3*

Milanov, Elias, Amparán, di Stefano, Warren, Clabassi, Previtali
cond.
Orchestra and Chorus of L'Accademia di Cecilia
3 discs
Victrola VICS 6101

If ever there were a singer's opera, it is LA GIOCONDA. The libretto (by Arrigo Boito writing under the anagram Tobio Gorria) is preposterous, the orchestral writing is subordinate, but given six fine, Italianate singers, this opera by Puccini's principal teacher soars. Understandably, GIOCONDA has always been a favorite of singers, and there have been several recordings of the work, two of which are distinguished all the way through in terms of casting, while two others are notable for the work of one prima donna, La Callas.

Whether one chooses the budget priced Victrola edition featuring Milanov, di Stefano, Warren, and Elias, conducted by Previtali or the London-Decca set will be a matter of personal preference as both are excellent. The Victrola set, made at the Rome Opera in 1958 finds in Zinka Milanov a mature yet sumptuous sounding heroine who recorded the "Suicidio" in one authoritative "take" and who lavishes a pianissimo on the Act One phrase "Enzo adorato, ah come t'amo" the likes of which has seldom if ever been equalled. True, the voice sounds tremulous at times, and little attempt at characterization is made, but the Milanov Gioconda remains a treasurable souvenir of a great diva's work. Backing Milanov up on this recording is Giuseppe di Stefano, a lyrical Enzo whose top tones are strained, but one whose velvety singing of "Cielo e mar" and the duets with the baritone and mezzo are noteworthy nonetheless. Leonard Warren is a uniquely fine Barnaba, impressing as much with his pointedly nasty characterization and frightening final scream as with his sonorous "O monumento" and "Pescator." Rosalind Elias is a creamy and rather sexy Laura, fitting the role almost perfectly, while Plinio Clabassi and Belen Amparan are more than acceptable in their respective roles of Alvise and La Cieca. Fernando Previtali conducts the willing and winning Rome Opera forces most knowingly.

London allowed Renata Tebaldi to record her Gioconda in 1967, which was shortly after the soprano completed her first of two New York seasons in this role. On stage, Tebaldi was an exciting Gioconda, although listeners wondered whether she was doing her voice any long range harm by taking on so demanding and heavy a role. The recording, which co-stars such estimable singers as Marilyn Horne, Carlo Bergonzi, and Robert Merrill, finds Tebaldi in strong vocal form. The high C's are labored, it is true, but are squarely on pitch, and Tebaldi's characterization is one of her most compelling. The quieter moments are marked by sustained beauty, and the "Suicidio" is appropriately desperate-sounding from the dramatic standpoint and is powerfully sung to boot. Bergonzi offers a firm voiced Enzo sung with more sensitivity than this operatic heel deserves or, for that matter, usually receives. Horne sings Laura with excellent vocal quality but is cold and uninvolved even when embracing Enzo or battling with Alvise or Gioconda. Nicolai Ghiuselev is somewhat dry voiced as Alvise, while Robert Merrill seems disinterested in the role of Barnaba. Like Marilyn Horne, he is content to sing nicely and offers little sense of characterization. Oralia Dominguez is a most ingratiating La Cieca. Lamberto Gardelli conducts the Chorus and Orchestra of the Santa Cecilia Academy with a lively and broadly theatrical beat, moving the work swiftly and vigorously.

The market is rich in modestly priced recordings of this opera, for in addition to the Victrola album, both Callas versions are available on budget labels, as is an older London-Decca set. On both the Cetra and Seraphim albums, Callas was surrounded by generally mediocre supporting casts (except for Barbieri on the older, Cetra set and Cossotto on the Seraphim version). The Seraphim album, recorded in 1959 finds her in disconcertingly rough voice, particularly in high passages where her famous wobble is all too obvious, but Callas' unique artistry and disciplined musicianship allow her some notably moving moments. Unfortunately, the La Scala forces led by Antonio Votto are not equal to the recorded competition. With Pier Miranda Ferarro being a particularly puny Enzo, and Piero Cappuccilli a rough voiced Barnaba, only Fiorenza Cossotto's Laura and Ivo Vinco's Alvise are worthy of Callas' company. The Cetra set is old and primitive, but on it Callas is a searing heroine and in better voice than on the Seraphim album. The Cetra recording also boasts having Fedora Barbieri as a particularly dramatic Laura. The Richmond set offers the huge, warm voices of Anita Cerquetti in the title role, Mario del Monaco as Enzo, Giulietta Simionato as Laura, Ettore Bastianini as Barnaba, and Cesare Siepi as Alvise in a performance that will undoubtedly please many listeners.

WAGNER: LOHENGRIN

Grümmer, Ludwig, Thomas, Fischer-Dieskau, Wiener, Frick, Kempe
cond.
Vienna Philharmonic and State Opera Chorus
5 discs
Angel S-3641*
UK: HMV SLS906

Janowitz, Jones, King, Stewart, Ridderbusch, Kubelik cond.
Bavarian Radio Orchestra and Chorus
5 discs
Deutsche Grammophon 2713005
UK: Deutsche Grammophon 2720036

Amara, Gorr, Konya, Dooley, Hines, Marsh, Leinsdorf cond.
Boston Symphony Orchestra and Boston Chorus Pro Musica
5 discs
RCA LSC-6710

Steber, Varnay, Windgassen, Uhde, Keilberth cond.
Bayreuth Festival Orchestra and Chorus
5 discs
Richmond RS65003 (Mono)

Of the three stereophonic LOHENGRIN sets available, the
Angel-HMV version conducted by Rudolf Kempe is the most
exciting, although, as will be seen, each of the other albums
has considerable merit. Leading the Vienna Philharmonic
Orchestra and State Opera Chorus with grandeur and scope,
Kempe creates a stunning aural canvas for Wagner's Brabant,

and his soloists work towards realizing the conductor's weighty yet vibrant conception of the opera.

Jess Thomas, who has recently emerged as a true helden-tenor, singing Tristan, both Siegfrieds, and Parsifal, is a manly, dark voiced Swan Knight who seems as capable of defending Elsa with his sword as with his prayers. Although Thomas has occasionally found top notes difficult to sustain in other performances, his voice is notably free of constriction here, and he is able to sing softly, as in "Meine lieber Schwan," with the same ease and finesse with which he can defy Telramund in the Second Act finale.

Elisabeth Grümmer is an old-fashioned dramatic soprano who is less maidenly than matronly as Elsa. Her large, evenly produced voice is, however, a very handsome instrument, and her authoritative singing and many moments of consummate beauty, as in "Elsa's Dream" or the scene in Act Two with Ortrud, add to the power of this performance.

Ortrud is sung by Christa Ludwig, an immensely intelligent actress who also happens to own one of the most fabulous voices of the century. In the art of Miss Ludwig, Ortrud may be a sorceress, but she is no Wicked Witch of the West! Ludwig is marvelously sweet-voiced as she seduces, so to speak, Elsa at the beginning of Act Two. The contrasting venom that pours out of her during the invocation of the gods is, therefore, all the more effective. Ludwig also understands the difference between playing evil and playing shrewishness. Thus, Ortrud's most dramatic moments are never marred by excessive shouting, chestiness, or shrillness of tone but are performed with the fine taste and outstanding vocalism that Ludwig has taught us to expect from her work.

Dietrich Fischer-Dieskau, the baritone of this album, is very much at home in Telramund's music and strives to present him as a blackhearted if blundering villain. Fischer-Dieskau's enormous intelligence coupled with his beautiful voice allow him to work out this somewhat self-limiting characterization successfully. Sometimes, of course, the most blatantly evil characters are less interesting than those with conflicting emotions or, at least, guilty consciences. Here, however, Fischer-Dieskau emerges as a dominant force in the performance.

Gottlob Frick is a sturdy King Henry, and Otto Wiener is a similarly stalwart Herald. The Vienna State Opera Chorus sings with infectious gusto, and the Vienna Philharmonic turns in one of its very best performances making this LOHENGRIN an unqualified success.

The recent Deutsche Grammophon LOHENGRIN is in many ways praiseworthy, too. The Bavarian State Radio Orchestra and Chorus do well under Rafael Kubelik's subtle, rather underplayed direction. Kubelik's LOHENGRIN is rather in the vein of von Karajan's Wagner performances—more lyrical and spiritual than one often finds Wagner played. From the first notes of the prelude, Kubelik establishes a hazy, dream-like feeling that filters through the opera. The Lohengrin, James King, has a smaller voice than Thomas and sings a rather cerebral, reserved Knight. His voice is often quite pleasant, although King occasionally has some trouble staying on pitch. King is very fine in the Bridal Chamber Scene and in the final moments of the opera, although one might look for more strength in his singing in the first act.

Gundula Janowitz is well cast as Elsa. Her sweet, youthful voice readily suggests Elsa's innocence and passiveness. Janowitz is not content with a bovine approach to her character and injects a sense of Elsa's rising fears and doubts. Musically, the soprano is top flight, singing squarely on pitch, with security of intonation, and a warm, soft tone that never hardens, even when she is singing fortissimo.

Gwynneth Jones reveals herself to be in severe vocal trouble here as Ortrud. Her wobble has by now crept into her middle register so that nearly every phrase is marred by tortured sound and unsteady production. Jones' top notes are all too often utterly devoid of beauty or even excitement which often can be a substitute for glorious sound. This Ortrud is strident and impotent, especially in comparison to that of Christa Ludwig on the Angel-HMV set.

If Jones disappoints, her partner in operatic crime, Thomas Stewart, impresses with his strong, honorable Telramund. Stewart's voice rides out the heavy orchestration, sounding a little tight only when he sings in his uppermost register. In contrast to Fischer-Dieskau's malign reading of virtually each of Telramund's lines, Stewart's Telramund seems to cling to his former reputation, as if doing evil only under his wife's influence. Karl Ridderbusch is a youthful and noble voiced King Henry—perhaps the best on records. Were it not for the glaring incompetence of Miss Jones in her assignment as Ortrud, this recording would be severe competition for the Angel-HMV LOHENGRIN. Even with this imbalance in the casting, it offers many pleasures to the listener.

RCA's LOHENGRIN commemorates a 1965 Berkshire Festival concert performance of the opera in which the Boston Symphony was led by Erich Leinsdorf. Soloists, Chorus (the Boston Chorus Pro Musica) adjourned to Boston's Symphony Hall to record the opera shortly after the concert. Leontyne Price had originally been announced for the role of Elsa, but withdrew several weeks before the concert took place. Her replacement was the Metropolitan Opera's ubiquitous Lucine Amara, more noted for her performances in lyric roles in French and Italian operas than for Wagnerian music drama. Miss Amara is perhaps not a first class artist, but she is an intelligent and hard-working singer who at her best can do some very fine work. Unfortunately, Amara is not well suited to Wagner. Her voice is not large, and has a distinct vibrato that can be used nicely in, say, LES CONTES D'HOFFMANN, where she doesn't need to worry about being heard over an immense orchestra. Here, Miss Amara seems constrained to force her voice, sounding strident and colorless in the upper ranges and none too secure throughout. Furthermore, Amara seems nervous and uncomfortable in the part of Elsa and thus sounds petulant and querulous rather than gentle and fearful. The first act aria does not, in truth, go badly, nor does a good portion of the Bridal Chamber scene, but nowhere does the soprano makes a distinctive or truly positive impression in the role. Sandor Konya, the Lohengrin, is supposed to have sung the opera more than 200 times in his career. With this background, he brings a certain well-routined authority to the role, but he has either ceased looking for, or has never found, means of characterizing the role. Mr. Konya sings the hero as if he were a kindly, patient, and very dull gentleman who rides a swan. Vocally, Konya sounds less tired than he often does in live performances nowadays, but his rather dull timbre and mechanical interpretation become boring on repeated hearings of the recording.

Rita Gorr, the Ortrud, is an artist of great intelligence who once had a brilliant mezzo soprano voice. Alas, even by 1965, Gorr had lost control of her top notes which emerge as harsh and ugly and which serve to make her Ortrud sound like an old crone rather than a beautiful sorceress. William Dooley is a forthright, musically accurate Telramund, but one who evidently doesn't find much of histrionic interest in the character. Jerome Hines is heard as the King. His still powerful voice, unfortunately, lacks security of intonation. Calvin Marsh as the Herald is also afflicted at times by vocal shakiness.

Leinsdorf conducts with a crisp, even beat and brings some sense of drama to the score. Somehow, though, his work here lacks thrust and excitement—all the climaxes seem a trifle on the tame side. This is too bad as the Boston Symphony, the first major American symphony orchestra to undertake an operatic recording since the days of Toscanini and the NBC Symphony, plays extremely well. The Boston Chorus Pro Musica, however, is a weak link in the performance. They produce a small, tentative sound that compares poorly to the precision and ease with which the choral groups on the other two sets perform. This RCA set presents a practically uncut version of the opera.

Budget minded listeners may acquire the Richmond monaural reissue of London-Decca's 1951 Bayreuth Festival LOHENGRIN. Eleanor Steber is a lovely Elsa, and Wolfgang Windgassen is an exemplary Lohengrin. Astrid Varnay is an impassioned Ortrud, while Herman Uhde is a sensitive, brooding Telramund. Joseph Keilberth leads an engrossing performance.

VERDI: I LOMBARDI
ALLA PRIMA CROCCIATA

Deutekom, Domingo, Raimondi, Lo Monaco, Gardelli cond.
Philharmonic Orchestra and Ambrosian Opera Chorus
3 discs
Philips 6703 032
UK: Same

Vitale, Bertocci, Petri, M. Wolf-Ferrari cond.
RAI Orchestra and Chorus
3 discs
Everest/Cetra S-454/3

Verdi's fourth work, an uneven pageant that offers some stirring music as well as an unwieldy and unconvincing plot, has
recently been treated to a new recording made by the adventurous Philips company and featuring Cristina Deutekom,
Placido Domingo, and Ruggiero Raimondi, with London's
Philharmonia Orchestra under the direction of Lamberto
Gardelli. The Philips set swells the number of LOMBARDI
albums to two, with a veteran Cetra set available at a budget
price.

The newer recording is deeply satisfying. The soloists and
the conductor approach the score with enthusiasm and a
superabundance of raw talent.

Cristina Deutekom has been widely hailed in Europe as the
latest major dramatic soprano d'agilità, with her repertoire
embracing such diverse parts as the Queen of the Night,
Elvira in PURITANI, and the title role in LUCIA DI
LAMMERMOOR. Due to the fact that Giselda in LOMBARDI
is one of Verdi's more florid heroines, one who looks backward

to Donizetti or Bellini creations rather than ahead to such later Verdian figures as Amelia or Aida, Deutekom finds her music mostly congenial. The Dutch artist's voice is not notably large, but it is bright sounding and evenly produced, sounding at its best rather like that of Beverly Sills. Unfortunately, Deutekom's vocal technique is far less secure than Sills' or Caballé's, with coloratura passages often being more bravely than brainily attacked. This sort of singing has brought Elena Souliotis to premature vocal decay, and one hopes that the same will not afflict Deutekom. For the moment, however, her vocal equipment bears up well under the heavy challenges it receives in this music. Deutekom's main weakness, besides her technical problems, is her inability to enunciate clearly. Even Joan Sutherland is far superior to her in this respect . . . however, the soprano produces consistently pleasant sound on this recording, and there is an undeniably electric quality to her work, even though many of her words are unintelligible. If she can come to terms with these weaknesses, Cristina Deutekom may well be destined for a great career. On the basis of this recording, one wishes her well.

The soprano is flanked by two young men with considerable operatic experience between them. Placido Domingo sings the role of Oronte with a marked smoothness of line and a glossier, more attractive tone than he has been demonstrating in other recent performances. Domingo sings warmly and with restraint, and the voice seems free from distortion even on the top of the staff. Ruggiero Raimondi emerges as the true hero of the set with his performance of Pagano, the lustful parricide turned religious hermit (this role is quite absurd dramatically and is made bearable only by the gorgeous music Verdi lavished upon it). Raimondi's voice suggests the qualities embodied in a good red wine—warmth, strength, and mellowness. The young bass' low notes tend to be a little raspy, but he compensates for this with his strong, secure top notes. Deutekom, Domingo, and Raimondi cap the performance with an idiomatic and magnificently sung account of the third act trio that somehow makes the entire fourth act seem superfluous. To my mind, the finest music in the opera, this trio, as performed by these artists, stands among Verdi's finest achievements, ranking with the RIGOLETTO quartet and, in its way, perhaps even with the great ensemble in the third act of OTELLO.

The supporting roles are successfully performed, with the young American tenor Jerome Lo Monaco due a special mention for his strong singing in the role of Arvino, the heroine's father. In addition to the excellent work by the Philharmonic Orchestra, the recording is helped by the stirring work by the Ambrosian Opera Chorus. Lamberto Gardelli succeeds in conducting one of Verdi's most rough and tumble scores with vigor but without a trace of vulgarity. No one remotely interested in Verdi's operas should miss this set.

Although the many excellences of Philip's I LOMBARDI all but rule out the Everest-Cetra version as a first-choice edition, those who already own the album need not feel too ashamed. While the performance is quite crude in comparison to the newer version, it is not without some satisfying elements. In the role of Giselda, Maria Vitale displays a wiry but by no means unpleasant soprano. In terms of diction, and strength of characterization, Vitale surpasses her smoother voiced rival in the Philips set.

Gustavo Gallo is more than adequate as Oronte, while Mario Petri is a strong if none too subtle Pagano. As is unfortunately usual in the Cetra albums, the minor and supporting parts are sung by a quite motley crew of artists, while the Chorus and Orchestra of RAI respond in a provincial manner to the workmanlike beat of conductor Manno Wolf-Ferrari.

DONIZETTI:
LUCIA DI LAMMERMOOR

Sutherland, Pavarotti, Milnes, Ghiaurov, Bonynge cond.
Covent Garden Orchestra and Chorus
3 discs
London OSA 13103
UK: Decca: SET528-30

Sills, Bergonzi, Cappuccilli, Diaz, Schippers cond.
London Symphony Orchestra and Ambrosian Opera Chorus
3 discs
ABC-Dunhill ATS-20006
UK: HMV SLS797

Callas, Tagliavini, Cappuccilli, Serafin cond.
Philharmonia Orchestra and Chorus
2 discs
Angel S-3601*
UK: Columbia SAX2316-7

Sutherland, Cioni, Merrill, Siepi, Pritchard cond.
Orchestra and Chorus of L'Accademia di Santa Cecilia
3 discs
London OSA-1327*
UK: Decca SET212-5

Moffo, Bergonzi, Sereni, Flagello, Prêtre cond.
RCA Italiana Orchestra and Chorus
3 discs
RCA LSC-6170

Scotto, di Stefano, Bastianini, Vinco, Sanzogno cond.
La Scala Orchestra and Chorus
2 discs (standard cuts)
Everest/Cetra S-439-2

Peters, Peerce, Maero, Leinsdorf cond.
Rome Opera Orchestra and Chorus
2 discs (Standard cuts)
Victrola VICS-6001

Callas, di Stefano, Gobbi, Serafin cond.
Orchestra and Chorus of the Maggio Musicale Fiorentino
2 discs (standard cuts)
Seraphim IB6032 (Mono)

Donizetti's psychotic heroine is certainly one of the most popular operatic crazy ladies to stand before the microphones, judging from the many recordings of LUCIA DI LAMMER-MOOR that have graced the catalogues of the recording companies. Even in this era of rediscovered Donizetti and Bellini operas, LUCIA seems to be the standard by which all coloraturas are to be evaluated.

The three major contenders for honors as the "greatest Lucia of our era" each have their partisans, not to mention qualifications for this title, so the words written here are not likely to change anyone's mind. However, having heard Sutherland and Sills in countless performances and Callas' two recordings of the role, as well as a few of that diva's LUCIA performances on tape, I will go down as admiring Sills' LUCIA the most, while maintaining a healthy respect for the work of Callas and Sutherland in the role.

Beverly Sills' LUCIA, released in the US on ABC Audio Treasury while available in the UK on the HMV label, is marred by weak conducting and an uneven supporting cast. Sills' voice is smaller than Sutherland's, and it is not as basically warm an instrument as that of her Australian rival.

However, the electrically charged Sills personality, and her skilled and abundantly creative use of her voice allow her to triumph. One senses in this Lucia, from her first appearance, the turmoil and rising hysteria that ultimately unhinge her. In addition to her affecting treatment of Lucia's character, Sills commands the musical gifts with which to meet every challenge that the composer offers her. Although the recording does not fully capture Sills' ethereal sound, her outstanding coloratura singing and her unfailingly real characterization serve her well here.

As for Sills Mad Scene, not even Callas, for all her technical virtuosity and dramatic fervor, achieves the degree of personal involvement that communicates itself from singer to listener that is apparent in Beverly Sills' work. Miss Sills' Mad Scene is made still more interesting through the use of the glass harp, called for in the original score but almost never heard in today's performances (a flute is generally used). The strange, eerie sounds produced by this instrument add a surrealistic touch to the scene which is lacking in all the other recordings.

Carlo Bergonzi, singing Edgardo, is, although dramatically neuter, the only truly distinguished member of the cast besides the soprano. Although the surprisingly dead recorded sound does him an injustice in veiling his normally bright, vibrant sound, Bergonzi's hero is sensitively sung with many finely spun notes and an ease of production at both ends of the tenor's range.

Piero Cappuccilli, the Enrico, is by no means a poor singer. Dramatically speaking, he captures his character's nastiness. The problem is that the baritone's voice is not large enough and not sufficiently pleasant to the ear to succeed in this sort of music. Cappuccilli pushes for volume and his singing often takes on an unattractive edge as a result. Justino Diaz is in distressingly rough voice in the role of Raimondo, and his singing hardly justifies the reinstatement of the chaplain's second act aria (as with most recent LUCIA sets, the score is performed complete, with the third act Storm Scene for tenor and baritone, all repeats, and many choral and miscellaneous passages restored). Thomas Schippers conducts the London Symphony Orchestra and the Ambrosian Opera Chorus with all the drive of an octogenarian in need of a physic. His flabby beat casts a further pall over a quirky performance that fails to provide the proper support for the fine work and gentle ravings of Sills as Lucia.

Joan Sutherland, whose Lucia has become the standard interpretation at both Covent Garden, where she first attracted international attention in the part, and at the Metropolitan, where she made her 1961 debut in the role, has recorded the opera on two occasions for London-Decca.

The earlier set, made in 1961, is eminently respectable. Miss Sutherland's huge voice and phenomenally effortless trills explode upon the ear as would a bombshell of brilliant sound. Sutherland's oft-noted faults, sliding into notes from below, less than perfect diction, and a blurred, generalized sense of character can easily be overlooked by those who would place gorgeous tone and pyrotechnics above all. My own preferences lead me to ask for more in a singer than the admittedly superhuman work that Sutherland at her best provides. This recording will probably not convert Callas or Sills aficionados into Sutherland fans, but those who do admire "La Stupenda" may use this set to support their praise for the soprano. The rest of the cast is more notable for the vigorous and smooth-voiced Enrico of Robert Merrill and the superbly wrought Raimondo of Cesare Siepi than for Renato Cioni's rather dry-voiced, provincial Edgardo. The uncut score is elegantly led by John Pritchard, who stands at the helm of the Orchestra and Chorus of the Accademia di Santa Cecilia.

Sutherland's second LUCIA was released shortly before this book went to press. This time, the soprano has been supported by the Covent Garden forces as well as by an international cast including Luciano Pavarotti, Sherrill Milnes and Nicolai Ghiaurov in the principal roles, and the soprano's husband, Richard Bonynge, on the podium. Although Bonynge's heavy, pedantic tempi do a great deal to mar the performance, the singing is of generally high quality. Miss Sutherland's voice has not sounded this bright in several years, and she scoops less than on many recent recordings. The voice has, surprisingly, grown richer in the lower register, and Sutherland actually exhibits some impressive chest tones. She has ornamented the music somewhat differently in this version than in her earlier recording which, unlike the new one, included an alternate aria for the heroine appended to the sixth side. Furthermore, Sutherland's diction is, while not nearly as incisive as Sills', Callas', or Scotto's, distinctly improved over most of her other recordings, and her characterization, while not finely etched, is at the very least appropriate and workmanlike. The ensuing ten years since her first LUCIA recording have in no way impaired Sutherland's ability to trill or to sing high notes. Again, to those who feel that a cardboard Lucia sung with consummate beauty is the ultimate approach to the role, this performance will be most rewarding.

Luciano Pavarotti is in something less than top form here, with a few high notes in the first two acts sounding slightly pinched, and his production seeming slightly constricted. However, Pavarotti in not quite best voice is still one of today's most gifted singers. The Tomb Scene finds the tenor in full command of his powers and is thus one of the most successful accounts of this music to be encountered on records.

Sherrill Milnes' Enrico Ashton is, unhappily, less praiseworthy. In spite of some magnificent, interpolated high notes, the baritone is plagued by sloppiness of intonation and a tendency to sing flat, which is distressingly apparent in the opening scene which contains Enrico's only aria. The duet with Lucia is more successful, but if this is typical of Milnes' current standards of performance, this young artist is headed for bad trouble.

More positively, Nicolai Ghiaurov's commanding, handsomely sung Raimondo is almost reason enough in itself to acquire this recording. The supporting cast, most notably including Ryland Davies and Hougette Tourangeau as Normanno and Alisa, respectively, is exemplary. Richard Bonynge's deadly conducting robs the music of much of its grace, and, though his handling of the finale to the Second Act is less lethargic, Bonynge fails to ignite the ensemble and thus must be blamed for the generally anemic, undynamic feeling of the performance.

Maria Callas has also recorded the opera twice. Her first version, the revered 1953 Florence May Festival performance led by Tullio Serafin is now available on the Seraphim label. Callas is in her own way chillingly effective in the title role. Her wiry, dark sound and intense characterization make for a womanly, quite naturally tragic Lucia, and, if the high notes are somewhat whitish in comparison with those of Sills or Sutherland, her singing of this music is still remarkable for ease and accuracy.

Giuseppe di Stefano is, on this set, a romantic and sweet-voiced Edgardo whose lyric tenor is heard in its early prime, with no hint of the strain that poor judgement would later inflict on his singing. Tito Gobbi is the fine Enrico, singing with style and elegance as well as providing a character as strong as Callas' Lucia is vulnerable. Nicola Rossi-Lemeni is a solid Raimondo. Serafin's handling of the orchestra and chorus is practiced and considerate. The only real flaw is that the score is heavily cut, conforming to the "standard" edition of the opera that muddles the drama and needlessly truncates the music.

Callas' second LUCIA, released in 1959 on Angel-HMV and made to allow the soprano to preserve her famous stage role in stereophonic sound, is disappointing on most counts. Again, the abridged version of the opera is used. Callas, although, if possible, more dramatically exciting than before as Lucia, had more or less lost control of her upper register when this set was made. As a result, there are many screechy moments and the Mad Scene is obviously a grueling challenge to the soprano. Still, the first act duet with Edgardo, sung by the none too youthful Ferruccio Tagliavini, is effective, and the duet with Enrico in Act Two is a powerful emotional experience. Piero Cappuccilli is heard on this set as Enrico and is in better voice here than he is on the Sills' recording. Serafin's conducting of the Philharmonia is efficient and appropriate, although rather routine.

A bargain-priced LUCIA that offers many rewards is Everest/Cetra's La Scala performance starring Renata Scotto as Lucia. Miss Scotto in 1958 was not yet the assured, often brilliant artist she is today. Her voice occasionally is pinched on top, but her technique is sure, and her tense characterization in the Callas mode is an interesting forecast of the marvellous Lucia that this Italian soprano was to become. Di Stefano is once again a nearly perfect Edgardo, while Ettore Bastianini is an arresting, strongly sung villain. Ivo Vinco is a decent if not especially distinguished Raimondo. Nino Sanzogno leads the cut version of the score with crisp tempi and a general awareness of the opera's many dramatic qualities.

The final LUCIA set I will discuss is on the RCA label, dating from the mid 1960's and featuring Anna Moffo as Lucia, with Georges Prêtre conducting the RCA Italiana forces in the complete version of the score. Moffo is an interesting actress who in her heyday had a lovely lyric soprano voice which she occasionally called upon to sing coloratura music. Her Lucia emerges as attractively if wanly sung in comparison to her more illustrious competition. There is a commendable earnestness to Moffo's Lucia and a sense of musical discipline, but the high notes are unbeautiful and the coloratura work is "catch as catch can" in the Mad Scene—in all honesty, Moffo has no real affinity for this sort of singing.

Bergonzi is an outstanding Edgardo, in even better form than on the later recording with Sills. Mario Sereni is competent but uninteresting as Enrico, while Ezio Flagello is a sonorous Raimondo. Prêtre conducts in a precise but uninteresting manner which makes this set of little appeal except for the work of Bergonzi.

DONIZETTI: LUCREZIA BORGIA

Caballé, Verrett, Kraus, Flagello, Perlea cond.
RCA Italiana Orchestra and Chorus
3 discs
RCA LSC-6176*
UK: RCA SER553-5

LUCREZIA BORGIA served as the vehicle for Montserrat Caballé's "surprise" New York debut in 1965 when she stepped into the title role of an American Opera Society concert performance of this rarely heard work when another artist cancelled. The acclaim that Caballé received that evening led directly to her Metropolitan Opera debut and her recording contract with RCA. One of her first complete opera sets on the RCA label was LUCREZIA BORGIA, a tribute both to the opera that had given her so momentous a success and to the awakening sensibilities of RCA executives who otherwise rarely venture away from "safe" repertory items in their choices for recordings.

These considerations set aside, the fact remains that RCA's LUCREZIA is one of that firm's best recent recordings, in which an almost matchless cast is supported by a highly competent maestro and a worthy chorus and orchestra. Donizetti's score is perhaps not among his best, although there are two brilliant arias for the soprano, "Com' é bello" in the Prologue and "Era desso il figlio mio" in the second act, and the familiar drinking song "Il segreto d'esser felice" for the mezzo in the last scene of the opera. The first act finale is a typically rousing piece that sounds like the musical relative to the second act Finale to LUCIA that it is. Elsewhere, some of the music, while graceful and rather pretty, is dramatically phlegmatic (as in the death scene of Gennaro) but the entire opera has its musical appeal to *bel canto* admirers and ought to be owned, at the very least in the highlights disc that RCA has also provided.

Turning to the singing, while Caballé may be the leading lady here, and a most distinguished one, her performance is but one of several superb ones. In more recent performances and recordings, the lady has done more in terms of characterizing her roles. Here Caballé is dramatically reserved. No one, of course, could describe a performance as gorgeously sung as this as dull. The Caballé technique is flawless, and the voice as limpid and soft as any that we have heard in this generation. Only when she is attempting very high notes *forte* does the soprano's voice harden. Caballé's pianissimi, on display in both of Lucrezia's arias and used for bloodchilling effect in the "Era desso il figlio mio," are beyond compare, and her frequent use of the *coup de glotte* is piquant and often exciting.

Shirley Verrett sings the "trouser role" of Maffeo Orsino, friend, in the opera's turgid libretto adapted from Hugo's play, of Gennaro, the illegitimate son of Lucrezia, and sworn, mortal enemy to that rather fearsome lady. The swaggering absurdities of a role such as this are legion, but the vibrant American mezzo makes these count as nothing with her singing. One wishes only that the (male) listener did not have to discount the allure of Verrett's artistry, though not to do so would serve only to confuse an already murky text!

Miss Verrett proves herself to be equal to the demands of *bel canto*, and her handling of the musical intricacies of her role lead one to hope that she will soon add Adalgisa in NORMA, and perhaps Rosina in BARBIERE and Leonora in LA FAVORITA to her stage and recorded roles. For heart-melting vocalism, listen only to Orsini's drinking song as handled by Verrett.

Alfredo Kraus sings the Gennaro, the ill-fated son of a Borgia about whom the plot revolves. As recorded here, Kraus' voice is smooth, velvety and tastefully handled, attributes which lead him to the forefront of today's lyric tenors.

He is a fine partner for both Caballé and Verrett, although he too might be more animated dramatically.

Ezio Flagello, singing Don Alfonso, Lucrezia's husband and a very villainous fellow, is in smoother voice here than on some other recent recordings. His dark, resonant basso voice is well suited to his music, and Flagello creates a properly nasty sense of character.

None of the supporting roles are particularly grateful to singers, consisting as they do of henchman for Lucrezia and Don Alfonso and four friends of Gennaro and Orsini. All of these parts are well handled by RCA's singers. Turning to conductor Jonel Perlea, if he does not infuse the opera with personal brilliance and a life force emanating from his baton, it may at least be said that he moves the music forward efficiently, and that his beat is strong and his tempi are always reasonable. The RCA Italiana Chorus sings with particular relish and that company's orchestra is entirely professional in quality. All in all, this is an outstanding recording of a beautiful work.

VERDI: LUISA MILLER

Moffo, Verrett, Bergonzi, MacNeil, Tozzi, Flagello, Cleva cond.
RCA Italiana Orchestra and Chorus
3 discs
RCA LSC6168*
UK: RCA SER5534-6

Kelston, Lauri-Volpi, Rossi cond.
RAI Orchestra and Chorus
3 discs
Everest-Cetra S-433/3

Verdi's LUISA MILLER, the first of the "middle-period" operas,
points ahead to the composer's most successful works in its
welding of note to word and in its treatment of the father-
daughter relationship so common in Verdi's operas. Still very
much a "number" opera, LUISA MILLER has its share of
fine scenes for soprano, tenor, baritone, and bass, with a less
grateful role for a mezzo. These scenes for the principals more
than counterbalance a few vapid choruses. Even though it has
been revived in recent years at the Metropolitan, La Scala,
and the Rome and Florence operas, LUISA has yet to establish
itself as an international repertory item. Thus, RCA's recording, far more than the old, inferior Cetra set, will serve to
introduce many listeners to one of Verdi's most interesting,
if not fully mature, scores.

RCA assembled a most attractive cast in its Rome studios
for this set, taped in 1964. On discs, Moffo is a warm heroine
who has the requisite flexibility for the role's difficult and
rather florid tessitura as well as the cutting power to soar
across the orchestra and be heard in ensembles. Her singing

is quite beautiful throughout. Moffo makes a commendable effort to get inside her role, and the result is an animated and moving Luisa. Shirley Verrett's fine voice is a sizeable asset to the recording, although the role of the Duchess hardly gives the mezzo an opportunity to shine. Still, when a less gifted artist might very easily have been assigned the part, RCA's generosity in engaging Verrett is all the more praiseworthy.

In the role of Rodolfo, tenor Carlo Bergonzi is in top vocal condition, sounding youthful and vigorous, spinning out the Verdian line with faultless taste backed up by sure technique and a voice of spun gold. Bergonzi's "Quando la sera al placido" provides documented evidence to support the claim that the aria ranks as the finest Verdi ever penned for tenor voice.

Cornell MacNeil sings Miller with more intensity than he usually musters. Although his voice is marked by a noticeable vibrato, MacNeil impresses with careful musicianship and an often handsome, burnished tone. Giorgio Tozzi and Ezio Flagello, as the Count and his henchman Wurm, respectively, are a fine pair of bass voice villains, with Tozzi sounding mature and guilt-ridden and Flagello being properly vicious in character and smoother vocally than on any of his other recordings. The late Fausto Cleva conducts with extreme sensitivity and a true feeling for the music, shaping an idiomatic, flavorful performance.

VERDI: MACBETH

Rysanek, Warren, Bergonzi, Hines, Leinsdorf cond.
Metropolitan Opera Orchestra and Chorus
3 discs
Victrola VICS6121
UK: Same as above

Nilsson, Taddei, Prevedi, Foiani, Schippers cond.
Orchestra and Chorus of L'Accademia di Santa Cecilia
3 discs
London OSA 1380
UK: Decca SET282-4

Souliotis, Fischer-Dieskau, Pavarotti, Ghiaurov, Gardelli cond.
Philharmonia Orchestra and Ambrosian Opera Chorus
3 discs
London OSA 13102
UK: Decca SETB510-2

Although this first of Verdi's Shakespearean operas is infrequently performed, it has been recorded three times in the past twelve years, once by RCA (now re-released as a Victrola budget set) and twice by London-Decca.

The Victrola album is the eldest, made in 1959 to preserve the Metropolitan Opera's first production of the opera, and, incidentally, one of the very few complete professional recordings made of a Met production. On this occasion, the orchestra and chorus are well drilled, although the intentionally pinched tones of the witches becomes annoying after a while. Erich Leinsdorf directs an incisive and lively performance. Leonard Warren's Macbeth ranks as one of his very finest creations.

His voice is as clear and ringing on top as in the lower registers, and his phrasing, diction, and vocal power add up to a stirring Macbeth.

The story of how Leoni Rysanek came to replace the fired Callas as Lady Macbeth in the work's Met premiere is by now all too well known. Fortunately, what the public lost in terms' of the Lady who never was, was largely made up for by Rysanek's clarion interpretation. Not without its flaws, Rysanek's voice soars upwards in complete security, but she finds the middle and lower registers more than mildly troublesome at times. In this recording, however, Rysanek's difficulties are minimal, and she is often extremely successful in this demanding role. It would be hard to surpass the first act aria, "Vieni, t'affretta," as sung by this Austrian soprano.

The many supporting roles are generously cast, featuring the vibrant Macduff(o) of Carlo Bergonzi and the brooding Banquo of Jerome Hines, to name but two.

London ought to have been content to allow its 1965 MACBETH to remain unrivaled in its catalogue, for it is superior in nearly every respect to its 1971 remake of the opera.

The earlier recording offers Birgit Nilsson as Lady Macbeth, a role which was one of her first major successes at the Stockholm opera back in the 1940's. Nearly twenty years later, the Nilsson sound was perhaps a little unwieldy in the more florid passages of the first act *scena*, but the Swedish soprano surmounts this problem with relative aplomb and goes on to impress with opulent sound and gorgeous top notes. As the word "gorgeous" might indicate, Nilsson does not realize in her singing the evil inherent in Lady Macbeth's character to nearly the extent that Rysanek does, but as pure singing, her performance is outstanding.

Giuseppe Taddei is a Macbeth of great musical and dramatic intelligence, but in this recording, his baritone voice is dry and harsh sounding, rendering him unable to do full justice to the role. What one does get from Taddei's Macbeth, however, is a sense of inner struggle and tension that make his performance valid and consistently interesting.

Bruno Prevedi performs the short role of Macduff with high competence, while Giovanni Foiani offers a Banquo notable for suppleness of tone. Thomas Schippers' conducting of the Orchestra and Chorus of the Accademia di Santa Cecilia is uneven, with certain sections, most importantly the second act finale, being sluggishly led, while others are whipped along almost too quickly.

The second London-Decca *Macbeth* ranks far below its predecessor. With the exception of the fine conducting of the London Philharmonic Orchestra by Lamberto Gardelli, the powerful Banquo of Nicolai Ghiaurov, and the brilliant singing by Luciano Pavarotti as Macduffo, this recording is a fiasco. Dietrich Fischer-Dieskau has neither the vocal power or proficiency in the Italian repertory to make him qualify as Macbeth. Musicianship and intellect are present to a large degree in his performance, but that considerable intelligence should have kept him away from the role in the first place. Macbeth's music must not sound like Schubert lieder, as it does in this case. Turning to the Lady Macbeth of Elena Souliotis, it had best be stated simply that this young woman is simply unqualified to even attempt this role. Her tone is pinched, and notes are lunged for, not sung.

One novelty of this recording, though, is that it includes the third act witches ballet that Verdi was obliged to write for the Paris Opera premiere of Macbeth.

Those interested in a great if incomplete Lady Macbeth ought to own the Callas recital known as CALLAS PORTRAYS VERDI HEROINES available on Angel-EMI, on which she performs the three great scenes allotted this heroine with customary vehemence.

PUCCINI:
MADAMA BUTTERFLY

Tebaldi, Cossotto, Bergonzi, Sordello, Serafin cond.
Orchestra and Chorus of L'Accademia di Santa Cecilia
3 discs
London OSA 1314*
UK: Decca SXL2054-6

Scotto, di Stasio, Bergonzi, Panerai, Barbirolli cond.
Rome Opera Orchestra and Chorus
3 discs
Angel S-3702*
UK: HMV SLS927

Price, Elias, Tucker, Maero, Leinsdorf cond.
RCA Italiana Orchestra and Chorus
3 discs
RCA LSC6160*
UK: RCA SER5504-6

de los Angeles, Pirrazeni, Bjoerling, Sereni, Santini cond.
Rome Opera Orchestra and Chorus
3 discs
Angel S-3604*

Moffo, Elias, Valletti, Corena, Leinsdorf cond.
Rome Opera Orchestra and Chorus
3 discs
Victrola VICS-6100

Petrella, Tagliavini, Questa cond.
RAI Orchestra and Chorus
3 discs
Everest/Cetra S421-3*

Tebaldi, Rankin, Corena, Erede cond.
Orchestra and Chorus of L'Accademia di Santa Cecilia
3 discs
Richmond RS 63001* (Mono)
UK: Ace of Diamonds GOM528-30

dal Monte, Palombini, Gigli, Basiola, De Fabritiis cond.
Rome Opera Orchestra and Chorus
2 discs
Seraphim IB 6059 (Mono)

Callas, Danieli, Gedda, Boriello, von Karajan cond.
La Scala Orchestra and Chorus
3 discs
Angel 3523 C (Mono)

Choosing from among the several recordings of this opera is
not a simple task, as there are four that can be recommended
with little hesitation, as well as two or three others that are
not without merit.

MADAMA BUTTERFLY is one opera in which the soprano
role is of paramount interest. Perhaps more than any other
opera in the standard repertoire, BUTTERFLY performances
are dominated by their leading ladies. Indeed, it would be
difficult to interest oneself in a BUTTERFLY only for the sake
of the mezzo, tenor, or baritone. However, the recording
companies have been quite generous in casting these roles,
and the various recordings feature some renowned artists in
the roles of Pinkerton, Suzuki, and Sharpless.

RCA's MADAMA BUTTERFLY is a rewarding listening

experience. Leontyne Price's robust voice is perhaps not the most likely medium for Puccini's child-bride, but even in Act One, Price sings with much delicacy. Furthermore, her ringing top notes and powerful vocalizing in the duet with Pinkerton, the second act set pieces, and the final moments of the opera are immensely appealing. What is lacking in Price's Cio-cio-san is a true sense of who and what this character is, but, for the beauty of singing, her Butterfly triumphs. The Pinkerton on this RCA recording is sung by Richard Tucker, whom these recording sessions found in mellow voice. Tucker's full-throated, almost naive approach to his music makes him a fitting partner for Miss Price in the love duet, but his "Addio, fiorito asil" is rather labored and 'hammy'. Rosalind Elias contributes a discreetly sung Suzuki, shaping her lines with beauty and contributing warm support to the drama. Philip Maero is a resonant and attractive Sharpless. Erich Leinsdorf conducts the Rome Opera Orchestra and Chorus with finesse, leading a musically distinguished if somewhat tame performance.

Renata Tebaldi is heard as Cio-cio-san in London-Decca's performance. Tebaldi is perhaps not one of nature's own Butterflys, since her huge voice is more suited to projecting adult passions than girlish innocence. However, the sheen of Tebaldi's sound coupled with her long-standing sympathies for Puccini combine to produce a charming, if somewhat mature, heroine. At her best in Butterfly's more emotional scenes, Tebaldi is predictably affecting when renouncing her child to Kate Pinkerton in Act Three and when singing a spellbinding "Un bel dì."

Carlo Bergonzi is the set's excellent Pinkerton. He opts for phrasing the lieutenant's music as if he were portraying Apollo instead of a shallow and bigoted officer. One gleans no sense of the man's viciousness from Bergonzi's portrayal, but one can certainly understand why Cio-cio-san fell in love with him.

Bergonzi's "Addio, fiorito asil" is a model of tastefully expressed operatic remorse, and even his final calls of

"Butterfly" are more compelling than those of other tenors who sing the role.

Fiorenza Cossotto, practically an unknown when this set was made in 1958, is a vocally luscious Suzuki. Cossotto and Tebaldi in the "Flower Duet" offer some truly outstanding singing.

The Sharpless, Enzo Sordello, best remembered as the baritone Maria Callas had fired from the Met not too long before she herself was discharged from that theatre, is plagued by a thick and disconcerting vibrato that weakens his performance.

Conductor Tullio Serafin leads a loving but slowly paced reading that emphasizes the sentimentality of this most tearful of Puccini's works. True Puccini fans (the writer among them) take little exception to this approach which allows them to savor the vocal gold for the maximum possible time, but it must be conceded that more cynical listeners might prefer a crisper performance. The Orchestra and Chorus of the Academy of Santa Cecilia are in particularly fine estate here.

Angel-HMV offers no less than four recordings of this opera in its current catalogue. Two of them rank with the best specimens in the operatic lepidopterist's collection: The Scotto-Bergonzi Rome Opera album conducted by John Barbirolli is an extraordinarily effective performance. The soprano offers a contrasting approach to the title character from that of Price and Tebaldi. Scotto's voice is steely and penetrating, and it lacks the sensuous beauty of the other two sopranos. A skillful and appealing vocal actress, Scotto achieves a far more vivid characterization than any of her rivals, with the possible exception of Dal Monte in the Seraphim set to be discussed below. Her Butterfly is captivatingly adolescent in Act One, pathetically deluded in Act Two, and, ultimately, majestically tragic in Act Three. Nowhere does Scotto's singing ravish in terms of pure sound, but her excellent musicianship and refreshingly direct approach to the dramatic content of the opera augment her more than adequate singing and transform her performance into a rare and enthralling experience.

Bergonzi is once again a suavely persuasive Pinkerton. Anna di Stasio is a disappointingly dull Suzuki, but Rolando Panerai's vivid and practised Sharpless is an asset. Sir John Barbirolli elicits clean and luminescent playing from the Rome Opera Orchestra, and his approach to the music is gentle but without the self-indulgent and saccarine excesses of Serafin.

Angel's Seraphim reissue of the 1939 BUTTERFLY, recorded in Rome with Toti Dal Monte and Beniamino Gigli and led by Olivero de Fabritiis, will not be to every listener's taste, but those willing to forgive the soprano's musical imperfections in the light of her uncanny interpretative abilities will be fascinated. Dal Monte was a favorite singer of Toscanini's who enjoyed success between the two World Wars. On the basis of this recording, her voice appears small, occasionally tinny, and quite strident on the top. Compared to Dal Monte, even Scotto seems opulent of tone. However, Dal Monte is a Cio-cio-san of delicacy and vulnerability. Her identification with the character impresses one as being almost mystical, and her communication of Butterfly's tragedy is all the more impressive in view of the limitations of her voice. Dramatically, Dal Monte's only important lapse is her excessive weeping in the last scene.

By contrast, Gigli sings Pinkerton with a particularly welcome sweetness of tone. Vittoria Palombini is a Suzuki with a darker voice than one usually encounters in that role, and the change is most welcome. Mario Basiola sings with no particular distinction as Sharpless. The dull, ancient recorded sound is not flattering to the Rome Opera Orchestra, but de Fabritiis leads a taut, nervous performance that fits most economically onto two discs.

Of the remaining BUTTERFLY recordings, budget-minded buyers may also choose the Richmond set, made in 1951, featuring Tebaldi and Giuseppe Campora, both of whom are in fresh, lyrical form here. Nell Rankin is the lovely Suzuki, and Alberto Erede conducts the Santa Cecilia force.

Angel's two other BUTTERFLY sets are less distinguished. One, with Victoria de los Angeles and Jussi Bjoerling is rather wanly conducted by Tullio Serafin. It will appeal to special admirers of those two artists, although both have been heard to better advantage elsewhere. This was the tenor's last studio recording, completed only weeks before his death.

The other Angel set is a 1956 La Scala performance led bloodlessly by Herbert von Karajan. Maria Callas scales down her voice to suggest Cio-cio-san's fragility, but the role doesn't seem to interest her greatly, and the result is a curiously detached, almost mechanical performance in which Callas' usual vocal weakness (arid or wobbly high notes) is, in this instance, unredeemed by her interpretation. Nicolai Gedda is an aristocratic though somewhat unromantic Pinkerton, singing pleasantly but coldly, while the supporting cast is below Scala's standard.

MASSENET: MANON

Sills, Gedda, Souzay, Bacquier, Rudel cond.
New Philharmonia Orchestra and Chorus
4 discs AUDIO TREASURY 20007
UK: HMV SLS800

de los Angeles, Legay, Dens, Monteux cond.
Orchestra and Chorus Opera-Comique
4 discs
Seraphim ID-6057

Although Massenet's MANON is generally conceded to be a better constructed work than Puccini's MANON LESCAUT, the French work has not proven to be as popular with record producers as the Italian opera. At present, there are but two complete MANON sets on the market, one a relatively new (1970) investiture with Beverly Sills in the title role (Audio Treasury), while the other is a Seraphim reissue of the 1956 recording that starred Victoria de los Angeles.

While the monaural Seraphim album has a number of impressive features, not the least of which is the enchanting work of soprano de los Angeles, the Sills recording, or more properly, the Sills-Gedda-Rudel recording, is the finer all-around performance.

First of all, the score is recorded complete by Julius Rudel and his cast. Rudel, who along with Miss Sills provided New York with the finest MANON in many years in their 1967 revival of the opera at the New York City Opera, animates the music with the skill of a truly musically-minded man of the theatre. Seraphim's Pierre Monteux may coax a slightly more glowing sound from his orchestra (that of the Opera-Comique) but Rudel's crisp, intelligent pacing of the opera highlights the sparkle of the score while providing a sensuous background for such moments as Manon's "Adieu, notre petite table" and the St. Sulpice episode.

In the title role, Audio Treasury has caught Sills in rare form. The soprano's voice here is softly burnished and evenly produced with none of the shrillness that occasionally works its way into Sills' tone. As an actress, Sills has never been more expressive than as the many-faceted Manon Lescaut. Act One finds her demure and innocent, with a genuine and uncloying sweetness, while the later acts show her as a woman of the world and as a consummate actress and manipulator of men's souls. The death scene is honest and touching. Throughout the opera, Sills' brilliant technique is very much in evidence. Not many sopranos could manage the elegant *fioritura* of the "Cours la Reine Scene" as well as the passions of the "St. Sulpice Scene" and the fifth act.

Fortunately (and here is the real strength of this MANON), Beverly Sills is not the only major singer in the cast. Des Grieux is sung with polish and a handsome line by Nicolai Gedda, remembered as an excellent Metropolitan Chevalier from the late 1950's and in the otherwise unsuccessful new production given Massenet's opera in 1963. Gedda, whose French diction is as precise as one might wish, brings off "La Rêve" without sounding as if the pianissimi were strangling him. He is also fiery and angry at the beginning of the crucial duet with Manon in Act Three then slowly melts away until he becomes her pliant toy by the conclusion of that scene. Throughout, Gedda's secure, strong singing is a source of pleasure to the listener.

Gerard Souzay offers a dashing and musical Lescaut, while Gabriel Bacquier is a dignified, sonorous Comte Des Grieux. Nico Castel, a "character" stalwart of both the New York City and Metropolitan Operas, recreates the Guillot that has been so stylish and amusing on the stage for several years. Michel Trempont is the De Bretigny. As noted earlier, the opera is given without cuts. Thus, one can hear the original closing scene of Act One (most productions, as well as the Seraphim set, end the act with the flight of the lovers in the stolen coach) and, in an "appendix" to the last side, the alternate version of Manon's *Cours la Reine* aria, complete with the Fabliau that Sills occasionally adds to her Manon performances on stage.

Turning back to the Seraphim version, all admirers of de los Angeles won't need any urging from this writer to acquire the discs since the Spanish artist has seldom been heard to better advantage. Her voice, in its prime, was at least as beautiful as Sills' and perhaps somewhat more naturally attractive. Lacking the fierce dramatic intelligence that has contributed so greatly to Sills' triumphs, Victoria de los Angeles often was content to sing prettily and more or less let the drama of her roles take care of itself. Here, however, the soprano is bewitchingly attractive as a rather more soft-hearted, less calculating girl than either Sills or Massenet probably conceived. Yet, no one can deny the radiance of the "Adieu, notre petite table" or the sincerity of the "N'est-ce plus ma main?"

Unfortunately, although the soprano's work is supported by the meticulously detailed conducting of Pierre Monteux, almost nobody else in the recording is in the same league as those in the rival version on Audio Treasury. Henri Legay is a typical example of all that is wrong with French singing; he is nasal, tremulous, unsteady of tone, and marked by a tendency to bleat out top notes. Legay would drive a Manon far less sensitive than de los Angeles to run off with the first available baritone! Michel Dens is a routine Lescaut, while Jean Borthayre has some decent moments as the Count. Giving credit where due, the Opera-Comique Chorus not only sings as well as does Audio Treasury's Ambrosian Opera Chorus, but pronounces the text with greater clarity. Thus, this MANON is an excellent supplement to one's library as it preserves the fondly remembered work of de los Angeles in the name part, but the Sills/Rudel version is unquestionably the finer performance.

PUCCINI: MANON LESCAUT

Tebaldi, del Monaco, Boriello, Corena, Molinari-Pradelli cond.
Orchestra and Chorus of L'Accademia di Sta. Cecilia
3 discs
London OSA 1317*
UK: Ace of Diamonds GOS607-8 (2 discs)

Albanese, Bjoerling, Merrill, Clabassi, Perlea cond.
Rome Opera Orchestra and Chorus
2 discs
RCA VIC 6127
UK: Same as above

Petrella, Beggiatto, Cupolo cond.
RAI Orchestra and Chorus
3 discs
Everest/Cetra S-461-3

Caballé, Domingo, Bartoletti cond.
New Philharmonia Orchestra and John Alldis Choir
2 discs
Angel SBL-3782
UK: HMV (Catalogue number not available)

Puccini's third opera, and his first true success has not been recorded as often as BOHEME, BUTTERFLY, or TOSCA, but three of the four versions of the score on disc that make up in quality for the insult dealt this charming opera in terms of quantity of recordings. One of these offers the additional virtue of being available at low cost, in a two-disc RCA Victrola album (VIC-6027). This set, made in 1954 at the Rome Opera features Licia Albanese, Jussi Bjoerling, and Robert Merrill, with the late Jonel Perlea at the helm.

Albanese enjoyed great success with Puccini's Manon on stage, and her portrait is nicely preserved by this recording. Her voice, although undeniably mature, was in near top form in 1954, and thus her Manon is sweetly sung with only the slightest hint of strain on top. Furthermore, Albanese's temperament ideally suited this most feminine of heroines. She captures the many sides to Manon's personality with commendable skill, being alternately shy, commanding, and ultimately pathetic.

Jussi Bjoerling leaves little to be desired as the Chevalier des Grieux. He brings a graciousness to the role that eludes del Monaco in the rival London-Decca edition, discussed below. Musically, Bjoerling is completely at ease in this spinto role, and sounds remarkably youthful, although he was in his mid-forties when this recording was made. Each of des Grieux's four arias (Puccini was much kinder than usual to the tenor in this opera!) is a model of fine singing.

Robert Merrill is completely satisfactory in the thankless role of Lescaut, and the supporting cast, consisting of Franco Calabrese as the sinister Geronte, Anna Maria Rota as the madrigal singer, and Mario Carlin and Enrico Campi dividing five roles between themselves is most commendable. Perlea conducts briskly, moving the music along as if spurred on by a spring breeze. The Rome Opera chorus is most helpful, but the orchestra sounds rather scrawny and the mono sound somewhat dull. Still, this MANON LESCAUT is a success on most counts.

A major alternative to the Victrola set is the London-Decca album, an early stereo set made in 1957 featuring Tebaldi and del Monaco.

Due to Molinari-Pradelli's staid tempi and, probably to her own inclinations, Tebaldi offers a stately account of the title role, missing just a little of Manon's girlishness in Act One, but offering a moving and somewhat larger than life impersonation of the unlucky Manon in the later scenes. Tebaldi's voice is richer and stronger than Albanese's, and she uses it with taste and feeling to create a rather highly strung heroine whose two major arias come off extremely well.

The huge sound produced by Mario del Monaco is less than ideally tailored to the requirements of des Grieux. Unfortunately, the tenor impresses the listener as a misplaced Otello in a number of scenes, most notably in the first and second act love duets, but del Monaco certainly imparts a sense of real anguish to des Grieux in the opera's later scenes, especially in "Guardate, pazzo son."

Mario Boriello is adequate as Lescaut while Fernando Corena offers a fine cameo portrayal of the only villainous role in his vast repertoire, Geronte. The Accademia di Santa Cecilia Orchestra and Chorus provide idiomatic support, while Molinari-Pradelli, approaching the score as if it were a heavier work, succeeds in making the orchestral writing sound almost as lush as that of the later Puccini operas.

Angel's recent stereophonic version of Puccini's opera in no way surpasses the monaural version it supersedes, although it offers a number of musical niceties.

Primary among these is the des Grieux of Placido Domingo who sings this most gratifying of Puccini tenor roles with sweetness of tone and lyric impetuosity. The tendency to push his voice for bigger sound that has been marring some of the tenor's recent recordings is far less in evidence here. A handsome partner to the Manon of Montserrat Caballé, Domingo provides the performance with its largest measure of vocal greatness.

As for Mme. Caballé, this is, to my mind, her least successful, commercial recording. While one has never been led to expect a tremendous depth of characterization from this artist, who is of course blessed with one of the most magnificent instruments of our time, it was still to be hoped that she would somehow find something in Manon's personality that would capture her—and our—imagination. Regrettably, Caballé has not done so, and thus dramatically, her Manon is flat and shallow, rarely rising to the emotional levels called for by the role. Even worse, the fabled Caballé voice was not in peak form during these recording sessions. Her *pianissimi* sound tired and shopworn, especially in "In Quelle trine morbide," and more than a few high notes seem to have been achieved through considerable effort. True, the great second act duet with the tenor comes off quite well, but in general, this performance is not up to Caballé's admittedly high standards.

The supporting cast is adequate, and the John Alldis Choir sings with a great deal of gusto. Bruno Bartoletti whips the score (played admirably by the New Philharmonia) along briskly enough to fit the opera onto two discs (both London's and the older EMI set take up three), but the opening of Act One seems a bit rushed. Therefore, while this set is by no means a total failure, it does not stand up to comparison with the competition, nor does it warrant its place in Angel's catalogue at the expense of the Callas-di Stefano version.

This last set can often be found in USA shops on one European label or another—Odeon, Pathé Marconi, or HMV (either in the original mono or in a recent electronically processed stereo pressing), and is well worth hunting for. It is said that Callas has never been fond of this set, since by the time it was issued in 1959, her voice had lost some of its early purity, and the notorious wobble was in evidence on high notes. However, looking back on this set in relation to the diva's later achievements, and indeed, in terms of her career as a whole, it seems that this MANON LESCAUT has been unjustly maligned. Lacking, of course, the sheerly gorgeous vocalism that Tebaldi brings to the part, Callas delves deeper into Manon's fascinating psyche than her Italian colleague, and the result is an intensely realized performance that ought to rank among her finest work. Even the high notes are often not really that bad, and her singing is always marked by extreme intelligence. As does Caballé, Callas offers her best work in the scene with des Grieux in the second act, but her work in Act Three and in the final scene is also breathtaking.

As des Grieux, one wishes that Giuseppe di Stefano could have commanded in 1958 the vocal brilliance that was his some five years earlier. He tends on this recording to bellow his high notes, and there is a variability of intonation in his singing, but he manages to create some beautiful moments anyway. He is especially compelling in the final two acts.

Outstanding among the supporting singers is Fiorenza Cossotto in the role of the Madrigal Singer.

Maestro Tullio Serafin shapes the score with his sympathetic, practised hand, and the La Scala forces perform with their usual precision.

DONIZETTI:
MARIA STUARDA

Sills, Farrell, Burrows, Quilico, Ceccato cond.
London Symphony Orchestra and the Ambrosian Singers
3 discs
AUDIO TREASURY ATS 20010

ABC's recording of MARIA STUARDA (the first on any commercial label) presents Beverly Sills in the second of her projected cycle of three Donizetti roles based upon English Queens. In the Spring of 1972, shortly after the release of this set, Sills sang STUARDA with the New York City Opera, thus leaving only Anna Bolena, to be done as a summer, 1972 recording project and a fall, 1973 New York production.

Evidently profiting from the expensive lesson of the ROBERTO DEVEREUX recording in which Sills was supported with but a minimum of excellence, ABC engaged a more distinguished cast with generally excellent results. MARIA STUARDA is really about two queens, Elizabeth as well as Mary, and the role of the English queen is of great importance. Eileen Farrell, never known for singing the bel canto operas, was engaged to sing Elizabeth, and this venture has proved to be most successful. Farrell's velvety dramatic soprano provides the proper contrast to Sills' lighter, smaller voice. Farrell, understandably, does not indulge in much ornamentation, but she meets her musical challenges admirably and sings with animation and power, providing one of the most pleasant vocal surprises of recent years. Stuart Burrows, the young Welsh tenor, is cast as Leicester, the courtier torn between the two queens in the Donizetti-Schiller historical pastiche. His sturdy technique and pleasant, light voice are both to be commended, although one wishes for a more stirring characterization. Louis Quilico, Sills' colleague at the New York City Opera, sings with characteristic artistry as Mary's friend Talbot. Quilico's baritone is not the most resonant or largest of such voices, but his intelligence and musicianship make him a valuable asset. Christian du Plessis, a young baritone from South Africa, makes an auspicious debut as Lord Cecil. He has a warm and easily produced voice that ought to take him far.

In the title role, Sills movingly portrays this romanticized version of the scheming and none too pleasant Mary. Adhering to the vision of Mary presented by the playwright and composer, Sills is alternately charming, vicious, and ultimately quite tragic. Her opening aria in Act Two is warmly expressive, while in the famous confrontation scene between the two queens, Sills is violently dramatic, hurling the notorious "Vil bastarda" line as if through clenched teeth. The death scene is regally sung, making this one of Sills' best recordings.

The London Symphony Orchestra and the Ambrosian Singers are conducted by Aldo Ceccato, a master of the lyric phrase, but a conductor who might do better if he dawdled less —Ceccato's tempi have a tendency to drift into listlessness. The recorded sound is a distinct improvement over the recent ABC LUCIA recording.

BOITO: MEFISTOFELE

Tebaldi, del Monaco, Siepi, Serafin cond.
Orchestra and Chorus of L'Accademia di Santa Cecilia
3 discs
London OSA 1307*
UK: Decca GOS591-3

Tagliavini, Neri, Questa cond.
RAI Orchestra and Chorus
3 discs
Everest/Cetra S-409-3*

Boito's opera has fared less well on discs than it deserves. As of the time this volume went to press, only two complete versions of the work had ever been recorded. (A new recording of this work featuring Treigle, Caballé, and Domingo, to be conducted by Julius Rudel is scheduled for release.) One is a fairly routine Cetra recording starring Giulio Neri in the title role, and the other (and by far the more interesting and superlative recording of the two) is a London-Decca release featuring Cesare Siepi, Mario del Monaco, and Renata Tebaldi, with Tullio Serafin conducting the forces of the Accademia di Santa Cecilia.

Hardly a "number" opera with the dazzling set pieces that abound in Gounod's FAUST, MEFISTOFELE is an Italian music drama painted in darker and more subtle colors than Gounod's musical palette contained. It requires a quartet (or at least a trio, when the roles of Margherita and Elena are duplicated) of artists capable of dramatic expression as well as musical virtuosity (only the latter is a must for FAUST) and an extremely fine chorus. Fortunately, the London-Decca set is strong in most of these aspects. The Prologue, essentially a dialogue between Mefistofele and a chorus representing the Heavenly Host is very well performed by the estimable forces of Rome's Accademia di Santa Cecilia and Siepi, whose commanding presence and rich, supple voice make him an ideal Mefistofele. (What a pity that he has not performed the role more often!) "Su Cammina" and "Ecco Il Mondo" are also excitingly vocalized, and Siepi's fiendish characterization is not only most rewarding in itself, but provides an extraordinary contrast to his equally famed Mephistopheles in FAUST.

In Gounod's work, Siepi is a cheerfully extroverted demon, capable, of course, of menacingly evil moments, as at the climax of the "Church Scene," but he is most comfortable when he is mockingly urbane, as in the Serenade or in the "Garden Scene" when pretending to woo Marthe. In Boito's opera, Siepi is, dramatically speaking, far nastier and less charming than is his courtly French alter ego. As Mefistofele he is a devil who can truly frighten sinners!

Mario del Monaco is not quite so well cast as Siepi. Boito's Faust demands a more introspective artist, and del Monaco's stentorian delivery is not nearly as effective in this opera as it is in PAGLIACCI or OTELLO. "Dai campi" is altogether too loud, and even the top notes lack their usual brightness and sound rather dry and constricted. Del Monaco sounds better in the "Helen of Troy Scene" and Epilogue than in the earlier portions of the music, but one still might wish for a less brassy interpretation.

Tebaldi offers some extremely fine singing in the role of Margherita. Sweet and girlish in the "Garden Scene" and fully capable of tragic projection in the "Prison Scene," Tebaldi could hardly be bettered, particularly in her harrowing account of "L'altra Notte." Strangely, as the diva was in full prime when this recording was made in the late 1950's, London did not see fit to allow her to perform Elena as well as Margherita. Since the latter role served as the vehicle for Tebaldi's professional debut, one would have thought that she would be eager to record the part. However, London chose a virtually unknown soprano, Florinda Cavalli, to perform Elena's music in the "Classical Sabbath." The studio was, it appears, mistaken in trying to launch Miss Cavalli as an internationally prominent artist, as she has dropped completely from sight in the operatic world. Furthermore, her small-voiced, squawky, and generally unsatisfactory account of Elena does nothing to create the impression that this singer has been unjustly ignored. Cavalli's performance suffers from direct comparison to Tebaldi's Margherita.

Lucia Danieli and Piero de Palma provide sterling support in the minor roles (each sings two), and the orchestra is more than adequate. Serafin's conducting is more scholarly and reverent than exciting, but his secure hand and understanding of the music is evident, and he may be given credit for directing an often memorable performance. London's recorded sound is quite acceptable for early stereo.

WAGNER: DIE MEISTERSINGER VON NURNBURG

Donath, Hesse, Kollo, Schreier, Adam, Evans, von Karajan cond.
Dresden State Opera Orchestra and Dresden and Leipzig Choruses
5 discs
Angel S-3776
UK: HMV SLS957

Gueden, Schoeffler, Treptow, Knappertsbusch cond.
Vienna Philharmonic and State Opera Chorus
5 discs
Richmond RS65002 (Mono)
UK: Ace of Diamonds GOM535-9

Schwarzkopf, Hopf, Kunz, Unger, von Karajan cond.
Bayreuth Festival Orchestra and Chorus
5 discs
Seraphim IB 6030

With the deletion of both the RCA and older Angel-HMV recordings of this opera and the removal from consideration of the Richmond performance starring Paul Schoeffler and Hilde Gueden as that is a disappointing and generally inferior one, there remains the interesting spectacle of two rival Karajan performances competing with one another: the older, monaural performance reissued by Seraphim, taken from an actual 1951 Bayreuth performance and the 1970 studio version made in Dresden on Angel-HMV.

The first performance, while hardly perfect, is preferable to the newer, stereophonic recording in any number of ways. Principally, von Karajan, in 1951, led a vital, animated MEISTERSINGER, in contrast to the bloodlessly lyrical performance he directed in Dresden nearly two decades later. While the conductor's cool, understated approach to the RING lends a welcome and fascinating new dimension to much of the music and serves to "humanize" the dramatic figures to some extent as well, such an approach to this most human, and earthy of Wagner's works robs MEISTERSINGER of much of its power. In the 1951 Bayreuth recording, for example, the Prelude to Act One is strongly directed, with the music surging forward to its climax, so that when the voices of the opening chorale enter as the final crescendo of the Prelude fades away, the listener is so caught up in the sweep of Wagner's music that a catch comes to his throat as the act begins. So lacadasical is Karajan's handling of the same moment in the second recording that one is scarcely aware of the chorus' entrance. Similarly, the marvelous ensemble at the conclusion of the second act, so vividly captured on the Seraphim set, is so flatly performed on the Angel-HMV version that one would never suppose that a public brawl were being depicted. In fact, the only moments where Karajan is suitably forceful on the newer set is in the third act, during the opening of the final scene where at last, aided by the excellent work of the combined Dresden Opera and Leipzig Radio Choruses, the performance takes wing.

Karajan's miscalculated approach to DIE MEISTERSINGER in 1970 is all the more frustrating given the excellent voices found in his cast. Theo Adam, although not possessing a really heroic sized instrument, offers a musical and three dimensional Sachs—pensive, at times angry, later mischievous, and always eloquent. "Wahn wahn . . ." is characterized by crisp diction and vocal adroitness, qualities that, in fact, distinguish Adam throughout the performance.

René Kollo, the popular singer turned heldentenor, displays a pleasant voice that is liable to desert him if he continues to push for power as unmercifully as he is apt to here. Kollo, at his best when singing quietly, suggesting Walther's youth, sounds a bit flinty during his two major pieces in the first act, and his Prize Song is less expansively performed than one might wish.

Helen Donath, who is assuming increasing prominence in new recordings of late, is a sweet, fresh voiced Eva, but one who exhibits few interesting personality traits. Eva is arguably Wagner's least rewarding soprano role, for even the ninny Elsa has some great music to sing, but this soprano doesn't much compensate for the composer's stinginess with any attempt at creating a spirited character for Eva.

Ruth Hesse, a very ingratiating Magdalene, succeeds in making Eva's companion a lot more interesting than the heroine herself!

The fifth member of this MEISTERSINGER quintet is Peter Schreier who makes David into a major personality of the opera and, given his pure, refined singing, a musically rewarding one as well.

Beckmesser is sung with a sure sense of comic theatricality by Sir Geraint Evans, whose roughness of voice is no major disadvantage here. Evans refrains from playing a grossly caricatured villain, but he does emphasize the town clerk's irascibility, making Beckmesser a funny, if hardly likeable fellow.

This recording is strongly cast in its Meistersingers. Among them are Karl Ridderbusch as a dignified and ample voiced Pogner and Zoltan Kéléman as a similarly persuasive Kothner, to mention but two.

As noted earlier, the huge combined chorus is outstanding, and the Dresden Opera Orchestra plays with surpassing clarity of sound. In the hands of another conductor—dare one mention Solti—this MEISTERSINGER might have been a complete success.

Returning to the 1951 set, here too, Karajan is lucky in his cast. Sachs is portrayed by Otto Edelmann, who in those days owned a large, rich voice well suited to Sachs' music. A skillful actor as well, Edelmann offers a sympathetic, gentle cobbler-

poet. Hans Hopf's weighty, baritonal timbre make him an
unlikely choice for Walther, sounding mature and heavy
where he should be youthful and spry of voice. Still, in spite
of troubled, wooden sound in the lower regions of Walther's
music, Hopf's high notes, particularly in Act One, ring out
pleasantly, and his work is reasonably animated. Since this
recording was made at one "live" performance, it is not surprising that Hopf's voice began to tire noticeably in the third
act, and the Prize Song is marred by an unsteady start and a
rather desperate, bleated finish.

Elisabeth Schwarzkopf is more outgoing than Donath as
Eva, but she pushes for greater volume and at times, particularly in her third act scene with Sachs, sounds shrill and
hard-toned. Schwarzkopf recovers her usual handsome sound
in time for the Act Three Quintet. Ira Malaniuk is a competent
Magdalena, but the David of Gerhard Unger is dry and
unsteady. Beckmesser is charmingly—indeed, almost too
charmingly—played and sung by Erich Kunz, who makes his
character seem almost too lovably eccentric. Even more than
Evans, Kunz sings Beckmesser without resort to overdone
distortions of sound. Never dull in the part, Kunz works too
hard at giving Beckmesser an unwanted slice of benevolence.

The various Meistersingers are, in the main, decently handled,
although the voices in the newer recording are, by and large,
more attractive. The postwar Bayreuth Chorus sounds a bit
the worse for wear, but its members perform with enthusiasm.
The Orchestra, if not the best in Europe, is nevertheless equal
to the music that it is called upon to play.

VERDI: NABUCCO

Suliotis, Gobbi, Cava, Prevedi, Gardelli cond.
Vienna Philharmonic and State Opera Chorus
3 discs
London OSA 1382*
UK: Decca SET298-300

Mancini, Gatti, Silveri, Capuana cond.
RAI Orchestra and Chorus
3 discs
Everest/Cetra S-455/3

Since NABUCCO is so rarely encountered in the opera house these days, one should be grateful for the London-Decca recording which outdistances the Everest-Cetra set made shortly after the Second World War. London-Decca offers a brilliant protagonist (Tito Gobbi), a fine conductor (Lamberto Gardelli), a great ensemble (the Vienna State Opera Chorus and the Vienna Philharmonic), an eccentrically exciting prima donna (Elena Souliotis), and a mediocre supporting cast.

Gobbi, whose still rich voice and galvanizing presence qualify him as today's automatic favorite for the role of Nebuchadnezzar, does not disappoint, delivering the mad king's arias with power and conveying a true sense of anguish in his duet with Abagaille (Souliotis) in Act Three. Elena Souliotis, even at the beginning of her career when this NABUCCO was made, never had a beautiful voice, but it was an exciting one. Her frequent register breaks do not fall lightly on the ears, but her low notes are powerful, and she copes with many of the superhuman demands of Abagaille's music about as well as any one else singing at the time might have done. However, when noting that this recording stands out as Souliotis' best recording to date, I cannot help regretting that this soprano never fully realized her potential for greatness and allowed her voice to deteriorate well before she reached the age of thirty.

Bruno Prevedi's rather dry tenor allows him to be a competent if not an outstanding Ismaele, and his second rate performance is evenly matched by the tentative, small scale Fenena sung by Dora Carral. Carlo Cava, the young Italian bass rushed into a major contract by London brings no particular virtues outside of a reasonably pleasant voice to the important role of Zaccaria, the Hebrew leader.

Fortunately, the sensitive conducting of Gardelli and the wonderful singing of the Vienna State Opera Chorus equal Gobbi's work, and thus the famous chorus "Va pensiero" comes off most successfully. Considering how rare NABUCCO recordings are, it's too bad that London-Decca didn't do quite as well with this opera as it has with any number of other productions, although Gobbi's performance and a fair amount of Souliotis' work make the set worth owning.

BELLINI: NORMA

Callas, Ludwig, Corelli, Zaccaria, Serafin cond.
La Scala Orchestra and Chorus
3 discs
Angel S-3615*
UK: Columbia SMS1011

Sutherland, Horne, Alexander, Cross, Bonynge cond.
Covent Garden Orchestra
3 discs
London OSA 1394
UK: Decca 424-6

Cigna, Stignani, Gui cond.
3 discs
Everest/Cetra S-423/3*

Callas, Stignani, Fillipeschi, Rossi-Lemeni, Serafin cond.
La Scala Orchestra and Chorus
3 discs
Seraphim IC 6037 (Mono)

Suliotis, Cossotto, del Monaco, Cava, Varviso cond.
Orchestra and Chorus L'Accademia di Santa Cecilia (abridged)
London OSA 1272*
UK: Decca SET368-9

Caballé, Cossotto, Domingo, Raimondi, Cillario cond.
London Philharmonic and Ambrosian Opera Chorus
3 discs
RCA LSC-6202

In 1953, there were two recordings of Bellini's NORMA, the
Cetra, with Gina Cigna and the Angel-HMV with Maria Callas.
A decade later, the only addition to this list was the second
Callas version, again on Angel-HMV, this time in stereo.
During the past ten years, however, four more NORMA's
found their way into the catalogues of the record companies,
and as an indication of the resurgence of popular interest in
the Bellini operas, another NORMA set, this one with Beverly
Sills, is projected for the coming year.

Unfortunately, none of the existing NORMA recordings
even comes close to being definitive. One must ultimately
make his choice based on personal preference, and understand
that no one set will satisfy him completely.

Of the two budget label NORMA's, the Callas mono version
(now available on Seraphim) is the most interesting. Maria
Callas was at the happiest vocal stage of her career when this
set was made. Her voice is fresh and equal to virtually all the
demands inherent in the role of the druid priestess. Although
she is well supported by the Scala forces led by Callas' mentor
Tullio Serafin, the other principals, with the exception of the
authoritative if hardly virginal Adalgisa sung by Ebe Stignani,
are far below Callas' level. Mario Fillipeschi's strident and
plebian account of Pollione makes one wonder why on earth
a woman of Norma's intelligence ever consented to be his
mistress. Nicola Rossi-Lemeni is competent but not especially
powerful as Oroveso.

The later Callas version, recorded in 1960, is perhaps the
best all-around version of the opera, although the years
between recorded NORMA's had cost Callas plenty in terms
of vocal security. What counts here, though, is Callas' special
intensity which allowed her Norma to be a viable stage creation
even at the end of her public career. Indeed, hearing Callas

sing "Casta diva" at a 1971 master class at Julliard was a more satisfactory experience than attending the 1970 Norma performances of Joan Sutherland at the Met. No one sings the "Bello a me ritorno" with more pathos than Callas, and no "Dormono entranbi" is more frighteningly desperate.

Christa Ludwig is the somewhat oddly cast Adalgisa of this set, but if not sounding completely at home in Bellini's music, she brings a youthful and creamy voice and a genuine "presence" to the role.

Franco Corelli turns in a powerful and vocally exciting performance as Pollione, while Nicola Zaccaria is an able Oroveso. The Scala forces are once again nobly conducted by Serafin.

Joan Sutherland and Marilyn Horne recorded NORMA in 1964, but did not get around to singing the opera at Covent Garden or the Met for another six years. This is too bad because lack of experience with the work is obvious on this recording. Although being in some ways a preferred version (due to its virtual completeness), the album suffers from a lack of involvement in the drama by Miss Sutherland and an excruciatingly bad job of conducting by Richard Bonynge, the diva's spouse and pet maestro.

The Norma-Adalgisa duets are beautifully sung however, and vocally, the "Casta diva" is flawless. Unfortunately though, in terms of diction, emotional projection, and bel canto style, the Sutherland Norma is close to being a disaster area. This recording, currently released by London-Decca should be junked and Mesdames Sutherland and Horne should re-record the opera with a stronger conductor. Completing the cast are John Alexander, an accurate but unthrilling Pollione, and Richard Cross, a weak Oroveso. The Covent Garden Orchestra and Chorus would sound better had their direction been stronger.

There is also the second London-Decca NORMA, a two-disc abridged version made in the late 1960's when Elena Souliotis' operatic star shone briefly. The sad account of the Greek soprano's mismanaged career that left her voice a wreck is too familiar to be gone into here, but even in 1968, she was in no condition to sing Norma. Her exciting but unbeautiful soprano may be a reasonable medium for the role of Abagaille, but Norma requires a great voice, not a flamboyant trickster. Her "Casta diva" is simply embarrassing, with wild lunges at notes and an utter lack of line. From there on, things go better for Souliotis, and in Norma's angrier moments, she is actually quite powerful, but in the lyrical phrases, Souliotis lacks the means to compete with Callas or Sutherland, not to mention Ponselle or Milanov who recorded scenes from the opera.

Although London calls the performance complete, that is not really the case. The libretto contains an essay explaining that the cuts in the choral passages and the omission of Oroveso's aria were made in the interest of dramatic cohesion, but basically, this is just a ruse to excuse the rushing into the market with a two-disc set designed to compete with the other NORMAs.

In spite of the tremendous weakness of Souliotis' Norma, this set offers at least one sterling performance: the Adalgisa of Firenza Cossotto, whose every note is gorgeously sung and sympathetically projected. She alone provides the great moments to be found in this recording, as Carlo Cava is unequal to the emasculated version of Oroveso that he is called upon to perform, and the veteran Mario del Monaco is loud but colorless as Pollione. Furthermore, the conductor, Silvio Varviso, rushes the proceedings to a ludicrous extent, particularly during the druids' procession in Act One. In spite of Varviso's third rate conducting, the Orchestra and Chorus of the Accademia di Santa Cecilia perform with their customary professionalism.

RCA's new NORMA set with Caballé, Cossotto, Domingo, and Raimondi, conducted by Cillario, was probably intended to deal death blows to a pair of celebrated pirated recordings of the opera with the above two ladies in their present roles. Unfortunately, this performance lacks bite, especially when compared to these two pirated sets, and certainly fails to triumph over either of Maria Callas' recordings of the opera.

Montserrat Caballé's stage performances of Norma seem to demonstrate a new found vein of dramatic awareness on the part of this soprano. This unfortunately does not transfer itself to these discs, for the Spanish artist sounds placid and untroubled throughout the opera. Vocally, however, Caballé has rarely been in better form, although the Act One *cabaletta* does not come easily to her. In virtually every other moment of her role, Caballé is in sumptuous voice, with silken *portamenti* and incandescent *piannissimi* to spare!

Fiorenza Cossotto's Adalgisa is equally well sung. The mezzo has, of course, recorded the part once before, on London's abridged version in which Cossotto was virtually the whole show in the absence of competence in her colleagues. Here, flanked by several first class voices, Cossotto matches Caballé and Domingo point for point in terms of vocal lustre. Dramatically, she is a sensitive and modest priestess, as called for by the composer.

Placido Domingo's Pollione is often exciting, singing as he does with a bright tonal palette, security of pitch, and a feeling for Bellinian line. At times, the middle and upper registers take on a slightly provincial, bleating quality, but this is reduced as soon as Domingo relaxes his voice and refrains from lunging for bigger sound.

Ruggiero Raimondi's Oroveso is intelligently sung but suffers from engineering that allows his voice to sound thinner than it actually is. The London Philharmonic and Ambrosian Opera Chorus work well, but the conductor, Carlo Felice Cillario, must shoulder a great deal of blame for dulling the level of the performance with his bland, bloodless conducting.

MOZART:
LE NOZZE DI FIGARO

Gueden, Danco, Della Casa, Siepi, Poell, Corena, Kleiber cond.
Vienna Philharmonic and State Opera Chorus
4 discs
London OSA 1402*
UK: Ace of Diamonds GOS585-7 (3 discs)

Moffo, Schwarzkopf, Cossotto, Taddei, Waechter, Giulini cond.
Philharmonia Orchestra
4 discs
Angel S-3648*
UK: Columbia SMS1010

Norman, Freni, Minton, Ganzarolli, Wixell, Davis cond.
BBC Symphony Orchestra and Chorus
4 discs
Philips 6707014
UK: SAME

Mathis, Janowitz, Troyanos, Prey, Fischer-Dieskau, Böhm cond.
Deutsche Oper Orchestra and Chorus
4 discs
Deutsche Grammophon 2711007
UK: SAME

Grist, Söderström, Berganza, Evans, Bacquier, Klemperer cond.
New Philharmonia and John Alldis Choir
4 discs
HMV SLS955 (UK only)

Gatti, Tajo, Corena, Previtali cond.
RAI Orchestra and Chorus
3 discs
Everest/Cetra S-424/3*

Rothenberger, Gueden, Prey, Berry, Sultner cond.
Dresden State Opera Orchestra and Chorus
3 discs
Sung in German
Seraphim S-6002

Among the oldest of the noteworthy stereo versions of Mozart's great comedy, the one found on London-Decca is the most pleasing. Cesare Siepi's Figaro has been an international treasure for more than two decades, and this recording captures his witty, mellow interpretation and his graceful handling of the music. Whether angrily sardonic as in "Se vuol ballare" or impishly teasing as in "Non più andrai" or heartsick and bitter as in "Aprite un' po' quegli' occhi," Siepi creates a very human and very charming Figaro. His Susannah, Hilde Gueden, is equally delightful. Youthful yet poised, Gueden is a sharply drawn heroine possessed of a strong will and a winsome voice, not afraid to let true feeling come through in her acting. There is a sense of poignancy in the third act ensemble "Riconosci in quest'amplesso" when this Susannah can't quite believe that Marcellina is Figaro's mother and thus no longer her rival.

Lisa della Casa is heard as the Countess, a role she has sung on stage with distinction for many years. Reserved yet affecting in her characterization, her voice is ideally suited to the Countess' music. Della Casa's delicately shaped "Dove sono" is a model of fine Mozart singing.

Unfortunately, Alfred Poell, the Count, is a rather gruff-voiced, uninteresting singer, and Almaviva thus suffers from his perfunctory handling of the role.

Suzanne Danco is a properly naughty Cherubino who sings

with sparkle. Fernando Corena is a wryly amusing Bartolo who does not allow his comic ideas to disturb his singing. Hilde Rössel-Majdan is an unshrewish Marcellina. The minor roles are deftly handled, and the Vienna Philharmonic performs in a superior manner under Erich Kleiber who leads a performance remarkable for lightness and grace.

Angel-HMV's FIGARO features an almost perfect cast and the Philharmonia Orchestra conducted by Carlo Maria Giulini. Only Giuseppe Taddei in the title role seems miscast. Not endowed with the most beautiful of baritone voices, Taddei frequently distorts his sound for what he seems to consider comic effect, and his Figaro is more *buffo* than it ought to be. He is broad where he ought to be sly, as in "Se vuol ballare" and raucous where he might better be ironic, as in "Non più andrai."

Anna Moffo is a fetchingly youthful Susannah, singing with ample tone and considerable charm. Elisabeth Schwarzkopf's tense, sad Countess seems modelled on her characterization of the Marschallin in *Der Rosenkavalier*. This is an interesting manner in which to approach the role, but one that robs the Countess of a little charm. The lady does, of course, have a sense of humor, or she would not consent to be drawn into all the intrigues so readily. Musically, Schwarzkopf is a mistress of her art, but high notes are often hard-toned and her voice sounds less comfortably produced than in, for example, Schwarzkopf's DON GIOVANNI recording.

Eberhard Waechter is an extraordinarily interesting Count who keeps the conflicting emotions and volatile temper of this character in play at all times. His rather light voice is somewhat taxed in the third act aria, but Waechter succeeds admirably in presenting the Count as a man and not an insensitive, pouty caricature. Fiorenza Cossotto sings a youthful, saucy Cherubino, seeming more comfortable in "Voi che sapete" than in "Non so più." Ivo Vinco is a snappish Bartolo, and Dora Gatta a suitably old-maidish Marcellina.

Giulini's tempi are rapid yet well-considered, and the *secco* recitatives are sped through in an attempt to give the illusion of spoken dialogue. This is an interesting idea, but listeners who are less than fluent in Italian may be left breathless. Except for the dubious choice of Taddei in the title role, this NOZZE DI FIGARO is a most satisfying recording.

Philips Records, which in recent years has become one of the most consistently interesting record companies, offers an altogether admirable LE NOZZE DI FIGARO whose total effect is rather stronger than some of its individual components. Although there is no lack of fine singers in the cast, the true "star" of the set is conductor Colin Davis who urges his BBC Orchestra into a white-hot, urgently exciting reading of the score that seems to emphasize the more dramatic elements of the opera. This is no frothy, bubbly comedy in Davis' approach, but a serious if often wry work in which considerable emotional tension is generated. Not perhaps a universally acceptable view of FIGARO, but a highly individual one that works quite well—never has the complex finale to Act Two seemed so grandly important as here . . .

The singers are readily disposed to accept Davis' outlook on the opera, and there is a minimum of vocal "mugging," sighing, and gasping. Vladimiro Ganzarolli has a light, intelligently used voice that makes him a serviceable if not brilliant Figaro. He lacks Siepi's invention, not to mention that artist's sonorous voice, but is able to make Figaro into a lively and likeable fellow just the same. Mirella Freni, whose voice becomes more beautiful with each passing year while losing none of its suppleness as it gains in strength, is a sweet, gentle, and adorable Susannah whose every phrase is a miracle of fine singing.

Jessye Norman, the Countess, may someday be considered a great soprano. Certainly the raw material of her voice is estimable—creamy and smooth, with secure high notes and a consistent opulence of tone. As yet, however, she is no actress, and thus here the Countess is a rather bland and uninteresting person. Miss Norman seems uncomfortable when negotiating the tricky passages at the end of "Dove sono."

To cast a relatively inexperienced artist such as Miss

Norman in a major recording of a role in which she has to compete with the likes of Della Casa and Schwarzkopf is perhaps unwise. Still, one is always glad to encounter as lovely a voice as this, and one hopes that Miss Norman delivers what she promises to at this moment. Ingvar Wixell is heard as the Count, and he too is an interesting "find." His well-placed baritone and consistently alert acting help to sharpen the theatrical values of the performance. Yvonne Minton sings Cherubino's music to perfection, yet she is rather cool in the part—perhaps a result of Davis' no-nonsense interpretation of the opera.

An interesting feature of the opera is the change of order of music in Act Three. "Dove sono" is placed before the ensemble, thus allowing the Countess time to go off stage and prepare her dictation for Susannah. This, in the view of the producers of the set, clears up some gaps in the logic of the time scheme of the third act which, according to legend, had to be mangled when, at the first performance, the singer of Basilio also sang Don Curzio and needed extra time for a costume change. The theory holds up, and even traditionalists will not be able to say that the act is hurt by this reversal of musical order.

The supporting roles are well taken, and the recording, if not perhaps to the taste of those who favor a joyous, *gemütlich* FIGARO, is an exciting and original event.

RCA's FIGARO (deleted but enjoyable), recorded in Vienna in 1958, has a number of musical virtues thanks more to the strength of many of the cast members than to Erich Leinsdorf's pale, lackluster tempi that dim the sparkle of the music. Giorgio Tozzi is competent, both musically and dramatically, in the title role, but his work suffers greatly in comparison to Siepi's as Tozzi lacks the former's suave authority in the role, nor is his voice as glowingly beautiful as Siepi's. Roberta Peters is an efficient, pert, and musical Susannah who fails to see a depth in Susannah that might lead her performance in directions similar to those taken by Freni or Moffo. Peters is coy and arch where she might be sensuous and a little wistful.

Lisa della Casa duplicates her London turn as the Countess,

singing and acting with admirable style, and sounding almost as well as on the earlier recording. George London is a rather blustery Count whose "Vedroi mentr'io sospiro" is powerful and menacingly effective.

Rosalind Elias as Cherubino offers what may be the best work of anyone in the cast. Her light mezzo voice is beautifully controlled here, and her sense of fun and skill as an actress help her to suggest boyishness. Both arias are sung with commendable feeling and a silky, appealing tone.

Sandra Warfield, who in this uncut performance has the opportunity to perform her character's rarely heard fourth act aria, is a rather youthful sounding Marcellina, while Fernando Corena, as might be expected, is excruciatingly funny—and eminently musical—as Bartolo. Not a brilliant FIGARO, this, but an acceptable and often thoroughly enjoyable one.

Deutsche Grammophon's 1970 FIGARO led by Karl Böhm has a great deal by which it might be recommended. Hermann Prey's graceful, mischievous Figaro is a decided asset, although some may prefer a darker voice in the role. If his grasp of the Italian language is not quite as idiomatic as native speaker Siepi's, his diction is more than adequate, and his handling of the music most noble. Edith Mathis is a beguiling Susannah, using her small but bright lyric soprano with agility and verve. Not a terribly warm Susannah, in the Sayao-Freni sense, Mathis is appealing if somewhat brittle in the part. Dietrich Fischer-Dieskau repeats his Count Almaviva, a holdover from an earlier DGG version no longer available. This is one of the German baritone's best roles, and he shades his voice knowingly, producing the right balance between bluster and insinuation. Gundula Janowitz' satiny voice and sensitive, regal manner enable her to be one of the finest Countesses yet recorded, but Tatiana Troyanos' somewhat reserved Cherubino hardly suggests the love-lorn youth who is one of the most endearing characters in opera. The remainder of the cast is acceptable, although one misses someone of the caliber of Fernando Corena as Bartolo.

Dr. Böhm's brisk and precise conducting gives the performance cohesion and power, and Böhm allows his singers proper
time in which to phrase with eloquence.

GLUCK:
ORFEO ED EURIDICE

Bumbry, Rothenberger, Pütz, Neumann cond.
Radio Leipzig Orchestra and Chorus
2 discs
Angel S3717

Horne, Lorengar, Donath, Solti cond.
Covent Garden Orchestra and Chorus
2 discs
London OSA-1285*
UK: Decca SET443-4

Verrett, Moffo, Raskin, Fasano cond.
the Virtuosi di Roma
3 discs
RCA LSC-6169
UK: RCA SER5539-41

Fischer-Dieskau, Janowitz, Moser, Richter cond.
Orchestra and Chorus of the Munich Bach Society
2 discs
DGH 2707033
UK: DGG 138268-9

UK ONLY:
Ferrier, Ayres, Vlachopoulos, Southern cond.
the Glyndebourne Festival Orchestra and Chorus
1 disc (Abridged)
Ace of Clubs ACL293

Gedda, Micheau, Berton, Froment cond.
Orchestra and Chorus of the Paris Conservatoire (in French)
2 discs
HMV OC179-80

Gluck's opera, often dubbed "the first modern opera," exists
in several versions and in three languages but is most frequently performed—and recorded—in its Italian incarnation,
and with the title role sung by a mezzo-soprano, although
baritone Dietrich Fischer-Dieskau recorded the role of Orfeo
for Deutsche Grammophon and tenor Nicolai Gedda once
recorded the French version for Angel.

The "standard" mezzo-soprano ORFEO has been served
quite nicely by recordings, and three current sets are worth
one's attention. London-Decca's album features the strikingly
sung Orfeo of Marilyn Horne, whose warm, deep-hued voice
is excellently suited to portraying the Greek hero whose song
was beautiful enough to bring his wife back from the dead.
Miss Horne, whose *forte* has been *bel canto* roles, handles the
part quite admirably, singing a noble "Che farò senza
Euridice" and, in general, seeming very much "at home" in
Gluck's music.

The Euridice, Pilar Lorengar, is attractive and persuasive
in personality and musically quite charming as well. The often
under-cast role of Amor is taken by Helen Donath, whose
bright, warm lyric soprano is most welcome. Sir Georg Solti,
leading the Covent Garden Orchestra and Chorus, makes a
profoundly moving contribution, animating a score that, by
twentieth century standards, can seem static to some listeners.
The ballet of the blessed spirits is performed by the orchestra
with particular clarity, and Solti's tempi are not only comfortable for the singers, but serve well enough towards moving the
very real and always touching drama along.

Angel's ORFEO is built around the "hero" of Grace Bumbry.
Miss Bumbry, always a forceful personality, communicates
Orfeo's grief quite vividly, and also conveys the joy of the
final moments when Euridice, twice taken away from him, is

restored to life by decree of the gods. In musical terms, however, Bumbry is less than totally successful, as the lower moments of her role tax her voice. The mezzo also often sounds breathy. Bumbry's "Che farò" is appropriately fervent, but it lacks regality of line.

The light and delicate voice of the Viennese soprano Anneliese Rothenberger makes for an immensely pleasant Euridice, but Ruth-Margret Pütz is not a terribly fresh of voice Amor, particularly in comparison to Donath on the London-Decca recording.

The Orchestra and Chorus is that of Radio Leipzig, and these are inferior to the Covent Garden forces, with the Leipzig Chorus' unclear Italian diction being a special nuisance to the listener. Moreover, the conductor, Vaclav Neumann, directs as if inside a vacuum, content to create a clean, neat rhythmic picture but imbuing the score with little dramatic vitality.

RCA's ORFEO is graced by the elegant, warm vocalism of Shirley Verrett in the title role. Her unaffected singing, clear and ample of tone, is always a joy to hear. The Euridice is Anna Moffo, whose once pure lyric soprano voice has become less than easily produced. Although Moffo can still manage to sound pleasant in the middle range, she does not compare well to either Lorengar or Rothenberger. Judith Raskin is an attractive, warm-sounding Amor. The Virtuosi di Roma provide splendid orchestral support under the direction of Maestro Fasano.

Residents of the UK, or travelers thereto, can also avail themselves of the previously mentioned, older Angel-HMV set featuring the French version of the opera with Gedda as Orphée and Janine Micheau as Euridice, as well as the single disc abridged version that is part of the recorded legacy of Kathleen Ferrier. Conversely, British readers will have to use contacts in the USA to obtain Angel's more recent version, which for some reason is not available in England.

VERDI: OTELLO

Tebaldi, del Monaco, Protti, von Karajan cond.
Vienna Philharmonic and State Opera Chorus
3 discs
London OSA 1324*
UK: Decca SET209-11

Jones, McCracken, Fischer-Dieskau, Barbirolli cond.
Covent Garden Orchestra and Ambrosian Opera Chorus
3 discs
Angel S-3742*
UK: HMV SLS940

Tebaldi, del Monaco, Protti, Erede cond.
Orchestra and Chorus of L'Accademia di Santa Cecilia
3 discs
Richmond RS63004 (Mono)

Broggini, Corsi, Guichandute, Mercuriali, Taddei, Capuana cond.
Radio Torino Orchestra and Chorus
3 discs
Everest/Cetra S-460-3

Perhaps the greatest Italian opera ever written, and certainly among the most powerful, OTELLO has fared well on records. Unfortunately, Toscanini's famous RCA recording is no longer generally available. Although two of his singers, Herva Nelli (Desdemona) and Giuseppe Valdengo (Iago) were not of first calibre, Toscanini's brilliant reading of the score and the eloquent, dark voiced Moor of Ramon Vinay make the set invaluable to the serious collector.

Among the more readily obtainable OTELLO recordings, one can choose between two London-Decca sets featuring the same trio of principals—del Monaco, Tebaldi, and Protti, led in the mono version, now found on the budget Richmond label, by Erede and on the newer, stereo set by von Karajan. The older version has as its primary asset the Desdemona of Renata Tebaldi. Few of her recordings surpass the richness or purity found in this early Desdemona. Her phrasing is gentle and lovely, and her interpretation is most touching. The love duet, Willow Song, Ave Maria, and the crushing lament in the third act ensemble are among the soprano's finest achievements. Although del Monaco eventually tempered his fiery and savage Otello, in the mid 1950's it had chiefly its great physical power to recommend it. Aldo Protti is a competent baritone who realizes little of Iago's villainy in his characterization. Chief among the supporting artists are Piero de Palma as Cassio and Fernando Corena, in a rare noncomic appearance, as Montano. Alberto Erede leads the Santa Cecilia forces with more abandon than customary for him, making this an altogether satisfactory performance.

The second London-Decca set, from 1960 or thereabouts, finds in del Monaco a more refined Otello and one who creates a true character rather than presenting a series of hysterical vignettes. Tebaldi sounds almost·as well as in her earlier Desdemona—which is very well indeed—while Protti shows little development (one wonders why he was re-engaged).

Von Karajan's precise and detailed account of the score, abetted by the wonderful Vienna Philharmonic and State Opera Chorus create an exciting framework for the tragedy.

The RCA-HMV set with Jon Vickers, Tito Gobbi and Leonie Rysanek, and the Rome Opera forces led by Tullio Serafin is marred by Mme. Rysanek's substandard Desdemona. In poor voice when the recording was made and perhaps not really well suited to Desdemona's tessitura, Rysanek sounds unsteady and vocally heavy throughout the disc. This is a pity, for both Vickers' restrained and beautifully sung Otello and Gobbi's definitive, excellently acted, and roguishly sung Iago are worth owning. Perhaps the highlight disc from this set is the best idea for the collector, as much of the Otello-Iago scene in Act Two plus three of Otello's monologues are included in addition to the love duet, Credo, and Willow song.

The most recent Otello is the Angel-HMV version in which the Covent Garden Orchestra and Ambrosian Chorus are conducted by the late Sir John Barbirolli. In the title role, James McCracken proves to be vocally the most powerful and opulent Moor around, outdistancing even del Monaco in terms of sheer size of sound. This Otello is no callow lover, indeed, McCracken is less at home in the first act duet than in the later scenes. He is a creature helplessly ripped open by his doubts and jealousies, and McCracken is overwhelmingly successful in communicating the Moor's great suffering. Gwynneth Jones is gifted with what is basically one of the most beautiful lyric soprano voices one could ever hope to hear. Unfortunately, the voice is rapidly losing security, particularly on the top of the staff, and, although there are some truly lovely moments— especially the Willow Song, some passages, such as some in the love duet, are spoiled by a vocal wobble reminiscent of those of Callas or Leonie Rysanek (in her Otello recording). Jones offers a rather diffident heroine in the first two acts, but builds to a moving and pitiable climax in Act Three in both the confrontation with Otello and the ensemble. One would like more vocal color in her work, though.

Dietrich Fischer-Dieskau undoubtedly has the brains necessary for Iago but, sadly, not the ideal voice for the role. In the softly insinuating measures of "Era la notte," this artist is in his element, spinning a deceitful but beautiful web around the unwary Moor's eyes and ears. However, whenever it becomes necessary to ride over the full orchestra, the baritone takes on a blustery, unpleasant sound that nearly puts him out of the running, especially when compared to Tito Gobbi.

Barbirolli, whose father and grandfather played in the first OTELLO performance along with Toscanini, favors broad sweeping tempi that create a pageant of gorgeous sound. If the soprano and baritone were as consistently fine as the tenor and conductor (not to mention the fine orchestra and chorus), this OTELLO could have been a milestone among opera recordings. As it is, McCracken and Barbirolli combine to make the set worthwhile.

Those interested in historic performances should pick up the Victrola disc of 1939 vintage excerpts featuring Giovanni Martinelli, Lawrence Tibbett, and Helen Jepson, with the Metropolitan Opera Orchestra and Chorus conducted by Wilfred Pelletier. The brilliance of Martinelli's Otello and the sonority of Tibbett's Iago transcend the limitations of 1939 sound. Miss Jepson's silvery Desdemona is worthy of her colleagues' performances, too.

LEONCAVALLO: PAGLIACCI

Carlyle, Bergonzi, Taddei, Panerai, von Karajan cond.
La Scala Orchestra and Chorus
3 discs (available only with CAVALLERIA)
Deutsche Grammophon 2709020*
UK: Same as above

Tucci, del Monaco, MacNeil, Capecchi, Molinari-Pradelli cond.
Orchestra and Chorus of L'Accademia di Santa Cecilia
2 discs
London OSA 1212*
(Available with CAVALLERIA OSA 1330)
UK: Ace of Diamonds (With CAVALLERIA)
GOS588-90 (3 discs)

Lorengar, McCracken, Merrill, Krause, Gardelli cond.
Orchestra and Chorus of L'Accademia di Santa Cecilia
2 discs
London OSA 1280*
UK: Decca SET 403-4

Caballé, Domingo, Milnes, McDaniel, Santi cond.
London Symphony Orchestra and John Alldis Choir
2 discs
RCA LSC-7090

Amara, Corelli, Gobbi, Von Matacic cond.
La Scala Orchestra and Chorus
2 discs
Angel S3618
UK: Columbia SAX2399-400

de los Angeles, Bjoerling, Warren, Merrill, Cellini cond.
RCA Orchestra
Robert Shaw Chorale
Seraphim IB 6058 (Mono)

Pacetti, Gigli, Basiola, Ghione cond.
La Scala Orchestra and Chorus
2 discs
Seraphim IB 6009 (Mono)

del Monaco, Petrella, Protti, Erede cond.
Orchestra and Chorus of L'Accademia di Santa Cecilia
2 discs
Richmond RSRS62009 (Mono)
(With CAVALLERIA) Richmond RS 63003)

Bergonzi, Tagliabue, Simonetto cond.
RAI Orchestra and Chorus
2 discs
Everest/Cetra s-411-2*

PAGLIACCI is one of the most frequently recorded of operas, with its three ingratiating roles for soprano, tenor, and baritone making it a favorite of firms wishing to show off the luminaries on their rosters.

Since there are probably six equally attractive PAGLIACCI sets available, as well as a number of other recordings interesting for one reason or another, choosing a favorite is impossible and individual taste will have to dictate the listener's choice.

The role of Canio has tempted every tenor from Caruso right on up to Domingo and McCracken. One of the finest Canios of recent years has been Mario del Monaco, who has sung the role before the microphones twice. While his earlier performance has survived on a low priced Richmond (Decca) release in a rather provincial reading featuring Clara

Petrella, Aldo Protti, and Afro Poli, this tenor's second PAG-
LIACCI set, still available on London-Decca is the more worthwhile set to own. This version, made in 1960, finds del Monaco
in enviable voice and in firm control of his dramatic talents.
The voice pours forth as searingly as a volcanic eruption, but
this raw power is tempered by a greater awareness of the need
for dramatic contrasts. Here del Monaco does not rely on
bellowing without relief, but works successfully towards
presenting the tormented actor as a sympathetic, real being.

Del Monaco is partnered by the Nedda of Gabriella Tucci
who is notable for clarity of production and sweetness of tone.

Cornell MacNeil, the set's Tonio, finds in the role a nearly
perfect vehicle for his dark hued baritone, although he is less
successful at projecting the hunchback's nasty personality
than at singing the "Prologo."

Renato Capecchi and Piero de Palma round out the cast as
Silvio and Beppe, respectively, and both perform ably. Francesco Molinari-Pradelli paces the score with a practised hand,
leading soloists and the Orchestra and Chorus of the
Accademia di Santa Cecilia in a robust and satisfying
performance.

A La Scala PAGLIACCI available in tandem with that
company's CAVALLERIA RUSTICANA (discussed elsewhere) issued by Deutsche Grammophon is distinguished by
Carlo Bergonzi's handsome singing of Canio's music. A more
reserved performer than del Monaco, Bergonzi manages to be
quite powerful when raging at Nedda and delivers a typically
winning "Vesti la giubba." Joan Carlyle, the young British
soprano, offers a technically accomplished Nedda, holding her
own with Bergonzi's articulate and self assured singing. Car-
lisle suggests that Nedda is a pretty and charming girl who
finds herself ensnared by emotions and events that she finds
herself unable to control, which is a fair enough manner in
which to play the part.

Giuseppe Taddei is an appropriately menacing Tonio,
making up for the lack of a truly great voice with his superior
musicianship and intense characterization. Rolando Panerai

is a mature sounding but full voiced Silvio, and Ugo Benelli does nicely with Beppe's music. The Scala forces prove their supremacy in Italian opera here, and Karajan offers what may be his most successful rendering of an Italian score to this date, never allowing his beat to become too slow or heavy and letting the drama build momentum as the opera progresses.

RCA's 1972 PAGLIACCI offers that company's three brightest young singers (Domingo, Caballé, and Milnes) in the leading roles, with the added attraction of opening a few cuts in the score. Under Nello Santi's rather slack direction, the performance is notable for some lovely singing, but the very real drama inherent in the score receives short shrift.

Placido Domingo's beautiful but essentially lyric tenor voice is not meant to sing so heavy a role as Canio in the opera house. Under studio conditions, Domingo carries it off without too much evident strain, but one hopes that he will resist offers to do the role at so large a theatre as the Metropolitan or Covent Garden, as even on discs, he seems to be pushing his voice rather cruelly while singing "Vesti la giubba." Domingo alone of the three principal singers captures the passions of his character.

Montserrat Caballé is one of the most generously endowed artists to undertake the role of Nedda on records. She sings as would the proverbial angel but is more lifeless than usual in her characterization. Sherrill Milnes is similarly golden toned and wooden hearted as Tonio, singing with dignity and little sense of expression. Barry McDaniel sounds ill at ease in Silvio's music, while Leo Goeke, a young Metropolitan Opera tenor, shows promise in the role of Beppe. The London Symphony Orchestra and John Alldis choir contribute greatly to the smoothness of the musical line, but the net effect of this performance may be likened to the barely smoldering embers left when a fire is drenched by a cold rain.

It might be mentioned in passing that while other PAGLIACCI sets fill the fourth side of their two disc sets with familiar arias, songs, or choruses, the Victor album takes the welcome and adventurous path of presenting Caballé, Domingo, and Milnes in excerpts from three virtually unknown Leoncavallo operas (or at least unperformed these days): ZAZA, CHATTERTON, and LA BOHEME.

London-Decca issued still another PAGLIACCI in 1969, this one built around the Canio of James McCracken who despite a tendency toward tight vocal production and a less spontaneous feeling for the music than del Monaco exhibits, creates a warmly sung and powerful hero. One wonders whether McCracken's true musical home might not be in German opera where sensuously beautiful sound (which is not a natural attribute of this intelligent and conscientious artist) is less important than powerful projection of score and text (a McCracken hallmark). Also featured on this set are Pilar Lorengar as a gracious and appealing Nedda and Robert Merrill as an experienced and smooth voiced Tonio. Tom Krause is the alert Silvio, while Ugo Benelli once again enjoys success as Beppe. The Santa Cecilia forces are conducted knowingly by Lamberto Gardelli.

Turning to two older, mono only, and budget priced editions of this opera found on the Seraphim label, the more recent set, dating from 1953, features an all star cast including Jussi Bjoerling as Canio, Victoria de los Angeles as Nedda, Leonard Warren as Tonio, and Robert Merrill as Silvio. These four artists combine their mighty talents to give an object lesson in just how Italian opera ought to sound. Bjoerling, who stayed away from the role of Canio in the opera house, is consistently idiomatic in his singing without resorting to vulgarity or excessive sobbing and he delivers a profoundly moving account of the all too familiar aria "Vesti la giubba," as well as reaching new interpretive heights in the opera's final moments. Leonard Warren is less flamboyant but equally strong vocally and dramatically as Tonio. De los Angeles, like her compatroit Caballé, is a ladylike Nedda, who sings the "Ballatella" with delicacy and the love duet with sensitivity. Merrill is in extremely mellow voice as Silvio (this seems to be the only time that he and Leonard Warren recorded together) while the Met's "star comprimario" tenor Paul Franke is an engaging Beppe. The RCA Orchestra is led with gusto by Renato Cellini, and the Robert Shaw Chorale performs with spirit. Well worth its modest price, this is one set that every opera fan would do well to own.

The older Seraphim set is a La Scala performance that dates from 1934 and is notable chiefly for the extraordinarily vibrant Canio of Beniamino Gigli. Another feature is the opening of the same cuts as are reinstated in the RCA set (and the later London-Decca one as well), however the other singers on the album are substandard.

The 1954 Scala set with Callas and di Stefano seems to be out of print, but the powerful singing of those two artists, as well as that of Gobbi as Tonio, make the set worth hunting for.

WAGNER: PARSIFAL

Windgassen, Mödl, London, Weber, Uhde, van Mill, Knappertsbusch
cond.
Bayreuth Festival Orchestra and Chorus
5 discs
Richmond RS65001
UK: Ace of Diamonds GOM 504-8

Thomas, Dalis, London, Hotter, Talvela, Neidlinger, Knappertsbusch
cond.
Bayreuth Festival Orchestra and Chorus
5 discs
Philips 835220/4
(Not in Philips UK catalogue)

King, Jones, Stewart, Crass, Ridderbusch, McIntyre, Boulez cond.
Bayreuth Festival Orchestra and Chorus
5 discs
DGG 2713004
UK: DGG 2720034

The oldest of the PARSIFAL sets dates from 1951 and is a
bargain on Richmond or Ace of Diamonds. It features, rarity of
rarities, Wolfgang Windgassen in prime voice. His sensitive
reading of the text coupled with an expressive and powerful
instrument make the tenor an almost ideal Parsifal. Marthe
Mödl is the set's Kundry. Mödl, of course, is a true singing-
actress and a respectable musician. Her voice, however, is of
itself rather unattractive, rough in the upper regions, and not
notably warm or rich elsewhere. Thus her Kundry convinces as
far as the woman's suffering is concerned, but her work in Act

215

Two, while at times dramatically gripping, is less than seductively beautiful.

The (then) youthful George London is an excellent Amfortas, virile of tone and supple of voice, while Ludwig Weber is a very sonorous Gurnemanz. Herman Uhde's Klingsor is dramatically exciting and quite well sung in the bargain. Hans Knappertsbusch paces the music well, never allowing the score to plod, and obtains particularly handsome work from his orchestra in the Prelude to Act One and the Good Friday Spell.

Knappertsbusch also leads the Philips version, made in 1961, which also finds George London, in less than perfect form, as Amfortas once more. This recording features the Parsifal of Jess Thomas whose flinty, not terribly exciting voice is not really well served by discs, as his electrifying stage presence cannot be preserved on that medium. He sings intelligently and has the stamina to last through a performance (singers recorded in actual performances lack, of course, the comforting studio convention of re-taking anything that goes wrong the first time).

The Kundry here is the Metropolitan Opera mezzo-soprano, Irene Dalis, whose fine top range and high-powered acting serve her well in the part. Not a subtle artist, Dalis provides a sense of raw emotion that can be quite effective. The majestic and authoritative Gurnemanz of Hans Hotter is still another value of this excellent set, while Gustav Neidlinger offers a malign but musical Klingsor, and Martti Talvela gives an impressive account of Titurel's music. Knappertsbusch once again provides seasoned and knowledgeable direction, although it appears that the decade between the two performances had not given him any special new insights into the score.

DGG'S 1970 PARSIFAL presents one of today's leading maestri, Pierre Boulez, as conductor. His intense direction and the fine playing he inspires in his orchestra places the recording squarely on a high level of achievement. James King is a youthful and musically gifted Parsifal, lacking perhaps the ultimate in authority for the role. His slightly tentative characterization is no great defect however. Gwynneth Jones, unfortunately, was in the depth of her vocal malaise in 1970, and her singing suffers in comparison not only to Dalis' work, but to the early high standard that the British soprano had set for herself. Thomas Stewart offers a very beautiful performance as Amfortas, and Karl Ridderbusch is an imposing Titurel. Franz Crass is not in the same league as Hans Hotter in the role of Gurnemanz.

London-Decca's new recording was unfortunately issued too late for inclusion here.

BELLINI: IL PIRATA

Caballé, Martì, Cappuccilli, Raimondi, Gavazzeni cond.
Orchestra and Chorus of the Rome Opera
3 discs
Angel S-35764
UK: HMV SLS953

Bellini's third opera has never enjoyed too much popularity, possibly due to its particularly lame libretto—not to mention the difficulty of Bellini's music. Callas performed it occasionally, in America most notably in a concert performance by the American Opera Society (which has survived as a "pirated" PIRATA set). It has, however, most recently been given attention by Montserrat Caballé, who has sung it on the stage, as well as on its only commercial complete recording (Callas recorded the opera's final scene quite beautifully in 1958, while her 1962 reading of Imogene's first act aria was released in 1972 on her "By Request" disc).

This HMV-Angel production from 1969 offers an ingratiating, often exciting interpretation by the Spanish soprano. Caballé's sensuously sweet, big voice is handled with refinement, and her tireless spinning out of the Bellinian line is a marvel to hear. However, Imogene's desperate predicament (she is married to a vicious character named Ernesto who imprisons and ultimately kills her lover, Gualtiero) is languidly realized by Caballé, whose sweet suffering is only occasionally marked by formidable moments of fire. On the whole, though, her characterization of the heroine is viable if not ideal, and her unfailing sense of personal dignity and musical accomplishment tend to mitigate her lack of power as an actress.

Although the work of Piero Cappuccilli as Ernesto is

excellent, and that of Ruggiero Raimondi as the hermit, Goffredo is equally distinguished (and all the more so in so relatively small a role), there is a major flaw in the casting— the engagement of Bernabé Martì as Gualtiero. The Spanish tenor (and husband of Caballé) has a basically fine voice which he has not as yet learned to produce with ease. High notes are strained and ugly, and even the middle register is often rather muddy in tone. Certainly no successor to Giuseppe di Stefano, Martì would be well advised to avoid Bellini in performance, and EMI's use of him here is a disservice to the public and to the tenor himself. Gianandrea Gavazzeni leads the Rome Opera Orchestra and Chorus with feeling, adding excitement to an often superb performance of an opera that seems unjustly neglected, as there is much music, particularly for soprano and tenor, that can hold its own with Bellini's later accomplishments.

BELLINI: I PURITANI

Sutherland, Duval, Capecchi, Flagello, Bonynge cond.
Orchestra and Chorus of the Maggio Musicale Fiorentino
3 discs
London OSA 1373*
UK: Decca SET 259-61

Callas, di Stefano, Panerai, Rossi-Lemeni, Serafin cond.
La Scala Orchestra and Chorus
3 discs
Angel 3502 C/L (Mono)

As of this writing, there are two recordings of Bellini's final opera (ABC is preparing a PURITANI featuring Beverly Sills and Philips is preparing one featuring Cristina Deutekom, but both were unavailable at press time). One, the Angel-HMV set, is a part of the original trio of Callas recordings that made the lady a major operatic personality in the USA months before she actually sang here, while the second, a vehicle for Joan Sutherland on London-Decca, was recorded during the height of that diva's popularity in the mid 1960's.

The Angel version, available only in monaural sound and in relatively limited quantities these days, is the one to own. Maria Callas brings to Elvira superior musical intelligence and the quality of poignancy that makes this rather feeble character live and breathe in Callas' hands. Her unique, reedy upper range was still, in 1953, able to contend with Elvira's coloratura flights of fancy, and Callas' "Qui la voce soave" is one of her greatest performances before the microphones.

Callas, despite her many excellences, is not the only strong singer found in the cast. Her Arturo is Giuseppe Di Stefano, whose lyric tenor was in full flower at the time he made this recording. Some consider him to be the finest Italian tenor since Gigli. Clearly, this recording helps to establish Di Stefano in that exalted position. Seldom has his voice seemed sweeter, more ardent, or less constricted, with high C's and even a high D flat in Act Three being produced as if without effort. The Callas-di Stefano combination has produced some memorable recordings, among which this PURITANI stands out as one of the very best.

Nicola Rossi-Lemeni had a singularly arresting voice— imperfectly produced and not truly beautiful, yet strong, vibrant, and imposing, and these three qualities are apparent in his singing of the role of Sir Giorgio. Rolando Panerai lends his solid, mahogany baritone to the role of Elvira's rejected suitor Sir Riccardo Forth. In that rousing duet "Suoni le trombe," these two artists make the most of the wonderful opportunity that Bellini provided them for stealing some of the thunder from the soprano and tenor.

Leading the Chorus and Orchestra of La Scala with great sensitivity and a sure command of *bel canto* support is Tullio Serafin. The chief problem with this set is that a number of standard cuts are honored and, the lovely "Rondo" which ends the work is among them. The Sutherland recording, for all its flaws, at least ends with this dazzling piece of coloratura composition.

Miss Sutherland, who very creditably followed in Callas' footsteps in resurrecting and performing neglected *bel canto* operas in the world's major opera houses had begun to exhibit the by now familiar faults in her singing in 1963 when her PURITANI set was recorded. Her voice is undeniably larger, more evenly produced, and sweeter to the ear than Callas', but, given her bland characterizations, tendency to scoop languidly, her problematical diction, and her fondness for slow tempi, Sutherland's often stupendous feats of trilling, proficiency in the stratospheric register, and the basically lovely sound she produces are often smothered in the torpor of her musical daze.

Where Callas made her voice embody the delicate emotions of gentle, insecure Elvira, Sutherland is content to sing prettily. Furthermore, her scooping and drooping becomes rather annoying very quickly. Sutherland is best in more rapid passages where it is impossible for her to indulge in her fondness for those mannerisms. "Son bel vergine vezzosa" comes off quite well, as does the previously mentioned "Rondo," "Ah sento mio bel angelo."

Sutherland's leading man on this album is the French Canadian tenor Pierre Duval, a young man who can indeed reach his high D's, but only with a great deal of obvious vocal strain and a strangulated sound. His singing is competent, but not even worthy of comparison to that of di Stefano. Renato Capecchi, though, makes a fine Riccardo, while Ezio Flagello offers a larger sounding Giorgio than Rossi-Lemeni, his Angel counterpart.

The estimable forces of the Florence May Festival would have benefited from a more lively conductor than Sutherland's husband, Richard Bonynge who must accept responsibility for the flabby, weak pace of this recording.

VERDI: RIGOLETTO

Scotto, Cossotto, Bergonzi, Fischer-Dieskau, Vinco, Kubelik cond.
Orchestra and Chorus of La Scala
3 discs
Deutsche Grammophon 2709014*
UK: Same

Moffo, Elias, Kraus, Merrill, Flagello, Solti cond.
RCA Italiana Orchestra and Chorus
2 discs
RCA LSC-7027*
UK: RCA SER 5516-7

Grist, di Stasio, Gedda, MacNeil, Ferrin, Molinari-Pradelli cond.
Rome Opera Orchestra and Chorus
3 discs
Angel S-3718*
UK: HMV SLS 933

Sutherland, Malagù, Cioni, MacNeil, Siepi, Sanzogno cond.
Orchestra and Chorus of L'Accademia di Santa Cecilia
3 discs
London OSA-1332*
UK: Decca SET 224-6

Pagliughi, Taddei, Questa cond.
RAI Orchestra and Chorus
3 discs
Everest/Cetra S-407-3*

Peters, Elias, Bjoerling, Merrill, Tozzi, Perlea cond.
Rome Opera Orchestra and Chorus
2 discs
Victrola VIC 6401 (Mono)
UK: Same

Callas, Lazzarini, di Stefano, Gobbi, Zaccaria, Serafin cond.
La Scala Orchestra and Chorus
3 discs (5 sides)
Angel 3537* (Mono)
UK: Columbia MWS 817

Sutherland, Tourangeau, Pavarotti, Milnes, Talvela, Bonynge cond.
London Symphony Orchestra
3 discs
London OSA 13105
UK: Decca (Catalogue number was unavailable at press time)

Although there is no completely satisfactory stereophonic
RIGOLETTO recording, several are relatively distinguished
and boast fine individual performances. Moreover, going
back to the older, monaural recordings of Verdi's opera that
are still available, one finds at least three performances that
are treasurable.

The best RIGOLETTO appears to be the EMI mono set
released in the USA on the Angel label and on the Columbia
banner in the UK. Made in 1955 at La Scala, this recording
features Tito Gobbi, Maria Callas, and Giuseppe di Stefano,
under Serafin's baton.

More than any other baritone who has thus far recorded the
jester, Gobbi communicates Rigoletto's vicious crudeness in
his behavior with the courtiers as well as his tender devotion
to his daughter. Vocally, Gobbi is strong enough, although
lacking ease on top. His "Cortigiani, vil razza dannata," is
perhaps one of the most electrifying moments in the annals of
recorded opera.

Callas, as have many others before and after her, found little dramatic vitality in Gilda's rather poorly drawn personality. Her high notes are weak, especially in the third act duet with Rigoletto, but her cleanly phrased singing and the darker, more interesting timbre that she brings to the music—especially in comparison to the songbirds who often chirp their way through the role—allow her to make her usual, singular impression in the role. One envies the theatre that La Scala must have been in the 1950's, in that it could provide an artist of Callas' stature for the role of Gilda in a performance that included Gobbi and di Stefano as well. As for the tenor, di Stefano has here all the attributes of a splendid Duke of Mantua: a graceful, easily handled voice with ringing top notes, an understanding of Verdian style, and a personality that is nothing if not ardent. One senses in the tenor's "La donna è mobile" the incredible impact that this song must have had upon the public at its first hearing. More than a century and countless renditions later, it emerges in di Stefano's account as a perfect musical expression of the sexual urge.

The three leading artists are joined in the fourth act quartet by the Maddalena of Adriana Lazzarini who sings gracefully if not particularly seductively.

The balance of the cast, drawn from the La Scala roster and including Niccola Zaccaria as Sparafucile and Plinio Clabassi as Monterone, is eminently satisfactory. Tullio Serafin's conducting lacks a degree of fire, to be sure, but his tempi are reasonably sound, and his work is never dull, especially given the blazingly fine singing of the principals.

A more recent La Scala RIGOLETTO may be found on Deutsche Grammophon, dating from 1965, featuring Dietrich Fischer-Dieskau, Renata Scotto, and Carlo Bergonzi under the guidance of Rafael Kubelik. Poor Fischer-Dieskau! An artist of tremendous merit in the German repertoire he rarely seems at home in the Italian works that he records with commendable perseverence if less than distinguished results. Fischer-Dieskau's Rigoletto is afire with sensitivity, and the baritone pays particular attention to his diction. He offers, unfortunately, barely a hint of the hunchback's violence, nor does he produce the large tone required if the role is to achieve its impact. For sweetness of voice and accuracy of pitch, this performance is unbeatable—but these elements alone cannot substitute for force of personality and command of the musical line.

Renata Scotto is, like Callas, a singer of proven dramatic ability, excellent taste, and a somewhat flawed soprano voice that is liable to become thin, reedy, and occasionally unpleasantly shrill in the upper reaches. This recording finds Scotto in particularly metallic voice, and in truth, she does not sing too prettily in most of her scenes. To Scotto's credit, she succeeds in capturing Gilda's despair in the later moments of Acts Three and Four, where, like Callas again, she refuses to let the character emerge as a sort of mechanical whimper box.

Where this RIGOLETTO succeeds best is in its Duke, Carlo Bergonzi, who offers a gallant, gracious portrayal more notable for stylish, tasteful singing than for unbounded passion. Bergonzi's Duke of Mantua may not be romantically convincing on stage, but as preserved on discs, it is a very creditable undertaking.

Fiorenza Cossotto was a full-fledged diva of the mezzo realm by the mid 60's and so her presence here as a sultry, glamorous Maddalena is an added delight. The mezzo's husband, Ivo Vinco, is heard as a forthright, no-nonsense Sparafucile.

Rafael Kubelik is not internationally regarded as a Verdi specialist, but on the basis of this recording, however, he ought to be more in demand as a conductor of Verdi's operas, for seldom has a more excitingly led, superbly clear account of RIGOLETTO been heard. One hears in this performance the great advances Verdi had made in orchestration by 1851. As conducted by Kubelik, the music seems to have more meaning in relation to the dramatic situations than in the hands of many Italian conductors who allow every phrase to sound as though it were indeed meant for an "oom-pah" band. Had there been a more idiomatic singer for the title role, this RIGOLETTO might have been the definitive recording—as it is, it emerges as uneven, but not without some magnificent moments.

RCA crammed an uncut RIGOLETTO onto two discs as opposed to the three required by Angel, Deutsche Grammophon, and London-Decca for their full length performances. The RCA set even restores the tenor's third act *caballetta* and numerous minor repeats. Under Georg Solti's strong if rather somber direction, principals Robert Merrill, Anna Moffo, and Alfredo Kraus eschew "traditional" interpolated high notes—a practice that, at least in the cases of Merrill and Moffo, may be due more to a reluctance to try, than to a commitment to Verdi's original intentions.

Merrill's Rigoletto is strongly sung, although he offers little subtlety of characterization, electing merely to sound efficiently distraught or angry from time to time. No one can fault, though, the oaken-solid sound that he produces—if only Merrill's acting were not cut from the same bough.

Moffo's Gilda is attractively sung, and since she refrains from high E's and other danger spots, her portrayal succeeds on musical grounds. Her acting in this role is more nervous and studied than genuinely youthful.

Alfredo Kraus has a lighter voice than one often hears as the Duke and one that requires more *slancio* and "ring" to make a fully superior impression in this music, but his natural elegance and good musicianship serve him well here, and he emerges as a youthful-sounding Duke and one whose romantic antics are entirely believable. The Metropolitan Opera's Rosalind Elias and Ezio Flagello make a lusty brother-sister team in Sparafucile's Inn, she impressing with her fluid, sensuous sound, and he with his deep hued, menacing impersonation of the assassin.

The RCA Italiana Orchestra and Chorus perform well under Solti. The conductor emphasizes the darker elements of the score, muting rather fascinatingly the primary musical colors of Verdi's Renaissance Mantua.

Angel's more recent RIGOLETTO (HMV in the UK) promises much in its assignments of the leading roles to Cornell MacNeil, Reri Grist, and Nicolai Gedda, but the performance led by Molinari-Pradelli somehow never gets off the ground, musically or dramatically. Although Cornell MacNeil has been singing Rigoletto around the world for nearly two decades, he has never penetrated the character's surface and thus always sings the role in a generalized, one dimensional manner. Worse, MacNeil's voice has in recent years taken on a heavy vibrato that often prevents him from staying on pitch for any length of time. These problems are in all too clear evidence on this recording.

Reri Grist, in spite of her elegant musicianship and delightful flair for operatic acting in comic roles, is a rather old-fashioned, twittering Gilda. Her light, silvery voice sounds small, especially when singing with MacNeil, and she, while singing with taste and certainly a pleasant sound, never fully comes alive in this performance.

Gedda's Duke of Mantua is the most fortunate element of this set, as he sings with his customary aristocratic bearing and bright voice. He too, though, is a trifle cold here. Perhaps the phlegmatic, impersonal conducting of the Rome Opera forces by Molinari-Pradelli impeded Gedda, and his colleagues as well, from breathing life into the opera.

Anna di Stasio is a routine Maddalena, with Agustino Ferrin contributing a rather bland Sparafucile. In sum, the most exciting aspect of this recording is the gripping color photograph of MacNeil and Grist in a moment from the third act which adorns the album cover. If only the performance were as arresting.

London-Decca's 1962 RIGOLETTO with MacNeil, Sutherland, and Cioni is now being replaced by a second Sutherland version in which the soprano is joined by Sherrill Milnes in the title role and Luciano Pavarotti as the Duke. The earlier version does find MacNeil in better voice than on the Angel set, while Sutherland offers dazzling trills and a gentle, shy characterization of Gilda. Cioni's Duke is less distinguished, as his voice is often dry sounding and unattractive, particularly in the upper register. Nino Sanzogno leads the Santa Cecilia forces in a somewhat listless performance.

London-Decca's latest RIGOLETTO is a showcase for the talents of Joan Sutherland, Luciano Pavarotti, and Sherrill Milnes, who performed the opera together at the Metropolitan in June, 1972 with Richard Bonynge conducting as he does here.

Sutherland's performance on this more recent RIGOLETTO is an improvement over her earlier one. She scoops less here and her diction is better. Thus, Sutherland's current Gilda ranks with her best recorded efforts. The immense Sutherland sound produces a more forceful Gilda than one often hears. Lacking the ultimate dramatic tension generated by Callas or Scotto, Sutherland is nonetheless an interesting and affecting heroine—and when does one get to hear so effortless a trill at the end of "Caro nome?"

Pavarotti's Duke is swaggering but graceful, with ample sound throughout and especially fine top notes in "La donna è mobile" and in the Quartet. Milnes' Rigoletto is conventionally characterized, and his originally stupendous voice occasionally falls prey to pitch problems and a noticeable raggedness near the top. Milnes' obsession with loud, long, interpolated high notes has already begun to affect his performances, and he would be wise to consider the possibility of permanent damage unless he reconsiders this practice. Also in the cast are Hougette Tourangeau, a rather raspy Maddalena, and Martti Talvela as her brother, the hired assassin, Sparafucile, who sings quite well. The comprimarii are quite acceptable, and Bonynge's conducting reveals some development in skill. Although Milnes' underacted and vocally spotty jester doesn't compare with the likes of Warren, Gobbi, or Bastianini, the ever-growing legions of Sutherland-Pavarotti fans will no doubt de delighted with the set in which, by the way, the score is presented uncut.

There are two interesting budget-priced monaural RIGO-

LETTOs currently available, one on Victrola and the other on Richmond.

The Victrola set was made at the Rome Opera in 1956 and finds Robert Merrill, Roberta Peters, and Jussi Bjoerling in the leading roles, and the late Jonel Perlea at the podium. Merrill's Rigoletto was, in 1956, even less well defined dramatically than it was 8 years later when he re-did the opera for RCA. Here, he is almost as poker-faced (poker-voiced . . . ?) as was Gary Cooper in High Noon, but he does, at least, sing the music with vigor and finesse. Roberta Peters manages a light-toned, slightly coy Gilda, adequately preserving one of her best and most frequently sung roles. Bjoerling is a shade below top form here, occasionally wandering from pitch and somehow not singing with his usual mellowness. I hasten to remind the reader that Bjoerling at 90% of top form offers more than many a tenor performing at the peak of his capabilities. At any rate, there can be no carping over the tenor's singing of "La Donna è mobile" or his participation in the Quartet. Rosalind Elias and Giorgio Tozzi perform efficiently as Maddalena and Sparafucile. Perlea, making all the traditional cuts, leads a briskly paced and reasonably effective performance.

Richmond's RIGOLETTO, a reissue of London-Decca's early recording of the opera, features a solidly professional if not exciting performance by Aldo Protti as the jester, a "macho" job by Mario del Monaco as the Duke (easily the most forceful of the recorded libertines) and a fine Gilda from Hilde Gueden. Cesare Siepi is a handsomely sung Sparafucile, and Giulietta Simionato is a worthy Maddalena. Alberto Erede's conducting is not terribly strong but he elicits some smooth work from both his singers and the Orchestra and Chorus of the Santa Cecilia Academy.

Another RCA RIGOLETTO was made in New York in 1950 with Leonard Warren, Jan Peerce, and Erna Berger, with the RCA Orchestra conducted by Renato Cellini. This was the first complete opera recorded in the USA (if one excepts the discs made from Toscanini broadcasts in the 1940's) and, in addi-

tion to that historical honor, featured an outstanding performance by Warren as Rigoletto, sung with urgency and a
great outpouring of beautiful sound. Peerce's Duke is a sunny,
bright personality and one of the American tenor's finest
efforts in the recording studio. Erna Berger's Gilda is entirely
satisfactory, a little cool dramatically, but sung with clarity.

A very recent reissue on the Everest label offers a late
1950's Florence May Festival recording that once appeared in
the United States on the Mercury label. The noteworthy cast
is headed by Ettore Bastianini in the title role, with Renata
Scotto as Gilda, Alfredo Kraus as the Duke, and Mr. and Mrs.
Ivo Vinco (she is Fiorenza Cossotto, of course!) as Sparafucile and Maddalena, with Gianandrea Gavazzeni conducting.

This is so fine a performance that it seems amazing that one
of the major labels never snapped it up. Now, doubly welcome
at its budget price, here is a RIGOLETTO that satisfies on
virtually every count.

Bastianini's Rigoletto is dark-voiced and sinewy, hardly the
likeable sentimentalist that many singers portray. Here is a
snappish jester who could all too easily incite the Duke of
Mantua's courtiers against himself. "Cortigiani, vil razza
dannata" is explosively, venomously delivered. "Si vendetta"
is not only properly ferocious, but, in the late baritone's
characterization, a perfectly logical expression of the hatred
that there is in Rigoletto all along.

Alfredo Kraus' Duke has become one of the tenor's most
popular roles at the Metropolitan Opera and at other
houses. His easy, stylish singing and unforced, pure high
notes make up for the absence of a warm or sensuous tone
from his pleasant if not terribly colorful voice. Kraus
includes the Duke's Act Three *cabaletta* (also found on RCA)
and makes it into quite a highlight of the performance—more,
of course, a compliment to the tenor than to Verdi, since this is
a rather banal piece of music.

Renata Scotto's Gilda is at times steely and thin on the high
notes, but her music is always sung with accuracy, and there
is a depth of characterization not often associated with Gilda in

the opera house or on other recordings.

Ivo Vinco's Sparafucile is satisfactory, while his (then) very youthful wife's Maddalena is quite the best on records, light of voice yet warm and enticing. All the supporting artists are satisfactory, and Gavazzeni conducts with an awareness of the dramatic tensions inherent in the score.

WAGNER:
DER RING DES NIBELUNGEN

1. DAS RHEINGOLD
Flagstad, Madeira, Watson, London, Svanholm, Neidlinger,
Waechter, Wolfhart, Solti cond.
Vienna Philharmonic Orchestra
3 discs
London OSA 13*
UK: Decca SET 382-4

Veasey, Dominguez, Mangelsdorff, Fischer-Dieskau, Stolze,
Kéléman, Kerns, Wolfhart, von Karajan cond.
Berlin Philharmonic Orchestra
3 discs
Deutsche Grammophon 2709023*
UK: Same

Hesse, Uhl, Polke, Kuhne, Swarowsky cond.
Sud Deutsche Philharmonie
3 discs
Westminster WGSO 8175-3

DIE WALKÜRE
Nilsson, Crespin, King, Hotter, Frick, Ludwig, Solti cond.
Vienna Philharmonic Orchestra
5 discs
London OSA 1509*
UK: Decca SET 312-6

Crespin, Janowitz, Vickers, Stewart, Talvela, Veasey, von Karajan
cond.
Berlin Philharmonic Orchestra
5 discs
Deutsche Grammophon 2713002*
UK: Same

Mödl, Rysanek, Suthaus, Frantz, Frick, Klose, Furtwangler cond.
Vienna Philharmonic Orchestra
5 discs
Seraphim IE-6012 (Mono)

Kniplova, Hesse, McKee, Polke, von Rohr, Swarowsky cond.
Sud Deutsche Philharmonie
5 discs
Westminster WGSO 8176-5

SIEGFRIED
Nilsson, Hoffgen, Sutherland, Hotter, Stolze, Neidlinger, Solti cond.
Vienna Philharmonic Orchestra
5 discs
London OSA 1508*
UK: Decca SET 204-8

Dernesch, Dominguez, Gayer, Thomas, Stewart, Stolze, Kéléman,
von Karajan cond.
Berlin Philharmonic Orchestra
5 discs
Deutsche Grammophon 2713003*
UK: Same

Kniplova, Kuhne, Swarowsky cond.
Sud Deutsche Philharmonie
5 discs
Westminster WGSO 8177-5

GÖTTERDÄMMERUNG
Nilsson, Ludwig, Watson, Valkki, Windgassen, Fischer-Dieskau,
Frick, Neidlinger, Solti cond.
Vienna Philharmonic and State Opera Chorus
6 discs
London OSA 1604*
UK: Decca SET 292-7

Dernesch, Ludwig, Janowitz, Brilioth, Ridderbusch, Stewart,
Kéléman, von Karajan cond.
Berlin Philharmonic and State Opera Chorus
6 discs
Deutsche Grammophon 2716001
UK: Same

Kniplova, Hesse, McKee, Knoll, von Rohr, Swarowsky cond.
Sud Deutsche Philharmonie and Vienna State Opera Choir
6 discs
Westminster WGSO 8178-6

THE SOLTI RING AVAILABLE AS ONE SET
19 discs
London RING S

DER RING DES NIBELUNGEN
Mödl, Frantz, Furtwängler cond.
RAI Orchestra
19 discs
Seraphim IS 6100

There are four complete RINGs available at this time, on
London-Decca, Deutsche Grammophon, Seraphim, and Westminster. I shall principally deal with the London-Decca and
Deutsche Grammophon RINGs, both of which are worthy,
indeed, heroic performances. The other two RINGS were

released too late for inclusion here. Each offers some fine singing, and, in the case of Solti's cycle, a magnificent directorial
conception executed with brilliance by a great orchestra.

The Solti RING took nearly seven years to record,
beginning with DAS RHEINGOLD in the 1950's and ending
with a GÖTTERDÄMMERUNG released in 1965. This RING
has the distinction of preserving all three of the Brunnhilde's
of Birgit Nilsson.

Solti's RING commences with a handsomely sung DAS
RHEINGOLD which finds George London in peak form as
Wotan. If London lacks some of Hans Hotter's vocal stature,
he still must be credited with a dignified, strong Wotan—a
formidable spouse for Flagstad's Fricka, and a fearsome enemy
to Alberich and the two giants.

Kirsten Flagstad, the legendary Sieglinde and Brünnhilde
of an earlier generation became a symbolic link with the past
through her participation in the recording as Fricka. She had
long since seen her finest days as a singer when this
RHEINGOLD was made, but she learned Fricka's music
especially for the recording sessions, emerging as a huge-
voiced, if rather hard of tone goddess. Never a tremendously
vivid actress, Flagstad is content here to sound matronly and
stern. More successful in making the transition from
heldentenor to character singer on this set is Set Svanholm,
who offers a smoothly sung and marvellously cunning Loge.
Alberich is sung with lusty craveness, if rough tone, by
Gustav Neidlinger. In Neidlinger's hands, it is not difficult to
believe that this character is loathsome enough to renounce
love for gold or vicious enough to place the curse upon the ring.
Paul Kuen is an able Mime, sounding distressfully whiny
without totally sacrificing musicality. Walter Kreppel and
Kurt Boehme make up a solid pair of giants, with Boehme's
Fafner being particularly well sung. How well the bass' rough,
unbeautiful, yet big voice fits this character! Eberhard
Waechter is somewhat light of voice for Donner, but he sings
with sure musicianship and a gracefulness not always found
in Wagnerian singers. Waldemar Kmentt is a more than satis-

tory Froh, while Claire Watson is suitably passive and fresh voiced as Freia. Jean Madeira, although afflicted with a marked vibrato, makes much of Erda's single appearance. The Rhine-maidens, sung by Oda Balsburg, Hetty Plumacher, and Ira Malaniuk, are an ingratiating trio. The Vienna Philharmonic is wonderfully helpful in bringing Wagner's "godscape" to life under the unfailingly sensitive, powerful leadership of Solti. The conductor never sacrifices clarity, all the while propelling the music drama forward with ever increasing dynamism, giving the listener first a majestic impression of the eternal Rhine, followed by a mammoth yet frail Valhalla, a murky nether world, and, ultimately, a god-like finale.

Solti's WALKÜRE set is one of the most moving perform-ances ever preserved through the medium of the phonograph. To begin with, there is the Brünnhilde of Birgit Nilsson. In nearly invincible form, Nilsson hurdles the Ho-jo-to-ho's with ease, sounding, as Brünnhilde should, youthful, strong, and fearless. Slightly and uncharacteristically uncomfortable in the lower register in the Act Two encounter with Siegmund, Nilsson nevertheless imparts her tragic message with dramatic urgency, soon regaining her standard vocal stride. Act Three finds Nilsson once more in complete control, spinning out high notes as if they were the simplest task that a soprano could be required to perform and acting with a fervor that even she has rarely achieved elsewhere.

The third hero of the recording, after Nilsson and Solti, is Hans Hotter who, although in the twilight of his career and occasionally unsteady when singing at full volume, still manages an heroic timbre and a mighty, noble charac-terization capped by a portrayal of the god's fatherly grief at the transgression and necessary punishment of Brünnhilde that must go down as one of the very finest single performances in the history of recorded opera.

Not far behind these achievements are those of Regine Crespin as Sieglinde and James King as Siegmund. Crespin, the Brünnhilde on Karajan's recording, is far better suited to Sieglinde, a role which does not tax Crespin's voice to its limits but, on the contrary, allows her to demonstrate her superb art in a gentle, lyrically conceived performance as touchingly acted as it is sweetly sung. King is a young, forthright Siegmund, whose Winterstürme is a joyous expression of love. Content with a less subtle, searching characterization than Vickers in Karajan's set, King is still a handsome, able Siegmund. Gottlob Frick is a more than capable Hunding, while Christa Ludwig's Fricka is impassioned and beautifully sung. Solti's work here is of the same standard of excellence that he exhibited in RHEINGOLD, culminating in an exquisite reading of "Wotan's Farewell" and the "Magic Fire Music."

It is interesting to note that on this recording, two of Brünnhilde's sisters are Helga Dernesch and Berit Lindholm, two current Brünnhildes of note.

SIEGFRIED introduces Wolfgang Windgassen in the title role. Not fully up to the fierce demands of the role, and indeed not the producer's first choice for the role, Windgassen does bring experience and a sense of purpose. If the voice never sounds terribly fresh, he at least husbands his dwindling resources with the skill of a true professional, finally mustering a fair measure of passion for the duet with Nilsson, who enters the proceedings as fresh as if indeed having slumbered for a generation or so on Brünnhilde's bed of rocks. Nilsson's ecstatic hailing of the young hero who has awakened her must count among her finest moments of song. Mime is sung by Gerhard Stolze with more musicality than he musters when he repeats the role for Karajan. The tenor performs with the gift for characterization that is perhaps his strongest suit in full evidence. Neidlinger continues his Alberich here with results similar to those of RHEINGOLD, while Erda is now sung by Maria Hoffgen. Joan Sutherland makes a vivid "guest" appearance as the Forest Bird.

GÖTTERDÄMMERUNG, the longest, most difficult, and complex of the four RING operas is so excellently performed by Solti, his musicians, and cast of singers, that it is perhaps the most impressive achievement in this RING cycle. To begin with, Nilsson's well nigh unbeatable Brünnhilde is, although the most spectacular vocal achievement in the set, but one of a number of outstanding performances. Taking up in the Prologue where they left off at the end of SIEGFRIED, Nilsson and Windgassen are marvellously ecstatic as the lovers. Windgassen is generally in better voice in GÖTTERDÄMMERUNG than SIEGFRIED, and his "death scene" is most heartfelt.

London-Decca's engineers resort to electronic trickery slowing the speed of the master tape in Siegfried's abduction of Brünnhilde in order to demonstrate the impenetrability of the Tarnhelm's disguise of the hero as Gunther, by making Siegfried sound as much like Gunther as possible. This practice may irk those who prefer that a performance stand or fall by an artist's personal skills, but in reality little if any harm is done to the music by this little prank.

Gunther himself is richly sung by Dietrich Fischer-Dieskau, while Gottlob Frick offers a properly vicious Hagen. Alberich is once more sung by Neidlinger, who places more emphasis on Alberich's wicked character than on singing the music smoothly. Claire Watson's limpid soprano is excellently deployed as Gutrune, while Christa Ludwig's strong, fervid Waltraute is a fine match for Nilsson in their scene together. The gentlemen of the Vienna State Opera Chorus make for a sonorous collection of vassals. The Norns include such distinguished artists as Anita Valkki, Grace Hoffman, and Helen Watts while the Rhinemaidens boast such singers as Lucia Popp, Gwynneth Jones, and Maureen Guy.

Solti's rendering of the score, most notably including, of course, "Siegfried's Rhine Journey," "Siegfried's Funeral March," and the final moments of the opera, is an incalculable wonder of virtuosity.

Thus Solti's RING, although flawed by some less than heroic performances by a few individuals, stands as a classic series of recordings, insured a place on any opera buff's list of favorite recordings.

The appearance of Herbert von Karajan's DGG RING cycle in the late 1960's created a rivalry between two expensive sets

of recordings, one that can only be resolved by personal preference. Karajan preserves on records his highly personalized
conception of the RING which he unveiled at the Salzburg
Easter Festival. (Karajan was supposed to both stage and
conduct this RING cycle in New York, but his participation in
that project was halted after the first two productions by a
strike at the Metropolitan.)

Basically, where Solti's RING is noble and mighty, Karajan's
is cooled and scaled down. His cast includes some very unheroic, if not downright small-voiced artists, and, although
much of the music is beautifully played under von Karajan's
direction, he never, to my mind, approaches the sonic wonders
tapped in every measure by Solti.

Von Karajan's RHEINGOLD features Fischer-Dieskau as
Wotan, in an intelligent, thoughtful performance that emphasizes Wotan's "human" frailties by playing down his power.
Fischer-Dieskau's Wotan is not notable for sonority or force.
The voice, when not pushed for volume, is most attractive,
and Fischer-Dieskau brings off in the recording studio that
which he probably could not undertake in a live performance
in a large opera house.

At the risk of being heretical, I find Josephine Veasey's
Fricka more successful than Flagstad's in terms of projection
of character. Vocally, the young British mezzo has an easier
time with the music than Flagstad, as well. Zoltan Kéléman's
Alberich is as malign as Neidlinger's, but richer of voice, too.
Erwin Wolfhart is not as interesting as Kuen in the role of
Mime, while Gerhard Stolze's nasal, dry voice is less pleasant
than Svanholm's as Loge. Stolze does, though, as is usual for
him, create a vivid, if unattractive character here. Robert
Kerns is a particularly good Froh, and Donald Grobe is a similarly fine Donner. Sylvia Mangelsdorff is a rather screechy,
white-voiced Freia, but Oralia Dominguez is excellent in Erda's
somber measures. Martti Talvela and Karl Ridderbusch, the
Fasolt and Fafner, are nicely cast, and the Rhinemaidens are
sweetly sung by Helen Donath, Edda Moser, and Anna Reynolds. In some ways, DAS RHEINGOLD is the finest of

Karajan's RING components, being excellently cast in most roles and finding the Berlin Philharmonic in finer form than in the other recordings where it sounds thin and threadbare in comparison to the Vienna Philharmonic.

Karajan's WALKÜRE finds Regine Crespin as an uncommonly feminine, sympathetic Brünnhilde who unfortunately must resort to scooping and lunging for powerful high notes in the "Ho-jo-to-ho". Crespin's characterization is more subtle and compassionate than Nilsson's, but she is unable to thrill the listener in Nilsson's manner—or indeed in her own accustomed way, as her voice takes on an unpleasant edge when forced. Thomas Stewart's Wotan, too, sounds uncomfortably dry and tight. It lacks Hotter's richness of sound. Stewart is dramatically cold and unbending here, as well, making his performance almost a liability.

Siegmund and Sieglinde emerge as the vocal winners of the performance. Jon Vickers, encouraged by the maestro to rein his considerable voice in to a near whisper in Act One, impresses with his ability to sing softly. The Winterstürme, for example, is taken mezza voce. Gundula Janowitz's lovely voice, used with taste and skill, makes her a pleasure to hear as Sieglinde. Karajan's controversial, underplayed approach to the music is at its most flagrant state here, offsetting the "humanization" of the score by robbing the meeting and recognition of the Wälsungs of much of its urgency.

Martti Talvela is a strong Hunding, while Josephine Veasey, continuing her portrayal of Fricka in Act Two, is once again well cast, standing up against Ludwig's competition on the rival recording. The eight Walküres are adequately performed in this recording, although these roles are even better sung on Solti's set.

SIEGFRIED introduces Jess Thomas in the title role. Beginning somewhat uncertainly, the American tenor loses the tenseness of voice and constriction of sound that bother him in Act One in time to sing impressively in Act Two and brilliantly in the final duet with Brünnhilde, portrayed here with musical competence but whitish, metallic, and none too pleasing tone by Helga Dernesch. While sounding more youthful than Nilsson in the part, Dernesch projects little of Nilsson's forceful character.

Thomas Stewart's Wanderer is a distinct vocal improvement over his WALKÜRE Wotan. The baritone sounds more sure of himself dramatically and far more sonorous, too. Gerhard Stolze's sniveling, grotesque Mime is quite interesting from a dramatic point of view, although his singing does make one wonder whatever led him to embark upon an operatic career. Kéléman and Ridderbusch repeat their roles of Alberich and Fafner with good results. Oralia Dominguez is once again a fine Erda. The Forest Bird is sung charmingly by Catherine Gayer. Karajan's slow pacing and the rather grainy sound of the Berlin Philharmonic do not work to the score's best advantage.

GÖTTERDÄMMERUNG boasts a new Siegfried, Helge Brilioth, who may be the heldentenor we have been waiting for. Singing with refinement and a fresh, truly beautiful voice that shows almost no signs of strain anywhere in the opera, Brilioth is a manly Siegfried and one whose power is more than merely legendary. Dernesch appears again as Brünnhilde, singing with a steady but often dull, steely tone and displaying little sense of character. Her Brünnhilde is a somewhat sulky, petulant creature, which is hardly what Brünnhilde is all about.

Christa Ludwig duplicates her London-Decca assignment as Waltraute, but her scene is less exciting here than with Nilsson under Solti's baton. Gundula Janowitz is a disappointing, dull Gutrune, but Thomas Stewart offers a sturdy Gunther matched by the malevolent, potent Hagen of Karl Ridderbusch.

The other singers include Kéléman as Alberich, Lily Chookasian, Christa Ludwig, and Catarina Ligendza as the Norns, and Edda Moser, Anna Reynolds, and Liselotte Rebmann as the very attractive Rhinemaidens.

Dernesch sings the "Immolation Scene" commendably while Karajan allows the orchestra to play with sufficient drive to suggest the end of the gods most admirably, concluding his

RING cycle with more power and musical eloquence than is found in many of the earlier sections. Thus, Karajan's RING is notable for some fine individual performances, while Solti's must triumph in terms of total conception and execution.

DONIZETTI:
ROBERTO DEVEREUX

Sills, Wolff, Ilosfalvy, Glossop, Mackerras cond.
Royal Philharmonic and Ambrosian Opera Chorus
3 discs
Audio Treasury ATS20003-3*
HMV SLS787

Donizetti's ROBERTO DEVEREUX is one of the several *bel canto* works that soprano Beverly Sills has helped reintroduce to opera audiences. Miss Sills first performed the role onstage at the New York City Opera in October, 1970 but recorded the work for ABC-Westminster a year earlier. However ungrateful this may sound, I wish that the soprano had waited to record the opera until after she had gained the authority that only can come after a number of actual, staged performances.

Still, Miss Sills' Queen Elizabeth is a most impressive achievement, as the soprano molds her light voice exquisitely to Donizetti's line, singing with purity and control throughout her full vocal range. Dramatically, Sills' recorded Queen Elizabeth pales only in comparison with her achievements in the role at the New York City Opera (this is particularly true in the second act confrontation with the erring Roberto), but she does capture much of the contradictory, even self-destructive character of the old monarch. Her "Vivi ingrato" (Act Three, scene three) and its haunting cabaletta, "Quel sange versato" are searing to the listener.

Even in ROBERTO DEVEREUX (indeed, particularly in this opera), the prima donna does not carry the entire responsibility for a successful performance. ABC has, in general, adequately cast the supporting roles, but does not provide any singer of the same special mettle of Miss Sills.

With such tenors as Placido Domingo (who sang the title role with Miss Sills in 1970 in New York), Luciano Pavarotti, and Carlo Bergonzi available, one wonders how ABC happened to choose a relatively obscure artist of no particular distinction, Robert Ilosfalvy for the strenuous part of Roberto Devereux. Ilosfalvy's rough tone and strained production hardly make him a favored contender for honors in the bel canto repertoire and it is a shame that Miss Sills could not have been given a more worthy partner in this recording.

Peter Glossop and Beverley Wolff are heard as the Duke and Duchess of Nottingham. Neither are blessed with first-class voices—his is big but rather dull while her's is less smooth than one might ideally wish, but both are skilled professionals who give reasonably good accounts of their roles. (Miss Wolff, by the way, recreated Sarah along with Miss Sills in that wonderful 1970 New York DEVEREUX.)

Most notable among the comprimario singers is the late Kenneth MacDonald who is heard as Lord Cecil. Charles Mackerras conducts the Royal Philharmonic with spirit, but his reading is a bit stiff, as if he were as yet unfamiliar with the score. He approaches the music respectfully, indeed perhaps too respectfully, for one misses a certain drive in his tempi. The Ambrosian Opera Chorus, as led by John McCarthy, is most commendable. A final weakness of the set is its cold, dry sound, unfortunately a frequent drawback of ABC recordings.

GOUNOD:
ROMEO ET JULIETTE

Freni, Corelli, Lombard cond.
Orchestra and Chorus of the Paris Opera
3 discs
Angel S3734*

GOUNOD's version of Shakespeare's tragedy has suffered a loss in popularity in recent years. Hardly ever performed in England, the opera was a staple of the Metropolitan Opera's repertoire for many years but went unperformed there for 19 years between 1948 and 1967 when a new production at the new Lincoln Center house restored the work to public favor.

Angel-HMV's 1968 recording transplanted the stars of the Met's revival, Franco Corelli and Mirella Freni, along with the opera's principal New York conductor, Alain Lombard, to Paris where a supporting cast was recruited from the members of the Paris Opera whose orchestra and chorus also took part in the recording.

A handsome and effective couple onstage, Freni and Corelli survive the change of medium from theatre to disc with most of their well-earned glory intact. Indeed, it would be difficult to find a more apt choice than Miss Freni for the role of Juliette from the entire list of lyric sopranos available today. Her warm, agile lyric soprano spins out Juliette's bubbly waltz song with ease, yet Freni packs the power necessary for projecting Juliette's emotional conflict and her love for Romeo. Carpers will find Freni's command of French less than perfect, but from the musical point of view, the soprano's work in this recording is most praiseworthy.

Franco Corelli possesses a "golden" voice capable of great

emotional impact. He overwhelms the listener with the basic beauty of his voice, which indeed has seldom been better captured on records, and his many sustained high notes are impressive. Corelli creates an impetuous and sympathetic Romeo. The tenor is, however, not a French stylist and is prone to some rhythmic excesses and an ostentatious display of every aspect of his vocal technique. With Corelli, a diminuendo or pianissimo always seems as much of a circus stunt as one of his fabled high C's. Still, I am pleased to concede that this is one of the Italian star's happiest recordings, and each of the long scenes for Romeo and Juliet are episodes for the record buff to treasure.

No one in the generally solid supporting cast reaches the same level of achievement of Freni and Corelli, but Xavier Duprez is a sturdy Frère Laurent, and Henri Gui is an able Mercutio.

The Paris Opera Orchestra and Chorus perform with high competence, with the orchestra sounding particularly good. Lombard's tempi are surprisingly swift, so swift, in fact, that one occasionally feels that the love scenes are rushed. Still, this approach creates an atmosphere of tension and unrest that is quite appropriate to the drama.

STRAUSS:
DER ROSENKAVALIER

Schwarzkopf, Ludwig, Stich-Randall, Edelmann, Gedda, von Karajan cond.
Philharmonia Orchestra and Chorus
4 discs
Angel S-3563*
UK: HMV SLS810

Crespin, Minton, Donath, Jungwirth, Pavarotti, Solti cond.
Vienna Philharmonic and State Opera Chorus
4 discs
London OSA 1435*
UK: Decca SET 418-21

Ludwig, Jones, Popp, Berry, Domingo, Bernstein cond.
Vienna Philharmonic and State Opera Chorus
4 discs
Columbia M4X-30652
UK: Columbia 77416

Schech, Seefried, Streich, Fischer-Dieskau, Böhm cond.
Dresden State Opera Orchestra and Chorus
4 discs
Deutsche Grammophon 2711001
UK: Same as above

Reining, Gueden, Jurinac, Weber, Kleiber cond.
Vienna Philharmonic and State Opera Chorus
4 discs
Richmond RS64001 (Mono)
UK: Decca 4BB115-8

ABRIDGED:
Lehmann, Schumann, Olczewska, Mayr, Heger cond.
Vienna Philharmonic
2 discs
Seraphim IC 6041 (Mono) (abridged)

Everyone has a "dream" ROSENKAVALIER cast, and it would
be useless to try to convince a Schwarzkopf fan that Crespin
or anyone else is as good or better in the role of the
Marschallin. I personally have a fondness that at times
approaches madness for the pre-World War Two, abridged
version of the opera with Lotte Lehman, Richard Mayr,
Elisabeth Schumann, and Maria Olczewska. Fortunately, one
need not be an atavist in order to find a decent ROSEN-
KAVALIER set, as there are at least three modern recordings
of more than passing interest.

London-Decca's 1970 release is my personal choice for the
most completely satisfactory performance of the opera. In
addition to the participation of Regine Crespin, one of the
finest Marschallins of recent years, the album is notable for
the high proportion of newcomers to the operatic scene in
leading roles: Helen Donath as Sophie, Yvonne Minton as
Octavian, and Manfred Jungwirth as Ochs, as well as a number
of old-timers who turn up in supporting ones: Emmy Loose
as Marianne, Anton Dermota as the Police Commissar, and, in
the miniscule role of the Notary, Alfred Jerger, one of Strauss'
favorite baritones, and one who excelled in Strauss' music
between the Wars.

In spite of the many excellences of the singers, the main force
behind this recording is Maestro Georg Solti. Aided of course

by the wonderful Vienna Philharmonic, Solti directs a shimmering, superbly controlled performance of this most enchanting opera. Allowing his singers every opportunity to savor the delicate emotional content of the score, Solti's hand is firm enough to prevent anyone from wallowing in sentimentality. If the glistening quality of Ochs' waltz as played in the final moments of Act Two in this recording doesn't bring a catch to the listener's throat, he ought to have both his stereo and hearing examined!

Returning to the singers, one finds Crespin's Marschallin mature, yet warmly vocalized and authoritative. Less concerned than Schwarzkopf with shading every syllable with enigmatic nuances, the French soprano lavishes her melting tone and powerful sense of character on the role. A delightfully humorous approach to the early moments of Act One is contrasted most effectively with the melancholy of the Princess' monologue, and the barely controlled heartbreak of the final scene.

Yvonne Minton, the Australian mezzo-soprano who established herself at Covent Garden and whose international career seems to be building steadily, is a triumphant Octavian. Her pliant and warm voice is a constant delight, sounding "manly" when called upon to do so, as well as providing an altogether delightful burlesque of girlishness when playing "Mariandel." Perhaps the most challenging facet of Octavian is for the singer to become convincing as a male lover, but whether pleading with the Marschallin or sharing tendernesses with Sophie, Minton is at least as successful as any other woman who sings the role could hope to be.

Helen Donath, a young soprano from Texas, reveals the appropriate freshness of voice desired for Sophie and prettily suggests that character's innocence and bland loveliness, contributing her full share to, among many other moments, the final trio and duet.

As Ochs, Manfred Jungwirth chooses a conventionally bumptuous characterization, and thus alone of the principal artists falls into the "routine category." The performance is undeniably funny, but Jungwirth's coarse vocalism becomes grating after a while, and his one dimensional portrait does not sit well on repeated hearings. Most importantly, the fact that Ochs is, after all, a baron seems to elude this bass-baritone.

The supporting roles are very well handled, with particularly fine work contributed by Murray Dickie and Anne Howells as Valzacchi and Annina, Otto Wiener, a marvellously theatrical Faninal, and Luciano Pavarotti who brings his customary yet nearly miraculous vocal grace to the Singer's first act solo, surely one of Strauss' most inspired moments.

In the Fall of 1971, Columbia (CBS in Europe) brought forth another Vienna Philharmonic-State Opera ROSENKAVALIER, this one directed and altogether dominated by Leonard Bernstein. Although this performance has some extraordinary qualities, it is on the whole not only inferior to the Solti and Karajan versions, but distinctly disappointing in its own right.

In the libretto brochure, the recording's producer, John Culshaw, describes the nearly chaotic conditions under which the set was made in the spring of 1971, with two principals, Walter Berry and Gwynneth Jones fighting illness, and with wholesale reshuffling of recording schedules resulting from their indisposition. While Culshaw insists that he is not apologizing for the recording, when faced with the results, it is difficult not to feel that these "acts of God" contributed to the failure of the performance to take off. With the myriads of splicing that evidently went on, it is no wonder that there is little continuity in terms of tempi, concentration, and even vocal estate.

Bernstein's tempi are so slow that although, unlike Solti, he observes most of the traditional cuts, the performance is approximately a quarter hour longer than Solti's. Under this languid conducting, the opening scene between the Marschallin and Octavian suggests two disembodied voices in space instead of two lovers sharing a bed. The final scene is also dangerously badly paced. Bernstein does, not surprisingly, elicit some beautiful playing from the Vienna Philharmonic, whose musicians are said to revere the American conductor, and his handling of many of Baron Ochs' scenes is more appropriately animated. Still in all, though, Bernstein's choices of tempi suggest nothing more than self-indulgence and a lack of true understanding of what the opera really is about.

Bernstein's choice of singers is less than perfect, too. Christa Ludwig has many qualities associated with great Marschallins—a beautiful voice, sensitivity, and fine histrionic skill. All of these attributes stand her in good stead, but, of course, Ludwig is a mezzo-soprano, and the basic "mezzo" timbre of her voice is not ideal for this character who is further benefited by the more ethereal, soprano sound which one hears in the performances of Crespin and Schwarzkopf. It cannot be denied, however, that Ludwig's performance is, on its own terms, distinguished and filled with many ravishing phrases. Interestingly, Ludwig's Marschallin emerges, largely due to her heavier voice, as being the earthiest one on discs, suggesting best the sensuality of her feelings for Octavian. Perhaps with a different conductor and a superior supporting cast, Ludwig would be heard to even better advantage in the role.

Gwynneth Jones' Octavian is by far the biggest disappointment in the set. Granted that she was suffering from a throat infection when the opera was recorded, it is nonetheless true that she ought to have withdrawn from the sessions completely rather than allow so unsatisfactory a reading of the part to be released. At times, as in the first act, Jones' voice is unsteady and unpleasant to hear. Elsewhere, as in the "Presentation of the Rose," the voice is fresher, but so feminine sounding and light in comparison to what one expects from an Octavian, that she seems musical but miscast. Jones lacks the sense of comedy needed to bring the Mariandel scenes off with the requisite humor. A final and deadly flaw (and this is not really her fault) is that the juxtaposition of soprano and mezzo voices is totally thrown out of kilter due to the casting of Ludwig as the Marschallin and Jones as Octavian, resulting in additional confusion for the listener.

A further disappointment is found in the work of the usually attractive Lucia Popp, in whose hands the role of Sophie loses sympathy, as Miss Popp is harsh-voiced, breathy, and generally far too abrasive, particularly in Act Two.

In the midst of all these problems, Walter Berry's Ochs stands out as the proverbial good deed in a very naughty world. Handsomely, cleanly sung with mellow tone and an ingratiating zest, Berry's Baron is the most cogent reason for owning the set, as he offers a charmingly roguish and never disgusting or gross characterization of the Marschallin's country cousin.

The supporting cast includes Emmy Loose and Murray Dickie, assuming the roles of Marianne and Valzacchi, while Margarita Lilowa is a capable Annina. Placido Domingo is the singer and offers a handsome if somewhat verismatic "Di rigori armati."

While I could not recommend this ROSENKAVALIER if it were to be the only one in the listener's collection, but those who already own the Solti or Karajan sets might be interested in Ludwig's Marschallin and Berry's definitive Ochs.

Turning to HMV-Angel's famous ROSENKAVALIER made in the late 1950's, one finds an altogether satisfying, often brilliant performance. Elisabeth Schwarzkopf will probably be best remembered for her Marschallin, and rightly so, for seldom has a singer brought more intelligence, grace, or feeling to a role. Some will criticize Miss Schwarzkopf's individual, idiosyncratic technique for excessive breathiness, but I have always found her to be a most rewarding and charming artist. The dazzling warmth of Schwarzkopf's recorded Marschallin stands up well to Crespin's competition, and to many, this performance will be untouchable by other singers. Certainly no one can attach more meaning to the Princess' final "Ja Ja" than Schwarzkopf.

The Octavian on this recording is sung by Christa Ludwig

in fine, youthful voice. She is quite the best exponent of the role on records, surpassing even Minton in opulence of sound and ardentness of characterization. Theresa Stich-Randall is an appealingly light-voiced Sophie, and Otto Edelmann is a close match for Berry as Ochs, with Edelmann's performance being a bit more clownish and less suavely vocalized than Berry's. Found in the supporting cast is Ljuba Welitsch as Marianne, while Herbert von Karajan conducts an elegant and often moving performance in which the Philharmonia Orchestra plays with grace and clarity.

In addition to these complete performances, the Seraphim ROSENKAVALIER set, a two disc abridgement dating from the 1930's must be mentioned. Roughly fifty per cent complete, the many huge cuts are terribly frustrating since the performances by Lehman (Marschallin), Schumann (Sophie), Mayr (Ochs), and Olczewska (Octavian) are beautiful. The sound quality is not very high and does scant justice to the Vienna Philharmonic as conducted by Robert Heger, but this budget-priced album is something to treasure.

RICHARD STRAUSS:
SALOME

Nilsson, Hoffman, Waechter, Stolze, Veasey, Kmentt, Solti cond.
Vienna Philharmonic
2 discs
London OSA-1218*
UK: Decca SET 228-9

Caballé, Resnik, Lewis, Milnes, King, Leinsdorf cond.
London Symphony Orchestra
2 discs
RCA LSC-7053
UK: RCA SER5582-3

Jones, Dunn, Cassilly, Fischer-Dieskau, Böhm cond.
Hamburg State Opera Orchestra
2 discs
Deutsche Grammophon 2707052
UK: Same

Goeltz, Patzak, Dermota, Krauss cond.
Vienna Philharmonic
2 discs
Richmond RS62007 (Mono)

Although there are four complete SALOME recordings on the
market, the old Richmond monaural version and the recent
DGG production pale in comparison to either the London-
Decca or RCA sets. The Richmond recording, featuring
Chrital Goltz with the late Clemens Krauss conducting the

Vienna Philharmonic, is a solid performance but one that simply cannot compete with the two sets cited above. The DGG SALOME preserves a vocally deficient Hamburg Opera performance, and even the conducting of Karl Böhm cannot offset the weakness of Gwynneth Jones in the title role.

Both the London and the RCA albums are solidly cast, with the London recording coming closest to the fulfillment of a Strauss-lover's dream. With Georg Solti presiding over the Vienna Philharmonic, the listener is assured of a fiery reading of the score and one that conjures up the oriental languor and depravity that characterize the opera. Without ever sliding into vulgarity, Solti and his musicians create what might be called a darkly lilting, slightly tipsy atmosphere that increases the rhythmic tension with which the Hungarian maestro infuses the opera.

The Salome here is Birgit Nilsson, whose very name should suffice to assure the listener that this Princess will have the vocal power to be heard over Strauss' crescendi. What is even more enthralling about Nilsson's singing is her complete mastery of the pianissimo. Her delicate handling of the scene with Jokanaan, as well as the final monologue's softest phrases, is as stunning as Nilsson's brilliant outpouring of sound in the "big" moments. If, in all truthfulness, the soprano does not sound adolescent, she compensates for this with her passionate acting and the burning ardor of her singing.

Jokanaan (John the Baptist) is sung by Eberhard Waechter. The baritone is hardly equipped by nature to provide a huge enough sound to either match the soprano's or to sound comfortable when heard singing in the distance from his cistern, but these considerations aside, Waechter delivers his lines with conviction and communicates the Baptist's suffering and his implacable righteousness.

Gerhard Stolze's noted impersonation of Herod is better sung on this recording, made in 1962, than in his recent stage appearances. His voice is light but musical, and his incisive portrayal of Herod as a real pervert is almost as vivid in this medium as on stage. The Herodias, Grace Hoffman, has a more attractive voice than one often hears in this part (which is a sort of burial ground, it seems, for aging mezzos), but she is unable to create a forceful sense of character.

Waldemar Kmentt is a handsome and lyric Narraboth (one wonders why this tenor's career never really blossomed), and the brief role of the Page is warmly sung by Josephine Veasey. Yet, in the last analysis, even with the generally excellent contributions of the supporting cast, the aural impression that lingers indelibly in this listener's mind is that of Nilsson singing of her lust for the Baptist's mouth on a wild summer night with her passion illuminated by Maestro Solti and his magnificent orchestra.

RCA's 1969 SALOME is less satisfying than London-Decca's, but this is less the fault of the singers than the conductor, Erich Leinsdorf. Leinsdorf's direction of the London Symphony Orchestra is neither slack nor dull, but he doesn't push for the lushness of sound heard on Solti's recording, nor does he create the torrid musical picture of Herod's court that Solti brings to life on discs. Leinsdorf's conducting is rigidly correct but as cool as an evening breeze in Vienna. The title role is sung by Montserrat Caballé. Surprisingly, and very gratifyingly, the lady sounds as fully at home in this opera as she does in the Italian works for which she is best known. Her pure, limpid voice is better suited for the portrayal of youth than Nilsson's, and there are many moments, particularly in the final scene, where this Salome is convincingly sixteen years old. High notes, too, come easily to Caballé, and little in Salome's nasty tessitura fazes her. However, the Caballé sound is regal, not sensuous. This Salome is more of a Persian kitten than a tigress, the princess' fixation with Jokanaan's body, at times, seems more spiritual than it ought. This coolness combined with the simple fact that the Spanish soprano's voice does not soar out over the orchestra in the Nilsson manner, make Caballé's Salome an interesting portrayal but one that while beautifully sung in all but a very few measures (her baiting of Herod, teasing for John's head suffers from hardness of tone and a matronly petulance) cannot be called definitive or even completely "right" for the role.

Sherrill Milnes has yet to sing the Baptist on stage, and his lack of experience in the role hinders his acting, although the mellow quality of Milnes' voice is very attractive. He is, though, simply too stolid and square. John is a zealot, not a mid-western churchman.

Richard Lewis is a competent Herod, although he lacks Stolze's skill as a character actor. Regina Resnik's vocally decrepit but fierce Herodias is an asset, as is James King's ringing Narraboth.

Leinsdorf's "Dance of the Seven Veils" is not nearly as sullenly intoxicating as the Solti version, and in general, he seems to scale down the orchestral climaxes, perhaps out of concern for the non-heroic voices in his cast.

SAINT-SAËNS:
SAMSON ET DALILA

Gorr, Vickers, Blanc, Diakov, Prêtre cond.
Paris Opera Orchestra and Duclos Choir
3 discs
Angel S-3639*

Stevens, del Monaco, Cleva cond.
The Metropolitan Opera Orchestra and Chorus (abridged)
1 disc
RCA LSC-2309

There is but one complete recording of this opera (which seems to be fading from popularity as evidenced by the paucity of opera house performances in recent years). Angel-HMV's 1964 album features several artists who have performed the opera in New York, including Rita Gorr who created Dalila in the first performance of the Metropolitan's most recent new production of that opera, Jon Vickers as Samson, and maestro Georges Prêtre.

Miss Gorr's powerful mezzo was captured at its peak by this recording. The voice has velvet, backed by steel, with a potent, exciting chest register. Her Dalila is a vivid, temperamental siren who may lack languid sensuality but atones for this by her earthy, direct appeal to Samson's (and the listener's) basic instincts. This Dalila is not perhaps characterized by the most beautiful singing imaginable, but Gorr is capable still of offering a highly respectable account of the role that achieves distinction through unswervingly intelligent and dramatic vocal coloration and fervor.

Jon Vickers is the poet of today's dramatic tenors. His ringing voice is less immense in size than, for example, those of James McCracken or Mario del Monaco, but his ability to sing with subtlety and dignity gives his work a special quality that places Vickers squarely among the great dramatic tenors of the century. His Samson is nobly sung, and his secure, vibrant high notes and ample power make Vickers a convincing "strong man." Samson's passion for Dalila is conveyed by the tenor with vocal warmth and lyricism. Not only is Vickers effective in Samson's clarion arias, but he captures Samson's mortal weakness for Dalila as well.

Completing the cast are Ernest Blanc who brings to the rather unrewarding role of the High Priest a mellow and pleasant baritone which he uses with fine style, creating, for a change, a dignified and intelligent character instead of a two-dimensional, stock operatic villain, and Anton Diakov who makes a satisfactory impression in the role of the Old Hebrew.

Georges Prêtre conducts the Paris Opera Orchestra and Chorus with verve and an authority that brings the rather phlegmatic if melodious score to life. Indeed, if all performances of SAMSON ET DALILA in the opera house were as fine as this one, the opera might regain its lost appeal to audiences.

An alternative to this recording is provided by a single disc, abridged version available on RCA, made in Boston during a Metropolitan Opera visit to that city in 1958. By sacrificing the familiar "Bacchanale," the producer manages to squeeze a great deal of important material from each act onto the disc, preserving the sensuously pretty Dalila of Risë Stevens who, in 1958, commanded less amplitude of sound than Gorr but who brought intelligence, musicianship, and a silky sweetness of voice to the role. Mario del Monaco is, in this recording, a brash Samson, again impressing with his magnetic presence and glorious top notes. His "Arretez o mes freres" has a crushing sense of suffering, and his singing in Act Two must surely have tempted Dalila to abandon her treachery and fall in love with him.

In this abbreviated version, the High Priest is heard only in the final ensemble, where his measures are competently sung by Clifford Harvuot. Also heard briefly is Ezio Flagello, beginning his Met career in such a secondary role as Abimelech. The Met's Chorus and Orchestra perform with vigor under the veteran baton of Fausto Cleva, who, like Prêtre, works hard to imbue the opera with a sense of urgency that is too often missing from staged performances.

VERDI: SIMON BOCCANEGRA

Gobbi, de los Angeles, Campora, Christoff, Santini cond.
Rome Opera Orchestra and Chorus
3 discs
Angel 3617 C/L

Silveri, Stella, Bergonzi, Molinari-Pradelli cond.
RAI Orchestra and Chorus
3 discs
Everest/Cetra S-434-3*

Angel-HMV's 1958 recording of SIMON BOCCANEGRA is the only modern vintage, stereo version of this opera which has been strangely neglected by the recording companies. Verdi's gloomy, complex work is redeemed by some enthralling and often powerful music, notably in the "Council Chamber Scene" (Act One, Scene Two) added by Verdi and librettist Boito when they revised the opera in 1881, some 20 years after its first production.

Angel's cast is headed by Tito Gobbi as the Doge of Genoa. Gobbi's Simon is sung with authority and a rare sense of character. The crucial scene where Boccanegra learns that Amelia is actually his own daughter lasts about fifteen minutes, and in that time, Gobbi, beginning as a cold and courtly Doge melts into a loving, tender father. His impassioned, anguished "Plebe, Patrizi" in the "Council Chamber Scene" is as riveting as Gobbi's death scene is racking. This exceptionally well acted characterization does much to compensate for the fact that the baritone was not in best voice here. Gobbi sounds harsher and more metallic than in most of his other work on recordings. High notes are powerful but want richness of tone. Still, Gobbi's articulate and very human portrayal of the Doge must stand as one of his major contributions to recorded opera, whatever the limitations of his singing.

Amelia, sometimes referred to as Maria, is sung by Victoria de los Angeles who offers one of her very best performances here. Her limpid soprano soars easily through Amelia's music, suffering little distress on top and ably carrying over the full ensemble in the first act finale. De los Angeles' trill at the end of the latter ensemble is nearly perfect, and the soprano manifests more of a sense of character as this generally passive heroine than one is accustomed to finding in her work.

The role of Jacopo Fiesco, Boccanegra's hated enemy, is taken by Boris Christoff, in rough voice here yet still a compellingly vivid, even frightening figure. Christoff's "Il lacerato spirito" turns this standard recital piece into the ultimate in gloomy, operatic introspection.

The tenor role in BOCCANEGRA, Gabriele Adorno, is, for a change in Verdi, subordinate to the baritone and bass (only *Falstaff* and the early *Nabucco* are similarly unkind to the tenor). Giuseppe Campora, whose once very handsome lyric voice had already begun to harden in 1958, bleats out his top notes but makes a competent although uninteresting "love interest" for the soprano. His second act aria is decently sung, but pales in comparison to the work of the other soloists. In the major secondary role of Paolo, Walter Monachesi sings acceptably but does not turn the character into a scene stealer, as Leonard Warren did in his Metropolitan debut.

The Rome Opera Chorus and Orchestra sound a bit less than their best under Gabriele Santini's thoroughly routine direction. The conductor fails to appreciate the dramatic vitality that courses through so much of Verdi's score. He makes what is essentially a music drama into a "number opera" by failing to vary tempi or to dynamically shape the music into the theatrically stunning experience that the opera can be. In sum, this BOCCANEGRA is imperfect, but, except for the even less satisfactory Everest-Cetra edition, it must, for the time being, suffice as the only reasonable way to hear the opera outside of live performances or pirated tapes.

BELLINI: LA SONNAMBULA

Sutherland, Monti, Corena, Elkins, Stahlman, Bonynge cond.
Orchestra and Chorus of the Maggio Musicale Fiorentino
3 discs
London OSA-1365*
UK: Decca SET 239-41

Callas, Cossotto, Ratti, Monti, Zaccaria, Serafin cond.
La Scala Orchestra and Chorus
European edition:
5 sides
EMI-Odeon C163-17648s/50M

Bellini's pastoral opera has enjoyed revivals in the major opera houses in the past two decades, being among the first of the neglected *bel canto* works to be resuscitated by Mmes. Callas, Sutherland, and, more recently, Scotto.

In addition to Cetra's reissue with Lina Pagliughi, there are two major SONNAMBULA albums. One of these, the EMI Callas set, has been withdrawn from Angel's USA list, but is commonly found in large city record shops as a European import in both the original monaural pressing and a 1972 electronically rechannelled stereo version.

London-Decca's recording of the opera with Joan Sutherland is still very much available on both sides of the Atlantic, which is well, as it remains one of the diva's happiest recordings. Made in Florence in 1962, the recording captures Sutherland in her fullest vocal bloom. The diva makes the passive girl whom she portrays into a sweetly appealing figure. More importantly, the soprano's singing is not marred by the excessive scooping that has become evident in her more recent performances—indeed, her vocalism is marked by clarity and sureness of pitch, and her incredible upper register has seldom been more brightly recorded. If her first act *scena* seems excessively bland, the "Ah, non credea mirarti" is sensitively done, and the "Ah, non giunge" is an example of the Sutherland art at its most brilliant.

The supporting cast includes tenor Nicola Monti as Elvino, a role which he sings on the Callas set as well. His voice is thin on top but reasonably agile, and his work is inoffensive if undistinguished.

Fernando Corena is not a *bel canto* specialist, but he copes decently with Count Rodolfo's music and makes him into an engaging and personable figure, too. Sylvia Stahlman is a stylish and pleasant Lisa, managing to remain interesting in a thankless role, and Margreta Elkins is a warm-voiced and properly matronly Teresa. Richard Bonynge, here conducting his first complete operatic recording, directs with a definite feeling for the music, although his work might hardly be termed inspired. Still, the music is paced attractively, and the Act Two ensemble is extremely well done. His orchestra and chorus, those of the Maggio Musicale Fiorentino, are most commendable, and the performance, on the whole, is charming and rewarding.

The EMI set, made at La Scala a few years before the Decca-London set was recorded, features the memorable Amina of Maria Callas. With a voice far more wiry than Sutherland's and with considerably less facility in the upper range, Callas still manages a riveting, exquisite performance, making far more of the text than Sutherland does and finding in the rather vacuous personality of Amina grace and courage. Vocally, Callas performs with a certain lack of spontaneity, but her *piano* singing is lovely, and unsteadiness is confined to a minimal number of *forte* or high notes. In Callas' hands, the "Ah non credea mirarti" becomes an unnervingly sad experience, impeccably sung and *acted* beyond endurance, thus giving the lie to those who claim that Bellini's music is devoid of emotional or dramatic power. If Callas' "Ah non giunge" is rather less abandoned than Sutherland's, it is perhaps even more moving in its electrifyingly swift release from tension into joy.

Callas' supporting cast is close in quality to Sutherland's. Monti is again adequate, if rather minimally so, as Elvino, while Nicola Zaccaria is an elegant Count Rodolfo. Eugenia Ratti is a rather twittery Lisa, but Fiorenza Cossotto's authoritative handling of Teresa is quite an asset to the recording. Tullio Serafin conducts more idiomatically than does Bonynge, although his tempi are a bit on the slow side, noticeably in the finale where he is obedient to Mme. Callas' every wish.

This SONNAMBULA will, of course, be enjoyed most completely by Callas partisans, but even to the more impartial, it is an important performance that offers documentation of the work of the most important personality in the post-war *bel canto* revival.

WAGNER: TANNHÄUSER

Nilsson, Windgassen, Fischer-Dieskau, Adam, Gerdes cond.
Deutsche Oper Orchestra and Chorus (Dresden version)
4 discs
DGG 2711008
UK: Same

Grümmer, Schech, Hopf, Fischer-Dieskau, Frick, Konwitschny cond.
Berlin Opera Orchestra and Chorus (Dresden version)
4 discs
Angel S-3620
UK: HMV SLS775

Dernesch, Ludwig, Kollo, Braun, Sotin, Solti cond.
Vienna Philharmonic Orchestra and State Opera Chorus (Paris version)
4 discs
London OSA 1438
UK: Decca SET 506-9

The three currently available TANNHÄUSER sets include a pair of "Dresden" versions (Angel and DGG) and a "Paris" version (London-Decca). Deutsche Grammophon's "Dresden" edition features Birgit Nilsson doing double duty as both Elisabeth and Venus, a feat which she duplicated at the Metropolitan in 1966. Nilsson sings superbly in both roles. She is pitch perfect, produces an enormous volume of sound, and her musicianship, as always, is consistently superior. What one misses in Nilsson's performance is a full sense of differentiation between the two women. In short, the soprano is *herself* rather than the innocent Elisabeth or the voluptuous goddess. Still, no one else who sings either role manages the power or musical electricity that Nilsson provides. Her "Dich teure halle" practically lights up one's phonograph. Nilsson's partner is Wolfgang Windgassen, once again recorded in post-prime condition. He struggles valiantly with the composer's demands, yet manages to remain musical if less than sonorous—this Tannhäuser is no match for the hefty persuasion of his Venus. Also featured prominently are Theo Adam, a Landgraf of stature and more vocal warmth than this bass often provides, and Dietrich Fischer-Dieskau, who sings Wolfram with consummate grace and nobility of phrasing. Hans Sotin, the London Landgraf, is heard here briefly as Reinmar. The (West) Berlin Opera (Deutsche Oper) Orchestra and Chorus contribute rousing work to a performance efficiently conducted by Otto Gerdes.

The lack of a suitable *heldentenor* for the title role that casts a shadow over the otherwise satisfying DGG album is even more of a debilitating factor in Angel's generally disappointing set which finds Hans Hopf in rough and unhandsome voice. Never a particularly brilliant artist, Hopf often made do with physical stamina and little else—managing to get through his music without illuminating any passages or otherwise demonstrating any interpretive merits. His dry, often unsteady singing is no advertisement for this recording. Elisabeth Grümmer's soft-timbred, gentle Elisabeth is a welcome asset. Grümmer also is able to muster the power needed for the part's heavier moments without strain.

Unfortunately, the Venus of Marianne Schech is quite dreadfully squally, shrill, and dramatically unappealing. This soprano is generally an embarrassment to the proceedings.

Gottlob Frick's Landgraf fairly crackles with authority, and Fischer-Dieskau repeats his assignment as Wolfram, delivering the "Evening Star" music with poignancy. An interesting "cameo" is the Walther sung by Fritz Wunderlich. The Berlin State Opera forces are heard again here, this time under the baton of Franz Konwitschny who creates an atmosphere of suitably romantic ardor. In spite of the several excellent performances found on this recording, the lackluster work of Hopf and Schech damage its viability in competition with the two other TANNHÄUSER sets.

London-Decca's edition, the most recent recording of the opera, and, as mentioned earlier, the only "Paris" version available, is also quite the finest. Revised in 1860, after Wagner had composed TRISTAN UND ISOLDE, the "Paris" version is most notable for the expanded Venusburg music and some post-TRISTAN harmonies in the orchestration, adding a further sense of decadence to the scenes between the hero and Venus. Georg Solti, leading the Vienna Philharmonic, builds an almost surreal cosmos of sound in the overture and keeping this alive throughout the entire work, imbuing the score with a sophistication that in large part atones for the murky and self-righteous philosophy of the text. Here, an old "warhorse" finally comes to life.

Solti's cast is headed by the young German tenor René Kollo as Tannhäuser. His is a rather lyrical voice, at times forced almost beyond endurance, as in the anguished third act monologue, but its basically pliant, fresh sound makes Kollo the most believable and successful Tannhäuser on discs. His Elisabeth, Helga Dernesch, is heard here to fine advantage, too. Her voice sounds warmer and more colorful here than on such recordings as FIDELIO, the RING, or TRISTAN. She sings with a noticeable, but not unpleasant vibrato that adds a touch of urgency to her work. Dernesch is the most affecting of the three recorded Elisabeths. Christa Ludwig generates great warmth as Venus, providing her two scenes with the excitement that comes from a great voice intelligently and judiciously deployed. No less excellent are Hans Sotin as the Landgraf and the relatively unknown Canadian baritone Victor Braun as Wolfram. Braun provides a generously sung "Evening Star," and it appears from the evidence displayed on this recording that he could become an important artist. As noted earlier, the Vienna Philharmonic's outstanding work is a major factor in the success of this set which belongs among the most cherished of Wagnerian recordings.

PUCCINI: TOSCA

Callas, Bergonzi, Gobbi, Prêtre cond.
Paris Conservatoire Orchestra
2 discs
Angel S-3655*
UK: HMV SLS917

Tebaldi, del Monaco, London, Molinari-Pradelli cond.
Orchestra and Chorus of L'Accademia di Santa Cecilia
2 discs
London OSA 1210*
UK: Ace of Diamonds GOS 612-3

Price, di Stefano, Taddei, von Karajan cond.
Vienna Philharmonic and State Opera Chorus
2 discs
London OSA 1284

Nilsson, Corelli, Fischer-Dieskau, Maazel cond.
Orchestra and Chorus of L'Accademia di Santa Cecilia
2 discs
London OSA 1267*
UK: Decca SET 341-2

Milanov, Bjoerling, Warren, Leinsdorf cond.
Rome Opera Orchestra and Chorus
2 discs
Victrola VICS-6000

Frazzoni, Tagliavini, Basile cond.
RAI Orchestra and Chorus
2 discs
Everest/Cetra S-408/2*

Tebaldi, Campora, Mascherini, Erede cond.
Orchestra and Chorus of L'Accademia di Santa Cecilia
2 discs
Richmond RS 62002* (Mono)

Callas, di Stefano, Gobbi, da Sabata cond.
Orchestra and Chorus of La Scala
2 discs
Angel 3508B
UK: HMV 33CX1094-5 (Mono)

Caniglia, Gigli, Bechi, Borgioli, de Fabritiis cond.
Rome Opera Orchestra and Chorus
2 discs
Seraphim IB-6027 (Mono)

Here is still another opera that is listed upwards of six times in current catalogues. Furthermore, TOSCA has fared well in several different performances, making a choice difficult.

Renata Tebaldi has recorded two TOSCA's for London-Decca. The first dates from 1951 and is now available as part of the low-priced Richmond series. Tebaldi's singing is predictably beautiful, although the high C's are shrill here. A softer, more romantic creature than Callas' sirenish protagonist, Tebaldi's conception of the heroine emphasizes Tosca's helplessness in Scarpia's hands. Her account of "Vissi d'arte" is peerless, and since Giuseppe Campora is an engaging and fresh-voiced Mario Cavarodossi, the love duets are stunningly sung. Only the scenes between Scarpia and the heroine are inferior, partly because Tebaldi's Tosca in 1951 was not the passionate girl she became in future performances and partly because Enzo Mascherini is not only too light a baritone to carry off Scarpia's music but also, on the basis of this recording, is an uninteresting actor as well. Alberto Erede's pacing is, unfortunately, quite slack, but the recording is further redeemed by two cameo performances, the inimitable Sacristan of Fernando Corena and the very fine Spoletta of Piero de Palma.

Seven years after her first TOSCA recording, Tebaldi redid the work, this time flanked by Mario del Monaco and George London as Mario Cavarodossi and Baron Scarpia, respectively, with the Santa Cecilia Orchestra and Chorus led by Francesco Molinari-Pradelli. The *raison d'etre* for this second version was the advent of stereophonic sound which is used well in this recording. 1958 was a good year for the soprano, who at that time was singing as well as ever and had further refined her dramatic sensibilities. Thus, Tebaldi's second Tosca is authoritatively sung with a new dimension of power and with no loss of vocal quality.

Del Monaco is a rugged and manly Cavarodossi, at his best in the "Vittoria, Vittoria" sequence in Act Two. At times, del Monaco almost overpowers the role, but the voice sounds freely produced, and the tenor colors his singing more skillfully than in certain later performances.

London is sonorous and mean in the role of Scarpia, but the voice is less supple than one would ideally wish for this role. Dramatically, one cringes before this Scarpia, but the villain's music is better served on other recordings. De Palma and Corena are again heard as Spoletta and the Sacristan. Molinari-Pradelli's hand is, alas, all too heavy, and the result is a slowly paced and stiff performance distinguished by the singing of Tebaldi and del Monaco.

London's catalogue rather incredibly boasts two more Tosca's. One was originally released in 1963 by RCA in the USA and by HMV in England. This album preserves what must have been a tremendously exciting series of performances at the Vienna State Opera. In almost every respect, this TOSCA excels, making it a fine choice for any collector. Leontyne Price is a Tosca notable for luscious tone and a rather generalized, "prima-donna-ish" conception of the role. Certainly Price is never actually dull in the part, but aside from the tremendous beauty of her singing, one still would like to feel more involvement in the role. Giuseppe di Stefano is not the freshest Mario possible, but his sense of Puccinian style is arresting, and like del Monaco, sings *con coglioni*. Giuseppe Taddei offers a masterful Scarpia, half-growling nearly every note, although allowing himself the option of delivering Scarpia's great monologue "Si, mi dicon venal" with the smoothest tone possible. Von Karajan, as might be expected, elicits first rate work from the Vienna State Opera Chorus and Vienna Philharmonic. His heavy approach is rather un-Puccinian but, in many places, particularly in the second act, is very effective.

London's fourth and, one rather hopes, last TOSCA for the present features Birgit Nilsson, Franco Corelli, and Dietrich Fischer-Diskau in the troika of leading roles, and Loren Maazel conducting the ubiquitous Santa Cecilia forces.

Nilsson's Tosca must be reckoned, with all due respect, a *success d'estime.* The voice lacks the sensuousness necessary in all Puccini heroines and never more called-for than in TOSCA. Nilsson sings the part with customary precision and imposing "presence," but what is needed here is less sheer size and more emotional commitment to the role.

Corelli sings rather well, but scoops between notes much too much. The voice is in good condition, though, and his fans will certainly find much to enjoy in his performance here.

Dietrich Fischer-Dieskau has never been associated with the role of Scarpia, and one understands the reasons for this after hearing the recording. Surprisingly uncomfortable in Italian, Fischer-Dieskay finds little in Scarpia's character that he can grasp onto, while his light baritone is out of its depth in Scarpia's music. One wonders why as intelligent an artist as Fischer-Dieskau would undertake a major recording of a role for which he is so clearly unsuited.

Maazel's conducting pays great attention to orchestral

detail but singularly lacks excitement, more or less completely placing this TOSCA out of competition.

Franco Corelli and Nilsson are often quite combustible together onstage, but this performance, while offering a number of pleasures to the listener, never truly takes flight. Perhaps a cause of the rather impersonal quality of the entire performance is the fact that Corelli and Nilsson recorded a number of scenes separately, leaving the engineers to mix their voices in the duets. This practice is an evil of the jet-age, and while offering the advantage of allowing singers to more neatly fit recording commitments into their busy schedules, should be condemned for robbing opera recordings of what little spontaneity is left to them, now that the engineers can quietly splice together fragment after fragment of music, synthesizing a finished performance.

Angel-HMV's 1965 stereo TOSCA was released at the time Maria Callas made her two-night return to the Metropolitan. Although the performance is often quite exciting, neither the soprano or baritone Tito Gobbi equal, let alone surpass, their work on the Angel monaural performance of a decade earlier. Callas' stereophonic Tosca impresses with its tremendous authority, as the diva certainly finds the heroine's personality congenial. Her brusqueness in the beginning of her Act One scene with Mario adds a humanizing, realistic touch to the otherwise romantic, heroic creature that Callas creates. Unfortunately, all this exciting acting cannot offset the fact that Callas' voice was at its lowest recorded ebb in late 1964. Virtually every note above the staff is strained and unsteady, and there is little sense of vocal ease anywhere in Callas' singing. "Vissi d'arte" for all its artistic sincerity, is almost painful to listen to here, and the less said about Callas' high C's, the more merciful!

Gobbi's Scarpia is brimming with nastiness and is forcefully yet subtly realized. Yet even he is not heard at his vocal best on this set. The tone is often dry and hollow, particularly on top. Gobbi still is the best of all Scarpias and of his many spine-tingling little touches, the most effective is his rendering of the line "Eh bene" when forcing Tosca to make up her mind at the end of Act Two.

Vocal abundance and glory is supplied on this recording solely by Carlo Bergonzi, whose vibrant lyric tenor has rarely been better recorded. Lacking only a little of Bjoerling's elegance in the role of Cavaradossi, Bergonzi sings with taste and ample power, creating a sympathetic if standard tenor-hero.

The supporting cast is more than adequate, and the Orchestra of the Paris Conservatoire is strikingly excellent under George Prêtre's firm and knowledgeable direction.

The older Angel TOSCA, still available in monaural sound only, is a La Scala recording led by the late Victor da Sabata whose frenzied pace makes the second act unbearably (and deliciously) tense. Callas, here in superb voice, creates a Tosca of rare quality: alluring, annoying, passionate, vicious— and sung with fiery tone. Tebaldi's and Price's Toscas are more warmly, even gorgeously vocalized, but this is undoubtedly the fiercest and most galvanizing Tosca ever recorded! Gobbi's voice is far fresher and warmer here than on the later set, but even this more youthful Scarpia lacks not one whit of vile wit or meanness. Added to these great performances is that of Giuseppe di Stefano as Mario and the excellent work of the La Scala comprimario artists, orchestra and chorus. This is a performance that ought to be a cornerstone of every opera buff's library.

Finally, there is the Victrola reissue with Zinka Milanov, Leonard Warren, and Jussi Bjoerling, made at the Rome Opera in 1956 with Leinsdorf conducting. The early stereophonic sound allows the voices to overpower a rather scrawny sounding orchestra, but what voices those were! Milanov is a mature Tosca, and indeed her gorgeous instrument is occasionally less secure here than in other recordings, but her *pianissimi* are as heavenly as ever, and, unlike Nilsson, Milanov is at home in this sort of music. Bjoerling is a perfect Mario. No one sings the role quite so enchantingly as that Swedish tenor whose lyric voice had all the stamina necessary to sustain the climaxes. Warren's Scarpia is undoubtedly the best sung on disc. Gobbi and London more successfully delineate every nasty aspect of the Baron's character, but Warren is dramatically acceptable in the role. Leinsdorf shapes the music well, but one would like a bigger, richer sounding orchestra. This recording is not the final word on TOSCA but still is a fine souvenir of three great artists of the recent past.

Since a choice of one TOSCA recording is practically impossible to make, one must be grateful that the opera consumes only two discs, and the collector can acquire several versions without seriously straining his budget.

VERDI: LA TRAVIATA

Caballé, Bergonzi, Milnes, Prêtre cond.
RCA Italiana Orchestra and Chorus
3 discs
RCA LSC 6180*
UK: RCA SER5564-6

Sills, Gedda, Panerai, Ceccato cond.
Royal Philharmonic Orchestra and John Alldis Chorus
3 discs
Angel S-3780
UK: HMV SLS960

Moffo, Tucker, Merrill, Previtali cond.
Rome Opera Orchestra and Chorus
3 discs
RCA LSC-6154*
UK: Victrola VICS6111

Sutherland, Bergonzi, Merrill, Pritchard cond.
Orchestra and Chorus of the Maggio Musicale Fiorentino
3 discs
London OSA 1366*
UK: Decca SET 249-51

Callas, Albanese, Savarese, Santini cond.
RAI Orchestra and Chorus
3 discs
Everest/Cetra S-425/3

de los Angeles, dal Monte, Sereni, Serafin cond.
Rome Opera Orchestra and Chorus
3 discs
Angel S-3623*
UK: HMV SLS957

Lorengar, Aragall, Fischer-Dieskau, Maazel cond.
Deutsche Oper Orchestra and Chorus
2 discs
London OSA 1279*
UK: Decca SET 401-2

Tebaldi, Poggi, Protti, Molinari-Pradelli cond.
Orchestra and Chorus of L'Accademia di Santa Cecilia
3 discs
Richmond RS63021 (Mono)

Scotto, Raimondi, Bastianini, Votto cond.
Orchestra and Chorus of La Scala
3 discs
UK: DGG 27809 010

It is axiomatic among opera fans that this most popular opera, while recorded at least a dozen times since the LP era began, has yet to receive a fully satisfactory, let alone definitive, recording. Certainly, there are any number of outstanding Violettas, Alfredos, and Germonts, as well as sympathetic and strong conductors, but unfortunately, they do not appear together in any single album. To narrow the field somewhat, eight TRAVIATA recordings are discussed below. These include two budget editions as well as six full-priced versions. No opera fan will be content with one only, nor am I satisfied that any of them fulfills the demands of this opera.

My personal favorite among TRAVIATA recordings is also the most recent: The Angel-HMV set issued in early 1972 starring Beverly Sills, Nicolai Gedda, and Rolando Panerai, with the Royal Philharmonic conducted by Aldo Ceccato, and with the participation of the John Alldis Choir.

Miss Sills is that rarity among Violettas, a soprano with the coloratura prowess to make more of the "Sempre libera" than an obstacle course for the voice and the vocal stamina necessary for the heavier music of the later acts. Added to this are Sills' gifts as an actress, and the result is a moving and musically exemplary heroine who, after dazzling the listener with an elaborate cadenza ending with a high E-flat at the conclusion of "Ah, fors'è lui," goes on to move him to tears in the second act, and build to a harrowing climax with a sensitively sung and acted final scene. Miss Sills' attention to musical detail and cleanness of phrasing is praiseworthy, while the skill and accuracy of her impersonation of the "Lady of the Camellias" is almost without equal in my experience. Miss Sills' colleagues, including Nicolai Gedda as a forceful Alfredo who creates a firm character at the expense of a little of his customary elegance and Rolando Panerai as a dry-voiced but quite serviceable Germont, do not quite equal her work, but the exceptionally graceful conducting by Ceccato which filters the music as if through a dream or memory of the past by means of unhurried, rather poetic tempi is an achievement of high order. The score is presented uncut, giving one the opportunity to savor both verses of "Ah, fors'è lui," "Addio del passato," and "Parigi, o cara," as well as Alfredo's second act *cabaletta* "O mio rimorso." Also included is Germont's Act Two cabaletta which is arguably the worst single piece the composer ever penned, and since Panerai sings it in a lifeless, harsh manner, its inclusion does little to help the performance. Still, this TRAVIATA offers much high calibre work.

Another Violetta of great ability in the coloratura department is Joan Sutherland who recorded the opera for London-Decca in 1963 in the company of Carlo Bergonzi as Alfredo and Robert Merrill as Germont with the Santa Cecilia forces led by John Pritchard. Unfortunately, this is not a successful performance for Miss Sutherland who sounds deathly ill even in the first act and is plagued throughout by pitch problems (particularly in "Ah, fors'è lui"), flatness of characterization, and bad diction. Fortunately, the "Sempre libera" turns out well, giving the listener a fleeting suggestion of the marvels that this soprano can accomplish when in form. Carlo Bergonzi's Alfredo is the best on disc, distinguished by easy, opulent tone and tastefullness. Robert Merrill, heard here in his third recorded Germont, is rather over-resonantly recorded, but note perfect and imposing. He exhibits no in-depth understanding of the part, however, with "Di Provenza" sounding as much like a travelogue narration for the French National Tourist Board as a plea to his erring son. John Pritchard's dragging tempi in this uncut version of the score make listening, at times, an ordeal even for the most ardent TRAVIATA fan.

RCA (HMV) has no less than three TRAVIATA sets in its catalogue. The most recent features Montserrat Caballé, Bergonzi, and Sherrill Milnes, with the RCA Italiana Orchestra led by Georges Prêtre.

Mme. Caballé is an exceptionally fine Violetta, and her beautiful, burnished soprano lavishes some truly immortal singing on the role. Even though not an overzealous actress, Caballé manages a sympathetic if slightly weepy characterization that might have been even sharper had Prêtre's conducting been less dreadfully harsh, speedy, and generally incompetent. Bergonzi's Alfredo is again notable, but, as opposed to the Sutherland recording, he is here mated with a soprano whose intelligent approach to the score is matched with his own. What a joy it is to hear these two artists together in "Un di felice" or "Parigi, o cara." Sherrill Milnes, on this his first complete opera for discs, favors a stiff and unfeeling Germont père, but the sheer pleasure of hearing this fine baritone is considerable. Despite the slights to the score committed by the unusually more conscientious Prêtre, this TRAVIATA is very much an asset to one's record library.

Another RCA set stems from the famous 1946 Toscanini

radio broadcasts of the opera featuring Licia Albanese, Jan Peerce, and Robert Merrill. For historical reasons the set is quite interesting, but as in later years, Toscanini had some bizarre ideas about the operas he directed. One must, therefore, be prepared to accept some wildly fast tempi which inhibit the soloists from projecting the music with any dramatic effect. Still, Albanese, in her happiest vocal estate, is a feminine and affecting Violetta, and Peerce and Merrill exhibit the vocal sturdiness that endeared them to the Maestro and a generation of opera-goers in the United States.

London-Decca's most recent TRAVIATA is a two-disc set that preserves the Deutsche Oper's recent production of the work conducted by Lorin Maazel and which featured Pilar Lorengar, Giacomo Aragall, and Dietrich Fischer-Dieskau in the main roles. Possibly more concerned with economic than musical considerations, London-Decca has opted in this case for the heavily cut, "standard" version which, of course, fits neatly onto two discs and thus allows the album to undersell most recent competition.

Pilar Lorengar's Violetta is musical but, in dramatic terms, not unmoving. Furthermore, her vibrato is annoyingly emphasized somehow by the recording process, and thus this most attractive young soprano never sounds fully comfortable in the music, and certainly she is not sufficiently strong to offset the competition of Sills, Caballé, Sutherland, et al. Giacomo Aragall is a graceful, light-voiced Alfredo whose vocal beauty is, from time to time, offset by his tendency to wander off pitch. Dietrich Fischer-Dieskau is, in this instance, an intelligent and musical Père Germont, seemingly more at home in this Verdian score than in other operas by the same composer. Maazel's tempi are too crisp and don't shed any particular new light on the score, but their unbending, cold pace is perhaps due to the necessity of completing the set in less than two hours time.

Deutsche Grammophon's TRAVIATA features Renata Scotto in the title role, with the under-rated Gianni Raimondi as Alfredo, Ettore Bastianini as Germont, and with the Scala forces conducted by Antonio Votto.

Scotto, whose unique artistry is at long last being appreciated by the American public, favors a somber, pensive characterization that is most appropriate and performs the death throes of the heroine with a gripping sense of hysteria. Vocally, the soprano is in smooth form here, gliding up and down the scale with ease, and with a minimum of strained or pinched high notes.

Raimondi's Alfredo is cleanly phrased and sung with animation. No tenor ever made his mark by singing roles such as Alfredo, but Raimondi performs most commendably. Bastianini is typically charismatic as Germont, singing a commandingly clear "Di Provenza." Votto's pliant, well-routined conducting moves the score adequately but not with the requisite feeling. Actually, considering the vocal talent present in this recording, a more capable maestro and a producer who reinstated all the standard cuts observed here might have made a good TRAVIATA into a great one.

Two budget sets feature the arch-rivals of the 1950's, Maria Callas and Renata Tebaldi. Interestingly, each recording offers an individualisitc interpretation from its diva, but, unfortunately, little else of value except its budget price. Callas is heard on an Everest-Cetra album which she dominates through her highly charged and often thrilling singing. Neither Franco Albanese as Alfredo nor Ugo Savarese as Germont arrive at anything nearly worthy of Callas' company. The veteran Gabriele Santini is the timid conductor of a performance further marred by all the traditional omissions (these are, regrettably, observed by Toscanini, too).

Richmond Stereo Treasury's recent re-release of Tebaldi's 1956 TRAVIATA, now processed for artificial stereo, offers that soprano in one of her more controversial parts. Never at ease in coloratura passages, Tebaldi opts for a transposition of "Sempre libera" one half tone down and still sounds somewhat uncomfortable. Elsewhere, she is more at home and contributes some lovely singing, particularly in "Un dì felice," the Act Two, Scene Two finale, and in Violetta's final moments.

Tebaldi's supporting cast is, like Callas', unworthy to be in the same studio with her. Gianni Poggi is an unsteady and frequently flat Alfredo, and Aldo Protti sings Germont as if from inside a vacuum. Francesco Molinari-Pradelli's conducting of the Santa Cecilia forces is of a higher calibre. These two sets are obviously inferior as total performances but are of interest because of the prominence enjoyed by their leading ladies.

WAGNER:
TRISTAN UND ISOLDE

Nilsson, Resnik, Uhl, Krause, van Mill, Solti cond.
Vienna Philharmonic and State Opera Chorus
5 discs
London OSA 1502*
UK: Decca SET 204-8

Nilsson, Ludwig, Windgassen, Waechter, Talvela, Böhm cond.
Bayreuth Festival Orchestra and Chorus
5 discs
Deutsche Grammophon 2713001*
UK: Same as above

Flagstad, Thebom, Suthaus, Fischer-Dieskau, Furtwängler cond.
Philharmonia Orchestra and Covent Garden Chorus
5 discs
Angel   *
UK: HMV RLS3

TRISTAN:
Vickers, Dernesch, Ludwig, Berry, Ridderbusch, von Karajan cond.
Berlin Philharmonic
5 discs
Angel SCL-3777
UK: unavailable at press time

Wagner's music drama, arguably his masterpiece, can be experienced on discs in four complete versions, two of which center upon the current era's great Isolde, Birgit Nilsson, while the third stars her immediate predecessor, Flagstad, and the fourth (and newest) features Helga Dernesch. The shortage of tenors able to cope with the role of Tristan is sadly apparent on the first three of these recordings, in each of which the hero remains in the shadow, vocally speaking, of the heroine.

Nilsson competes with her own early 1960's studio recording on the London-Decca label in a live Bayreuth recording made by Deutsche Grammophon in 1966. Under Karl Böhm's razor sharp direction of the latter performance, the soprano is perhaps a more commanding actress than she is on Solti's more contemplative, inner-directed, London-Decca set. Certainly her delivery of the "Narrative and Curse" is unrivaled for steely thrust and vehemence in the Deutsche Grammophon performance. Of course, one of the most miraculous elements of the Nilsson Isolde is her transformation after drinking Brangaene's potion, manifested not only by her enunciation of the text but by her softened vocalism, culminating in an unearthly pianissimo at the close of the "Liebestod" and expressed in an ecstatic second act "Liebesnacht." Furthermore, the Bayreuth performance is blessed in its supporting cast. One is tempted to think that Christa Ludwig is wasted in the role of Brangaene, but her luscious, warm tone and strong dramatic involvement in this secondary part is not only a major asset of the set, but further proof of Ludwig's stature as an artist in accepting a role that is all too often undercast and making it so important a figure in the music drama.

The Tristan in this recording is Wolfgang Windgassen, a sterling Wagnerian who by 1966 lacked the stamina for this most demanding role. The tenor is musically eloquent, but, except when singing quite softly, his voice sounds threadbare and lacking in quality. In the love duet, Windgassen pales before Nilsson. Eberhard Waechter is a first rate Kurvenal, strong of voice and authoritative in characterization. Even more remarkable is the King Marke of Martti Talvela, a bass whose voice is as dark and seemingly infinite as a summer night. Talvela makes the King's monologue a dignified and arresting lament, instead of the excruciating bore into which too many lesser artists turn it.

Urging this fine cast onto ever greater achievement is Maestro Böhm who captures every passionate nuance of Wagner's score and drives it home. This nine-sided TRISTAN set is the shortest of the three albums, but the music is neither heavily cut nor rushed. Instead, Böhm creates an atmosphere of utterly palpable tension that engulfs the music and carries it forward.

Solti's TRISTAN is, in its way, equally fine a performance and is perhaps even the more listenable one. Böhm was, after all, conducting an opera house performance in which the physical and visual elements contributed greatly to the final result, while Solti and his Decca colleagues work only with the medium of sound and create an even more aurally impressive cosmos than does Karl Böhm. Indeed, Solti's peerless Vienna Philharmonic, coupled with the richer recorded sound that the engineers were able to provide for this studio production surpass the work of Bayreuth's orchestra. Solti's conception of the score is somewhat less turbulent than Böhm's. In his hands, the opera emerges as rather a more lyrical experience.

As stated previously, Birgit Nilsson's first Isolde is a shade more benign than her later effort. As far as her singing is concerned, Nilsson's facility with literally every note of the role will be forever astounding.

The Tristan here is Fritz Uhl who, while falling far short of Nilsson in terms of ease of singing and eloquence or intensity of characterization, nevertheless does reasonably well with an impossible role. At the very least, he sounds both younger and more virile than Windgassen.

In the role of Brangaene, Regina Resnik's voice has never sounded more beautiful, although Ludwig is even lovelier on the Deutsche Grammophon set. Resnik matches the German mezzo, however, in terms of interpretation, and her handling of Brangaene's "Warning" is especially poignant.

Tom Krause turns in still another strong performance, this time in the role of Kurvenal, but Arnold Van Mill is a reedy, thin-voiced King Marke who suggests the character's age but not his nobility.

Turning to the Flagstad recording made in the early 1950's, originally for RCA but now available on Angel-HMV (with highlights on Seraphim), the soprano's work is remarkable, considering that she was nearly sixty. The voice is as bright and warm as ever (it is true though, that the high C's in this performance were sung by Elisabeth Schwarzkopf and later dubbed into Flagstad's tapes) and her characterization, while less complex than Nilsson's is extraordinarily feminine and moving.

Ludwig Suthaus is a Tristan of tact and good musicianship, although, like most of his competition in the role, he is not a true *heldentenor*. Blanche Thebom is a decent if uninspired Brangaene, and Dietrich Fischer-Dieskau contributes a handsomely sung Kurvenal. Wilhelm Furtwängler's intense direction of the Philharmonia Orchestra combined with Flagstad's heroine make this recording a true classic that deserves its place along with the more recent two recordings.

Herbert von Karajan's 1972 TRISTAN UND ISOLDE is the first complete recording of TRISTAN to feature a real Tristan. Jon Vickers embodies every one of the knight's virtues, including nobility of characterization, vocal beauty to win Isolde's (and the listener's) affection, and vocal strength to survive his nearly four-hour ordeal. Of course, singing Tristan in the recording studio is vastly different from a live performance, but the two other studio Tristans on the rival recordings (Windgassen sang in a live performance) pale in comparison to Vickers' work.

Christa Ludwig duplicates her Bayreuth Brangaene with even happier results, while Walter Berry is a stirring Kurvenal, and Karl Ridderbusch is an effective King Marke.

As for the contributions of Helga Dernesch as Isolde and von Karajan's conducting, these are not to my taste. The soprano performs her arduous task with professionalism, but her voice is cruelly taxed in the Liebesnacht and Liebestod, with Karajan rather unchivalrously allowing the orchestra to overpower her so that Dernesch is nearly inaudible at the climax of the Liebestod (exactly where Nilsson is at her strongest). Interpretively, Dernesch is feminine but tame and devoid of any special attractiveness. Karajan's quirky tempi make for a frustratingly cold Liebestod and a terribly slow first act, but he does elicit magnificent playing from the Berlin Philharmonic, and brings out a wealth of orchestral detail, particularly in the second act love scene. This is a "Tristan's TRISTAN" that ought to be owned in conjunction with either of Nilsson's "Isolde's TRISTAN." How sad that the soprano and tenor could not have recorded the opera together.

A final note: Those wishing a different perspective on Isolde's "Liebestod" should hear the Italian versions of that piece sung by Tebaldi (London—Tebaldi Festival) and Callas (Everest—Maria Callas Prima Donna). While not "authentic" stylistically, these performances provide a contrast to the usual singing of the "Liebestod" as well as giving a glimpse of what the Isolde of two great Italian(ate) artists might have been like. Actually, Callas did sing the role in Italy (and in Italian) early in her career. Tebaldi never sang Isolde complete, but in her recording of the "Liebestod," one senses an understanding and perception of this character transliterated into a somewhat different musical idiom.

PUCCINI: IL TRITTICO

1. Boxed Collection of IL TABARRO, SUOR ANGELICA and GIANNI SCHICCHI

Tebaldi, Simionato, del Monaco, Lazzari, Merrill, Corena, Gardelli cond.
Orchestra and Chorus of the Maggio Musicale Fiorentino
3 discs
London OSA 1364
UK: Decca SET 236-8

Simonetto, Petrella, Carteri, Bertocci, Baroni, Taddei, Corena, Previtali cond.
RAI Orchestra and Chorus
3 discs
Everest/Cetra S-464/3

2. Individual Recordings of the Three Operas

IL TABARRO

Tebaldi, del Monaco, Merrill, Gardelli cond.
Orchestra and Chorus of the Maggio Musicale Fiorentino
1 disc
London OSA 1151
UK: Decca SXL6122

Price, Domingo, Milnes, Leinsdorf cond.
New Philharmonia Orchestra and John Alldis Choir
1 disc
RCA LSC 3220
UK: RCA SER5619

SUOR ANGELICA

Tebaldi, Simionato, Gardelli cond.
Orchestra and Chorus of the Maggio Musicale Fiorentino
1 disc
London OSA 1152
UK: Decca SXL6123

de los Angeles, Barbieri, Serafin cond.
Rome Opera Orchestra and Chorus
1 disc
Angel 35748
UK: World Record Club ST934

GIANNI SCHICCHI

Tebaldi, Lazzari, Corena, Gardelli cond.
Orchestra and Chorus of the Maggio Musicale Fiorentino
1 disc
London OSA 1153
UK: Decca SXL6124

Gobbi, de los Angeles, dal Monte, Santini cond.
Rome Opera Orchestra and Chorus
1 disc
Angel S-35473

The three one-act operas known collectively as IL TRITTICO have been recorded twice in recent years, and there is also an old, Cetra set still available.

London-Decca recorded all three operas in Florence in 1962, anchoring the project around conductor Lamberto Gardelli and soprano Renata Tebaldi who perform in each of the three works. Angel-HMV recorded SUOR ANGELICA and GIANNI SCHICCHI at the Rome Opera some years earlier, featuring

Tito Gobbi and Victoria de los Angeles, while RCA in 1972
released a lone IL TABARRO with Price, Milnes, and Domingo.
The three operas will be considered separately, although the
London-Decca recordings are available in a single boxed set
as well as individually.

IL TABARRO

Although Puccini is grouped with the verismo composers, he
is not truly a member of that group, as his operas are, in general,
far too lyrical and sentimental. TABARRO, with its drab
setting of a Parisian barge, its lower class characters, its
swift-moving, violent plot, and its strong language is probably
the only real verismo opera that Puccini penned. Although
most critics have praised it as a near masterpiece of musical
expression, this opera has never, at least in the USA and
Britain, found the favor that the universally adored GIANNI
SCHICCHI has gained. This is entirely unjust, for there is
some first rate writing for the protagonists, as well as some
of Puccini's most adroit atmospheric touches (the barge whistle
that accompanies the opening music and the organ grinder's
musical puns on LA BOHEME being but two).

London's recordings finds Tebaldi a passionate Giorgette,
admirably lyrical when dreaming of a new love with Luigi
(sung by Mario del Monaco) and vividly frightened during the
closing moments. At the time of these recordings, the soprano's
voice was beginning to take on certain characteristics of
Tebaldi's later work. Youthful freshness had begun to fade,
replaced by a darker quality in her voice. Luscious chest tones
became more prominent, and a heightened dramatic tension
had developed in her artistry.

Mario del Monaco's Luigi hardly suggests a 20 year old
youth, but the tenor's fervent, authoritative performance
makes up in vigor and sensuality what it lacks in musical
velvet. Del Monaco and Tebaldi in their long, desperate love
duet document one of the greatest eras in Italian singing—that
of the 1950's and early 60's. Robert Merrill's dark, scowling

Michele is one of the baritone's best dramatic turns, and he sings the role with ease, as well. Piero de Palma is heard briefly as the song-sheet vendor, adding his accustomed charm to a cameo role, while Lucia Danieli is a witty Frugola. The Orchestra and Chorus of the Florence May Festival respond well to Gardelli's crackling, highly tensed direction, adding up to a gripping performance.

RCA's TABARRO, led by Erich Leinsdorf, features singing that is at least as admirable as the alternate version, but what one misses here is the powerful sense of melodrama that Gardelli and his singers capture so well. The New Philharmonia plays excellently, and Leinsdorf's pacing is more than reasonable, yet the performance does not ignite. Some of the fault must go to Leontyne Price and Sherrill Milnes who are in eminently fine voice here but who make little effort to penetrate their roles. Price's heavenly voice seems rather disembodied from Giorgette's torment, while Milnes is a placid though mahogany-toned Michele. He, like Merrill, is allowed to perform the alternate version of Michele's soliloquy, "Nulla, silenzio" (as an appendix to the opera).

Ironically, it is tenor Placido Domingo, whose radiant lyric voice makes him a convincingly youthful Luigi, who attempts most of the acting, yet who, lacking del Monaco's *machismo*, falls short of achieving that which he so earnestly attempts to do. Still in all, the singing on this disc is impressive, and given its relatively modest cost, deserves a place alongside the London set in a collector's library.

SUOR ANGELICA

Puccini's all-female opera set in a Renaissance Italian convent can be heavy going for those who don't particularly care for Puccini. Its weak, slow start depicting vignettes of convent life is tiresome and cloying. Then too, the syrupy, religious "miracle" that is the climax of the opera will strike many as hopelessly naive. Yet the opera is worth hearing for its central incident, the brutal confrontation between its heroine, Sister

Angelica, and her hard-bitten elderly aunt—Puccini's only great scene for two women. Furthermore, the Aunt is Puccini's only interesting role for a mezzo-soprano, with the possible exception of Suzuki in MADAMA BUTTERFLY. Then too, there is the aria "Senza Mamma tu sei morto" for the soprano.

Tebaldi, is happily cast as Angelica, for she not only manages high notes with little strain, but enters into the "spirit" of the opera, finding a depth of character entirely missed by de los Angeles in the Angel-HMV recording. Buoyed by Giulietta Simionato's searing portrayal of the unbending Aunt, Tebaldi makes the nun an articulate and forceful personality, giving the spoken line "Sorella di mia madre voi siete inesorabile" an unbearable pathos. The supporting voices are entirely pleasant, and Gardelli prevents the music from sounding too lacrimose by means of flexible yet firm conducting.

Angel-HMV's Rome Opera set finds de los Angeles in lovely voice except when trying for high C's which emerge pushed and tentative. The Spanish artist holds an aurally appealing line in "Senza Mamma" but is apparently quite unmoved by and uninterested in the girl's plight, sounding self-contained and calm throughout, rising to a heightened emotional pitch only during the finale when the dying Angelica is comforted by a vision of her son and the Virgin Mary. Fedora Barbieri is an imposing Aunt, but her singing lacks Simionato's regality, sounding shrewish and common at times. It is further marred by unsteadiness in the lower register. Serafin's excessively slow tempi also serve to retard the drama and dull the music's appeal.

GIANNI SCHICCHI

GIANNI SCHICCHI, the sly comedy with which IL TRITTICO concludes is nicely served by both recordings. The Angel-HMV set offers Gobbi as a Gianni Schicchi who is far less a clown than London's Corena paints him. Gobbi emphasizes the peasant's real loathing of the greedy relatives of Buoso Donati, and his shouts of "Niente" to Lauretta (which of course lead to her aria, "O mio babbino caro") are more fearsome than Corena's. Gobbi's taut baritone serves to make Schicchi a figure of great dramatic interest, especially in the "Addio Firenze" which could not possibly be sung in a tarter, more pungent manner. This is the only Puccini opera not completely dominated by the heroine, so de los Angeles' cool demeanor is less important here than elsewhere in the Puccini canon. She sings Lauretta's one moment of musical glory in a polished if frosty manner. Carlo Del Monte is adequate as Rinuccio, and the supporting cast is at least decent. Gabriele Santini leads the Rome Opera forces in a sprightly, nicely animated performance.

The London-Decca set is dominated by Fernando Corena's ebullient, good-natured *buffo* interpretation of the title part. His Schicchi is a zany, inspired practical joker who does not need to be won over by the "O mio babbino caro" so sweetly sung by Tebaldi. Rinuccio is sung rather lightly and not too well by Aggostino Lazzari, but the supporting singers are quite good, and Gardelli supplies an atmosphere that most properly exudes *asti spumante*. Thus the listener has a choice between an ironical, "black comedy" SCHICCHI found on EMI (Angel in the USA, although the set originally was released on Capitol Records, and HMV in the UK) and the brightly humorous performance issued by London-Decca. Since neither version is precisely the "last word" and since each compliments the other, the dedicated Puccini aficionado will undoubtedly want both recordings.

VERDI: IL TROVATORE

Price, Cossotto, Domingo, Milnes, Giaiotti, Mehta cond.
New Philharmonia Orchestra and Ambrosian Opera Chorus
3 discs
RCA LSC 3023*
UK: RCA SER5586-8

Price, Elias, Tucker, Warren, Tozzi, Basile cond.
Rome Opera Orchestra and Chorus
3 discs
RCA LSC 6150*

Tebaldi, Simionato, del Monaco, Savarese, Tozzi, Erede cond.
Orchestra and Chorus of L'Accademia di Sta. Cecilia
3 discs
London OSA 1304*
UK: Ace of Diamonds GOS614-6

Tucci, Simionato, Corelli, Merrill, Schippers cond.
Rome Opera Orchestra and Chorus
3 discs
Angel S-3653*
UK: HMV SLS916

Stella, Cossotto, Bergonzi, Bastianini, Vinco, Serafin cond.
La Scala Orchestra and Chorus
3 discs
Deutsche Grammophon 2709011

Callas, Barbieri, di Stefano, Panerai, von Karajan cond.
La Scala Orchestra and Chorus
3 discs
Angel 35545s/2 (Mono)

Mancini, Lauri-Volpi, Previtali cond.
RAI Orchestra and Chorus
3 discs
Everest/Cetra S426/3

The most recent TROVATORE, found on RCA, is also one of
the most enjoyable recordings of this mad, tuneful work.
Leontyne Price, in her second Leonora before the microphones,
reveals further mastery of her art in a performance distinguished by glorious high notes (note the high C thrown in in
Act Four as Leonora prepares to drink poison) and a uniformly
handsome account of the music. Price's acting is not exactly
spine tingling, but in such a part as this, one must be grateful
for the vocal splendor that the soprano provides. As the
opera is performed complete, one is able to hear both verses
of "Di tal amor" (here Price encounters some rough going in the
florid passages and in low lying measures), and Leonora's
beautiful, rarely done cabaletta "Tu vedrai che amore in
terra" that follows the "Miserere."

Fiorenza Cossotto is little short of perfect as Azucena. The
only complaint that one might (unreasonably) register about
her singing is that the mezzo produces a far too beautiful
sound for this old crone, but this seeming inconsistency
between character and artist is made up for by Cossotto's
vivid vocal acting. From the opening measure of her superbly
controlled and powerful "Stride la vampa," one senses that
this Azucena is someone special.

Placido Domingo, here in his first complete operatic recording, sings with innate sensitivity and cultivated grace, and
while impressing with a beautiful voice, the tenor is perhaps
miscast in so heavy a role as Manrico. Young tenors who

push their voices in such heroic parts don't always get to be old tenors. Sherrill Milnes, on the other hand, is in no danger of harming his voice in the role of Di Luna, singing with eloquence and power, although offering little expression of the Count's villainous nature.

Bonaldo Giaiotti is effective and sinister in Ferrando's narrative, while Ryland Davies of Covent Garden is quite impressive in the pitifully thankless role of Ruiz.

The Ambrosian Opera Chorus handle the varied assignments of gypsies, soldiers, and monks with ease. Zubin Mehta, a quirky opera conductor in live performances, here creates a brooding, tense atmosphere suitable to the drama, enlivened by energetic tempi and a definite feeling for the music.

London-Decca issued its TROVATORE in 1957 in primitive stereo. Primitive is also the word for the style embodied in the singing of its tenor and baritone, Mario del Monaco and Ugo Savarese. However, since del Monaco at that time was in peak form, the fact that his approach to the entire role of Manrico is that of one, long "Di quella pira" may be overlooked to a fair degree. The tenor's performance of that *cabaletta* is about as stirring as they come, and he is also quite effective in the final scene. Savarese as Count Di Luna, though, offers no particular virtues either of voice or interpretation. In fact, his rather blustery reading of the Count's music is the set's weakest point.

Renata Tebaldi never sang Leonora in the opera house, but, aside from some discomfort in the most florid passages of her two cabaletta's, Tebaldi makes one wish that she had done the role on stage. Leonora is a rather uninteresting character, always gloomy (she does, of course, have little reason to be otherwise), and Tebaldi does far less with this role dramatically than with, for example, Aida, but there is no denying that her voice is one of the most beautiful to have graced the role on discs. Giulietta Simionato offers a richly vocalized and vibrant characterization of Azucena. Her Act Two duet with del Monaco is a high point of the performance. Giorgio Tozzi, in this early recording, is an exceptionally strong Ferrando, and the Orchestra and Chorus of the Accademia di Santa Cecilia respond well to the crisp conducting of Alberto Erede. This performance is also nearly complete, including Leonora's fourth act *cabaletta*, the full version of the first act trio, and a number of other passages too often omitted elsewhere.

Angel-HMV's 1965 stereo IL TROVATORE with Tucci, Simionato (her last recording), Corelli, and Merrill, conducted by Schippers is not strong enough competition to outshine the earlier Angel (mono) version that featured Callas, Barbieri, di Stefano, and Panerai, conducted by von Karajan.

Tucci, usually a fine singer, is plagued by a heavy vibrato in this set and simply cannot surpass her stiff competition from other Leonoras. Still, her fourth act is most affecting, and there are any number of lovely individual passages. Simionato is not as good vocally in this recording as she is on the London album made ten years or more earlier. However, what little her voice had lost in freshness by the time this set was made, Simionato makes up in terms of musicianship, accuracy, and a penetrating characterization. Corelli, of course, has a glorious voice, but one which he has never learned to husband properly. "Di quella pira" is brilliantly sung, but otherwise, Corelli's work is plagued by continual scooping, bad diction, and failure to observe the niceties of the art of *bel canto*. Robert Merrill's Di Luna is dark-hued and persuasive. Maestro Schippers, unfortunately, has a tendency to confuse speedy tempi with dramatic excitement, and his headlong rush into the score is irritating. The Rome Opera Orchestra and Chorus are quite good. Although this recording takes up three discs, most of the "standard" cuts remain unopened.

The older Angel set employs five sides of a three disc format and is practically complete. Maria Callas' Leonora is properly desperate sounding (dramatically) while vocally strong although shrill on the top. Her phrasing and musicianship are unparalleled. Giuseppe di Stefano offers one of his best recorded performances, as Manrico. (Of course, singing dramatic roles like this contributed to the early decline of this once sterling lyric tenor.) Fedora Barbieri provides a rather hard-bitten gypsy, but one that is not without many powerful moments. Rolando Panerai is somewhat dry sounding as Count Di Luna, but Herbert von Karajan's handling of the estimable Scala forces is above reproach.

Victor's two TROVATOREs released prior to 1970 are each worth acquiring. The 1959 recording with Leontyne Price, Richard Tucker, Rosalind Elias, and Leonard Warren (his last recording) is an even finer triumph for Price than the second version discussed previously. Nothing in Leonora's music posed any problems for Price in those days, and this recording, particularly in the fourth act, gives credence to those who claim that Leonora is Price's best role. Tucker, who had not as yet sung Manrico on the stage when this was made, offers some powerful yet finely shaded singing. Elias is a competent, if less than brilliant, Azucena. Her singing can't be faulted, but she is basically a lyric mezzo and thus lacks the power and thrust necessary for the part. Warren's handling of Di Luna's music in this set unfortunately reveals him in less than top form, particularly compared to his 1951 RCA performance. Arturo Basile's conducting is solid but routine.

The earliest RCA Victor LP TROVATORE is a two record, mono performance that is becoming increasingly difficult to find in the shops. One hopes that it will soon reappear on the Victrola label. The cast features Zinka Milanov, Fedora Barbieri, Jussi Bjoerling, and Leonard Warren. The conductor is Renato Cellini.

Milanov has called this the best of her recordings, and indeed, it is hard even to imagine Milanov in more radiant voice than that revealed in this album. Barbieri is, once more, a rousingly sung Azucena, and Warren's singing practically melts the record with its glowing warmth. As for Bjoerling, although this lyric tenor wasn't associated with the part of Manrico in the opera house, his warmly sung account of the role is thoroughly within Verdi's idiom. His "Di quella pira" ranks with the best, and furthermore, his "Ah si ben mio" is perhaps the finest on discs.

Renato Cellini conducts a New York pick-up orchestra

lustily, and the Robert Shaw Chorale offers some fine work,
particularly in the "Anvil Chorus."

BERLIOZ: LES TROYENS

Lindholm, Veasey, Vickers, Glossop, Davis cond.
Chorus and Orchestra of Covent Garden
5 discs
Philips 6709002*
UK: Philips—same as above

Opera recordings perform perhaps their greatest service when they bring to the public works rarely if ever performed by opera companies.

Philips Records has in the past few years built for itself the reputation of a company that is unafraid to commit itself to the huge expenses involved in making major recordings of unfamiliar operas, whether they be contemporary ones or forgotten operas of earlier times. Foremost among this firm's achievements is the five disc set of Berlioz's LES TROYENS, one of the most spectacular and musically worthwhile "grand operas" ever composed.

With its five acts filled with mammoth ensembles, choruses, ballets, and complex stage effects, it is understandable that few opera companies have the resources to do LES TROYENS well. The Royal Opera, Covent Garden, however, has made the work a part of its repertoire since 1957, and it is this production that Philips has chosen to preserve.

Conductor Colin Davis deserves a great deal of credit for bringing to the opera a driving sense of energy and a sensitive understanding of the music. Evoking from the Covent Garden Orchestra a varied and luminescent reading of the score, Davis, furthermore, goes on to prove himself to be an excellent "singers' conductor" as well, showing his cast every consideration and keeping a firm yet sympathetic balance between soloists, orchestra, and chorus.

Turning to the singers, Berit Lindholm is a firm-voiced, often exciting Cassandra. The soprano's work is characterized by a rather steely, none too pliant sound, but the top notes are perfectly secure, with the sort of stoic, no-nonsense air that one associates with Birgit Nilsson. Lindholm conscientiously works towards communicating Cassandra's despair, but the bigness of her voice and the unfalteringly heroic manner in which she sings, tend to work against the establishment of Cassandra as a pathetic character. However, Lindholm's "Malheureux roi" is about as exciting a piece of vocalism as one is liable to hear in a great many sessions by the phonograph!

Cassandra is, of course, killed off at the end of Act Two, and the leading female role for the remaining three acts is Dido, sung here by Josephine Veasey. This British mezzo-soprano has a handsome voice and a secure technique. What Veasey lacks, though, is vocal weight and an heroic ring to her voice. Her voice also tends to take on a heavy vibrato when pushed for volume. Still, Veasey is a noble queen here and is capable, as in the famous love duet with Aneas, "O nuit d'ivresse," of sounding appealingly feminine. Personally, though, I would prefer to hear a voice such as Ludwig's or Cossotto's in this role.

Aneas is sung on this recording by Jon Vickers who has made the role something of a specialty since 1957 and who is undertaking the role in the new Metropolitan Opera production. In top voice here, Vickers manifests the physical strength of the Trojan hero as well as the subtlety of character given him by Virgil and Berlioz. Vickers' slightly reedy, unique sound may not be sensuously beautiful, yet, this tenor's work is marked by extremely fine musicianship and a sense of dramatic appropriateness unmatched by any other tenor singing today.

The large supporting cast in this recording features a number of the Royal Opera's best younger singers, including Anne Howells as Ascanius, Ian Partridge as Iopas, Heather Begg as Anna, Elizabeth Bainbridge as Hecuba, and Ryland Davies as Hylas. Also most welcome is the participation of

Peter Glossop as Corebus and Roger Soyer as Narbal.

The Covent Garden Chorus, if slightly deficient in terms of clear French diction, has never been more musically distinguished than in this recording. All told, this set of LES TROYENS is a rare treat for the listener and ought to go far towards popularizing an unjustly neglected opera.

PUCCINI: TURANDOT

Nilsson, Tebaldi, Bjoerling, Tozzi, Leinsdorf cond.
Orchestra and Chorus of the Rome Opera
3 discs
RCA LSC 6149*

Nilsson, Scotto, Corelli, Giaiotti, Molinari-Pradelli cond.
Orchestra and Chorus of the Rome Opera
3 discs
Angel S-3671*
UK: HMV SLS921

Borkh, Tebaldi, del Monaco, Zaccaria, Erede cond.
Orchestra and Chorus of L'Accademia di Santa Cecilia
3 discs
London OSA 1308*
UK: Decca SXL 2078-80

Cigna, Olivero, Merli, Ghione cond.
3 discs
Everest/Cetra S-427/3

Puccini's last opera has, since the advent of Birgit Nilsson, whose ability to vanquish the title character's frighteningly high tessitura has made the opera possible to cast adequately, been heard frequently in the world's opera houses. Although other current sopranos can and do sing the role with success, Nilsson has become uniquely identified with the cruel Princess in the public eye and ear. Not surprisingly, Nilsson has recorded the role twice. The 1959 RCA recording finds the

Swedish diva in excellent form musically. All the high C's, whether *forte* (as in "In questa reggia") or *pianissimo* (as at the end of the third act duet) are there and are produced seemingly without effort. Nilsson's complete mastery of every phrase of this short but killingly difficult role is breathtaking. Often criticized for an alleged lack of warmth in Italian roles, the soprano is in this case "type cast" even from her detractors' point of view as the icy heroine and successfully makes the dramatic transition from cold goddess to loving woman at the end of the opera.

Jussi Bjoerling, the Calaf on this recording, also sings gloriously, with the warmth emanating from his throat being sufficient to melt a dozen Turandots. Will anyone surpass Bjoerling's "Nessun dorma?" I doubt it.

Renata Tebaldi is heard as Liù, singing with customary radiance. Although TURANDOT is supposed to be graced by two leading sopranos, this recording is especially fortunate to bring two so enormously talented singers together. Giorgio Tozzi completes the list of principals with an eloquently sung Timur. Erich Leinsdorf leads the Rome Opera Orchestra and Chorus in a lush and colorful performance.

Nilsson re-recorded the opera for Angel-HMV in 1965, flanked by Franco Corelli and Renata Scotto. The Rome Opera forces again are employed, this time under the most sensitive guidance of Francesco Molinari-Pradelli. If possible, Nilsson is even more impressive than on the RCA release. Her singing is now shaded with more variety, and the pianissimi are even more superbly controlled than in the earlier performance. Furthermore her characterization is more intense than on the RCA set. Franco Corelli lacks Bjoerling's grace but surpasses him in terms of power and excitement. The many fully documented Nilsson-Corelli duels of windpower in opera house performances of TURANDOT have become legendary already, and a good deal of the combustibility of this pairing of soprano and tenor transmits itself from stage to disc. One senses a rivalry between artists here, similar to that between Calaf and Turandot.

Scotto is a winning, delicate Liù, making an impression alongside the larger-than-life work of Corelli and Nilsson. Bonaldo Giaiotti is the set's moving, mellifluous Timur.

In addition to these two fine recordings, there are two other editions of the opera on disc. London-Decca's has many fine points, including the powerful Calaf sung by Mario del Monaco and Renata Tebaldi's youthful Liù. Competing with her own RCA rival version, Tebaldi benefits on the London set from the complete ease of production that was hers in the mid 1950's.

Unfortunately, Inge Borkh, although a fine singer and a better actress than Nilsson, is no match for the latter's vocal prowess. While pleasant in the middle range and when singing quietly, Borkh's voice whitens, becomes reedy, and loses body on the top of the scale and during *forte* passages. Thus, in the absence of a Turandot able to cope with the many challenges of her role, London's supporting cast, which also includes Nicola Zaccaria as Timur and Fernando Corena as Ping, is unable to make the performance as a whole succeed. Alberto Erede's sympathetic conducting of the Santa Cecilia forces is most helpful, but one comes away from this performance with the feeling that the most crucial part has been left unperformed.

Everest-Cetra's budget TURANDOT is from the 1930's. In addition to the forthright work from Gina Cigna in the title role and Franco Merli as Calaf, the performance boasts (and is chiefly memorable for) the Liù of the very young Magda Olivero who projects the slave girl's wounded heart with tenderness and a silvery, pliant voice.

CATALANI: LA WALLY

Tebaldi, del Monaco, Cappuccilli, Diaz, Cleva cond.
Monte Carlo Opera Orchestra and Chorus
3 discs
London OSA 1392*
UK: Decca SET 394-6

Alfredo Catalani, Puccini's melancholy contemporary and friend of Toscanini, has languished in the affections of opera lovers who thrive on the works of Mascagni, Giordano, Puccini, and Leoncavallo. Dying of tuberculosis at an early age, Catalani left behind several works, of which only LA WALLY, a favorite of Toscanini (indeed, the maestro named his daughter after the heroine), has achieved any sort of international recognition. Even so, performances of the opera are rare, and the only well known music consists of two soprano arias, "Ebbene, ne andrò lontano" and "Ne mai avrò la pace."

With London-Decca owning the almost exclusive services of Renata Tebaldi, and given that artist's fondness for late 19th century Italian opera, it was perhaps inevitable that a LA WALLY set starring Tebaldi would someday appear. This 1968 recording is a welcome release, as Catalani's score proves to have vitality, and a singularly haunting, alpine flavor which pervades the darkly melodious writing.

The libretto sketches a slightly unsavory tale of a neurotic village heiress' love-hate relationship with a handsome hunter. (Believing that Giuseppe Hagensbach has insulted her, Wally instructs his rival, Gellner, to throw him from a cliff). Conscious stricken, Wally nurses the miraculously saved man, then retreats to the mountains where Hagensbach is finally killed in an avalanche after coming to declare his love and forgiveness. The distraught soprano ends the merry proceedings by hurling herself from a cliff. The opera, however, offers fine musical opportunities to the soprano and baritone, but a relatively thankless role for tenor (no arias, but rather a collection of amorous phrases alternating with screams of terror). There is also an interesting trouser role for a mezzo.

Fausto Cleva's seasoned conducting urges a richness of sound from his principals who in addition to Tebaldi include Mario del Monaco, Piero Cappuccilli, Lydia Malimpietri, and Justino Diaz.

Tebaldi is in satisfactory "late-middle career voice." Although the voice does not soar as freely as it did in the 1950's, the sound is ample, and, as the role of Wally does not lie very high, Tebaldi sounds quite comfortable in all but a very few passages.

By 1968 Tebaldi had become a truly "dramatic" dramatic soprano, and on this recording, she makes full use of her chest register which endows Wally's several spoken lines with old-fashioned yet wonderfully appropriate emphasis. "Ebbene, ne andrò lontano" is sung with some degree of caution but is sensitively phrased and quietly powerful. In the third act aria, "Ne mai avrò la pace," Tebaldi is less inhibited and more successful. Only in the frantic moments in the fourth act when Wally hears her lover approaching does Tebaldi show serious signs of strain. However, she rallies, and ends the opera with a fine high A.

Mario del Monaco retains his remarkable vigor in this performance, but his singing is rather tightly produced, and his dynamic rigidity threatens to grow tiresome in some passages. However, the tenor is irresistible in the second act waltz scene with Wally, and the final scene finds both him and Tebaldi in near top vocal shape.

Piero Cappuccilli's rich baritone dominates every scene in which Gellner appears. This is his best recorded performance to date. Justino Diaz is heard briefly as Wally's unpleasant father, an ungrateful role which he handles decently. Lydia Malimpietri is a fresh-voiced Walter, making most of the opportunities provided in her (his) first act yodel-

ling song (the opera is set in Switzerland). The Monte Carlo
Opera Orchestra and Chorus play stylishly, making for an
effective recording debut for an unjustly neglected work.

MASSENET: WERTHER

de los Angeles, Gedda, Mesplé, Soyer, Prêtre cond.
Paris Opera Orchestra and French Radio Children's Chorus
3 discs
Angel S3736
UK: HMV SLS945

Tassinari, Tagliavini, Molinari-Pradelli cond.
RAI Orchestra and Chorus
3 discs
Everest/Cetra S436/3

Highlights: Elias, Valletti Souzay, Leibowitz cond.
Rome Opera Orchestra
1 disc
Victrola VICS 1516

The only stereo, complete recording of this opera is the 1969 Angel-EMI set that features Nicolai Gedda in the title role, with Victoria de los Angeles as Charlotte, under the baton of George Prêtre. The fact that Nicolai Gedda lost out to Franco Corelli when the Metropolitan revived WERTHER in 1971 is one of the scandals of the Rudolph Bing administration, but Gedda, fortunately, has had the opportunity to record the neurotic if melodic Massenet-Goethe hero, giving fans a souvenir of this tenor in a role that he is ideally suited for, although he seldom gets to perform.

Gedda is one of the brainiest tenors ever to hit a high C and hold on to it and thus not only commands the raw vocal material necessary to sustain the role of Werther (as Cesare Valetti, who sings the role in the abridged Victrola edition, does not) but also is an extraordinarily tasteful artist who gives notes their proper value, obeys the dynamics of the score, and has mastered the French language, all the while creating a dramatic personality for Werther as well.

The recording is less fortunate in the choice of Victoria de los Angeles for the role of Charlotte, often sung by a mezzo-soprano. Charlotte does not lie very high, but de los Angeles sounds uncomfortable in the role's upper reaches, furthermore, her lower register lacks size and ease of production. Excellent musicianship and beautiful diction mitigate de los Angeles' purely vocal problems to a considerable extent, but with Regine Crespin and (dare I suggest this?) Maria Callas under contract to EMI, one can't help feeling that Charlotte might have been better cast.

Charlotte's younger and happier sister, Sophie, is sung on this recording by Mady Mesplé, who seldom seems to venture outside of France. This is a decisive loss to opera-goers elsewhere as Mesplé possesses a silvery, light (but not chirpy) voice which ennobles a part that can all too often become treacly.

Roger Soyer is a particularly ingratiating Albert who succeeds in making this stuffed shirt interesting. Rarely has Albert's first act aria "Elle m'aime" sounded this well! Jean-Christophe Benoit also makes the most of his opportunities as the Bailiff.

George Prêtre, not always the most sympathetic operatic conductor, in this instance offers strong support, treating the score delicately but shaping it nonetheless into a musico-dramatic entity, and L'Orchestre de Paris plays for him superbly. The recorded sound is as fine as one would expect from so recent an effort.

Those interested in a "highlight" edition of WERTHER will find one, and at a budget price, too, in the Victrola catalogue. This disc dates from the early 1960's and finds in Rosalind Elias a high spirited and velvety Charlotte. Not nearly as subtle an artist as de los Angeles, the American mezzo still provides a thoughtful "Letter Scene" and a convincingly taut finale, and is, in general, up to the role's vocal demands.

Cesare Valetti, a lyric tenor of great ability was, however, out of his proper depth in the *spinto* role of Werther. He overused head tones at the top of the staff and was unable to summon sufficient strength to animate Werther.

Gerard Souzay, heard briefly as Albert, sings "Elle m'aime" decently, but without illuminating Albert's character at all. Rene Leibowitz is a most competent conductor in these excerpts.

MOZART:
DIE ZAUBERFLÖTE

Janowitz, Popp, Gedda, Berry, Frick, Klemperer cond.
The Philharmonia Orchestra and Chorus
3 discs
Angel S-3651*
UK: HMV SLS912

Lear, Peters, Wunderlich, Fischer-Dieskau, Crass, Böhm cond.
Berlin Philharmonic
3 discs
Deutsche Grammophon 2709017*
UK: Same

Lorengar, Deutekom, Burrows, Prey, Talvela, Solti cond.
Vienna Philharmonic and State Opera Chorus
3 discs
London OSA-1397
UK: Decca SET 479-81

Gueden, Lipp, Simoneau, Berry, Boehme, Böhm cond.
Vienna Philharmonic and State Opera Chorus
3 discs
Richmond SRS63507
UK: Ace of Diamonds GOS501-3

Donath, Geszty, Schreier, Adam, Sultner cond.
Rundfunkchor, Leipzig and Staatskappelle, Dresden
3 discs
Eurodisc 80 584 XR

The three modern, stereophonic recordings of THE MAGIC
FLUTE are, incredibly, almost uniformly strongly sung and,
in at least two cases, superbly conducted. Although a choice
between the London-Decca, DGG, and Angel-HMV sets is
difficult, the one that, to my mind, seems definitive is the
London-Decca version led by Solti. Although the cast is virtually unanimously delightful, first honors must go to the
Maestro and his orchestra, the Vienna Philharmonic, whose
supple playing under Solti's buoyant, meticulously detailed
direction propels the recording into the realm of the truly
great sets of the past two decades. Under Solti, the opera's
gentle radiance melts the hearts of even those who take the
dimmest possible view of the FLUTE's libretto. The
ensembles glide forward, and all the music is performed
under an aura of grace and perfect ensemble. Nowhere else
does the quintet in Act One, Scene One, to cite but one example,
shimmer so deliciously in the air. Georg Solti's soloists do not
let him down either. Stuart Burrows is an uncommonly
tastefully, youthful Tamino. That his voice may be somewhat
on the cool side is of less importance here than is the intelligent
manner with which it is deployed. Hermann Prey is a winning
Papageno, singing handsomely and with the lightest, easiest
tone of any Papageno yet recorded, as well as performing
with an impish charm that serves the character well. As for
Martti Talvela in the role of Sarastro, he is undoubtedly the
most majestic interpreter of the role singing these days.
Talvela, as has been previously noted in these pages, is gifted
with one of the most enormous voices one might reasonably
expect to hear in a lifetime of opera-going, and he handles his
instrument with a full measure of decorum.

Pilar Lorengar revives memories of the Metropolitan's 1967
staging of this opera in which she was one of the loveliest
Papminas imaginable. When singing the "Bei mannern" with
Prey, also featured in that production, the joy is positively
contagious, as Lorengar's lyric soprano is effervescently
pleasing and strongly matched by the baritone's graceful
work. Lorengar's voice, though, is marked by a vibrato that

in an opera house is not at all unpleasant but somehow always seems more obtrusive on her recordings, masking pitch and robbing her singing of clarity. Thus, the Spanish soprano's work here is slightly disappointing in a few places, but her gentle characterization and superior work in the second act work toward her credit.

Cristna Deutekom sings the Queen of the Night with a large, authoritative voice but is not fully in command of the brutal coloratura passages, particularly in the first act aria in which she seems to almost yodel at times. Furthermore, the singer would do well to improve her diction.

Smaller roles are taken by artists of the stature of Dietrich Fischer-Dieskau, DGG's Papageno, who here performs the Speaker, Gerhard Stolze, a nasty but very dry-voiced Monostatos, Renate Holm, an appealing Papagena, and René Kollo and Hans Sotin who are heard briefly as the two armed men. It should also be noted that the Vienna Opera Chorus sings very beautifully indeed.

London-Decca's producers have opted for use of the complete spoken dialogue, which will surely please German-speaking listeners who revere the text as well as the music of this opera.

The Deutsche Grammophon FLUTE features such artists as Fritz Wunderlich, Evelyn Lear, Roberta Peters, Fischer-Dieskau, and Franz Crass, with the Berlin Philharmonic under the experienced hand of Karl Böhm. If Dr. Böhm's FLUTE is not quite as infectiously joyous an experience as Solti's, it is made memorable by its precision and grace. Vocally, Böhm's cast in most cases equals Solti's, and one or two performances are even better than their London counterparts. The late Fritz Wunderlich was a tenor of such stuff as an opera buff's dreams are made. His voice was not only as warm as Bjoerling's, but his musicianship and versatility were also on a par with that of the Swedish tenor's.

Wunderlich sings Tamino's "Die Bildnis ist bezaubernd schön" with an endearing glow, and throughout the opera, he is an aristocratic yet human character. His tragic death at the age of thirty-six left a hole in the ranks of lyric tenors that no one has, as yet, stepped in to fill.

Evelyn Lear is a dramatic soprano who can scale her voice down sufficiently to sing lyric roles successfully. Her Pamina is silvery-toned and girlish, although her highest notes are steely.

Dietrich Fischer-Dieskau is a comically ebullient Papageno, demonstrating his superiority in this repertory where he does not need to force his beautiful but not very large voice. His witty characterization is even a step more animated than Prey's, making Fischer-Dieskau quite a formidable bird catcher!

Roberta Peters is at her absolute best here as the Queen of the Night, singing the two arias with bravura assurance, tonal accuracy, and a sense of what the Queen is all about. Peters is unquestionably the finest Queen of the Night on discs at this time, handling her music with authority, and with her light voice emerging unscathed from the cruel ordeal to which Mozart subjects it.

Franz Crass' Sarastro is lighter-voiced and consequently more human than Talvela's. Crass, unfortunately, is not as forceful as he should be. His singing lacks color and his words lack authority.

Hans Hotter is heard as the Speaker, and other notable performances are contributed by Lisa Otto as Papagena, Friedrich Lenz as an uncommonly fine Monostatos who manages to perform an absurd role effectively without resorting to unmusical silliness, and (talk about superior casting) James King and Martti Talvela as the armed men.

The Angel-HMV set is also not without some outstanding singing from its leading artists, not to mention a trio of Ladies that includes Elisabeth Schwarzkopf and Christa Ludwig, but Otto Klemperer's conducting, however regal, is entirely too placid. Even without the dialogue, this perform-ance lasts over two hours, and there is absolutely no dramatic tension generated from first scene to last. The Philharmonia Orchestra, though, does play beautifully.

The directorial sluggishness is all the more pitiable because the vocal achievements are many. Nicolai Gedda is an ideal Tamino (how well cast this role has been on records). Musically polished, with a manly, lyrical voice that never fails to thrill the listener with its purity and strength, Gedda is strong competition even for Fritz Wunderlich, although the latter's voice had a throbbing ring to it that Gedda's does not naturally possess.

Walter Berry, a dark-voiced Papageno, is less mischievous than either Fischer-Dieskau or Prey, but is a gentle and charming bird catcher nonetheless. Perhaps if Klemperer had been more co-operative, Berry might have been more energetic.

Gottlob Frick is the set's imposing, rather stern Sarastro, fitting in with the austere vision of the opera evidently held by the conductor.

Gundula Janowitz, surely among the finest of Mozart singers currently to be heard, is a soft-voiced Pamina, distinguished by creamy top notes and a sense of melancholy that seems appropriate for this character.

Lucia Popp is a highly competent singer, but her cold, somewhat metallic voice does not fall pleasantly upon the ear, even though she negotiates the two arias with no trouble. Certainly a skilled singer, Miss Popp is not, however, a particularly vivid musical personality.

Franz Crass turns up here as the Speaker, also doubling as a Priest, and tripling as an Armed Man. In sum, this is a very well sung MAGIC FLUTE, but one that lacks a sense of drama as well as musical drive. Admirers of the individual artists would do well to acquire this recording, but those who wish a truly cohesive performance had best look to one of the other sets.

INDEX